IMAGES
of America

FORSYTH COUNTY
1849–1999

IMAGES
of America

Forsyth County
1849–1999

Cindy Casey on behalf of the
Forsyth County Genealogical Society

ARCADIA
PUBLISHING

ISBN 978-0-7385-1547-2

Published by Arcadia Publishing
Charleston, South Carolina

Printed in the United States of America

For all general information contact Arcadia Publishing at:
Telephone 843-853-2070
Fax 843-853-0044
E-Mail sales@arcadiapublishing.com
For customer service and orders:
Toll-Free 1-888-313-2665

Visit us on the Internet at www.arcadiapublishing.com

Contents

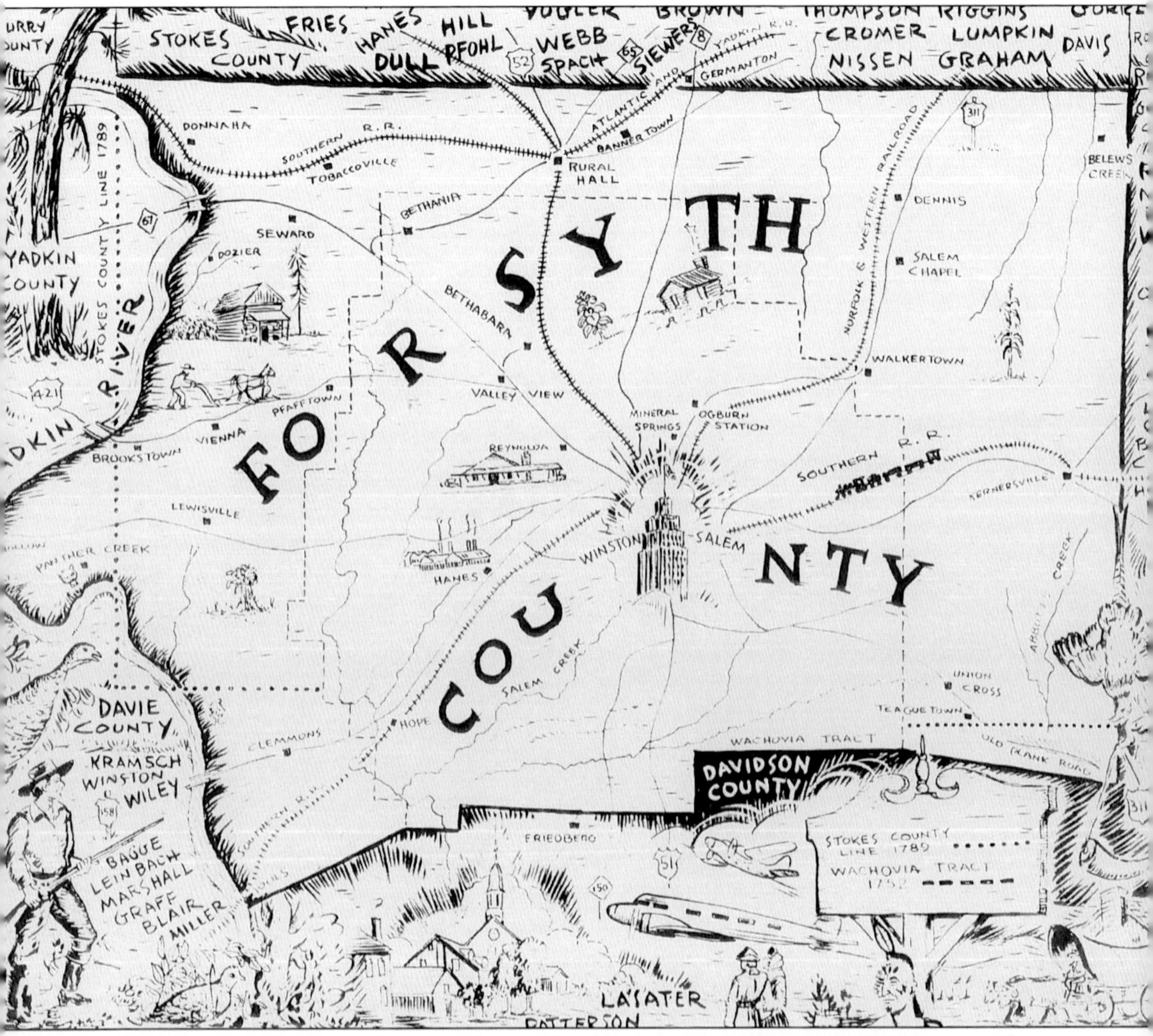

CREATED FOR ADELAIDE FRIES'S BOOK, *FORSYTH, A COUNTY ON THE MARCH*, BY WINSTON-SALEM ARTIST JOE KING. Mr. King captured the small communities of Forsyth County on this wonderful little map.

Acknowledgments

The collection of photographs and images in this publication were made available by the Lewisville Historical Society, the Tobaccoville Historical Society, volunteers of the Forsyth County Genealogical Society, and a number of private collectors.

Special thanks go to Jerry Carroll and Mrs. Molly Rawls of the North Carolina Room of the Forsyth County Library.

And to Mr. Edwin Welch—thanks for making an idea into reality!

Introduction

During the latter half of the eighteenth century, a number of non-Moravian settlements appeared in what is now Forsyth County. They were as follows: Rural Hall, *c.* 1750; Clemmons, *c.* 1757; Lewisville, *c.* 1777; and Kernersville, *c.* 1756. Eventually the surrounding agricultural communities grew, resulting in even more townships. Abbot's Creek, *c.* 1753; Belews Creek, *c.* 1753; Town Fork, *c.* 1755; Salem Chapel, *c.* 1768; Pfafftown, *c.* 1786; Brookstown, *c.* 1790; and Waughtown, *c.* 1806, were among these new townships.

The purpose of this book is to celebrate 150 years of Forsyth's existence and the lives of those who built these small farming communities into thriving, self-supporting townships and villages that still exist. This endeavor focuses on the smaller communities of Clemmons, Kernersville, Pfafftown, Lewisville, Rural Hall, and Tobaccoville, which also contributed to the rich heritage of Forsyth County. Not all of the wonderful leaders of this community have been featured. Instead, some of the "unsung heroes" who were instrumental in the development of Winston-Salem are the subjects of focus.

Most of the photographs are from the Frank Jones Collection of the Forsyth County Library. However, there are some special photographs from private collections. In absence of a photograph, a sketch has been provided. Due to limited space, all the wonderful photographs available to our society could not be used in this publication.

The Forsyth County Genealogical Society hopes this pictorial view of the county portrays the stories of the lives, dreams, and realities of the residents of Forsyth County. This book will surely rekindle memories, as well as awaken new curiosities of the county. In each image, no matter how minute, there is a story to tell.

Cindy H. Casey
Editor

Legend to Photo Credits

BO	Beverly Oates
CC	Clara Caldwell
CHC	Cindy H. Casey
FCL	Forsyth County Library, North Carolina Room—Frank Jones Collection
FF	Gwynne Stephens Taylor, *From Frontier to Factory, an Architectural History of Forsyth County*
FJM	Faye Jarvis Moran
GPM	Georgianna Page McCoy
HRH	Rural Hall Women's Club, *History of Rural Hall*
JC	Judy S. Cardwell
JK	Christian Baumann, *Joseph Von Kernersville*
JOK	Jules Gilmer Korner, *Joseph of Kernersville*
JRH	Jewell and Ronald Hauser
KB	Kernersville, NC Bicentennial
LHS	Lewisville Historical Society, Lewisville, North Carolina
SIW	Charles Crossfield Ware, *Star in Wachovia*
THS	Tobaccoville Historical Society, Tobaccoville, North Carolina
TW	William J. Wall and Helen J. McMurray, *Tanglewood: Historic Gem of Forsyth County, North Carolina*
WM	Willard McCloud Sr.

One

Clemmons

The Town that Keeps on Growing

Peter Clemmons, a Quaker from Delaware, founded Clemmons in 1802. With other settlers in the area, and more still to arrive, Clemmons eagerly opened his first store and came to be known as "Peter Clemmons, Merchant of Clemmonsville." Some of the early settlers he served were John Douthit Sr. and John Douthit Jr. (1761), George McKnight (1762), Evan Ellis (1758), William Johnson (1757), and Lewis Mullican (1780s). William Johnson bought 1 square mile of land (640 acres) on the east side of the Yadkin River. This tract is now the site of Tanglewood Park, located west of Winston-Salem and 3 miles west of Clemmons.

The Peter Clemmons House is located west of the United Methodist Church on Clemmons Road (U.S. 158). From this location, his great-grandson, Edwin T. Clemmons, started a stagecoach line to points such as Salem, High Point, Raleigh, Asheville, and Wytheville, Virginia. Upon Edwin's death, he left money to start the construction of Clemmons Moravian Church and a school.

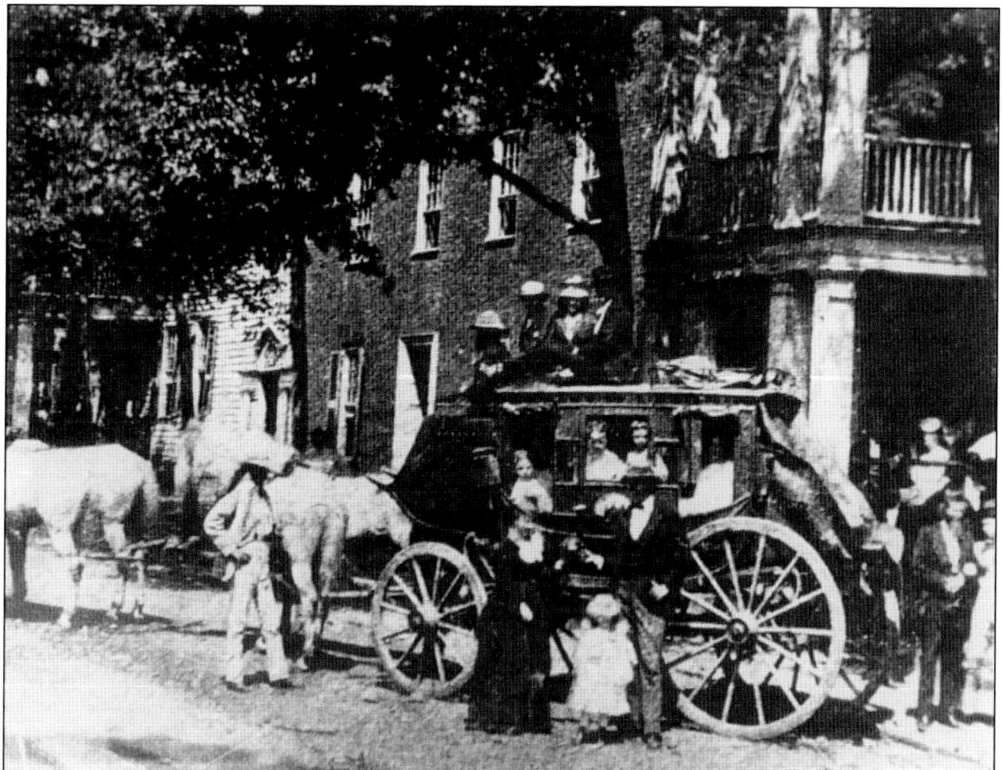

HATTIE BUTNER STAGECOACH. It was named for Edwin Clemmons's wife and provided transportation from Clemmons.

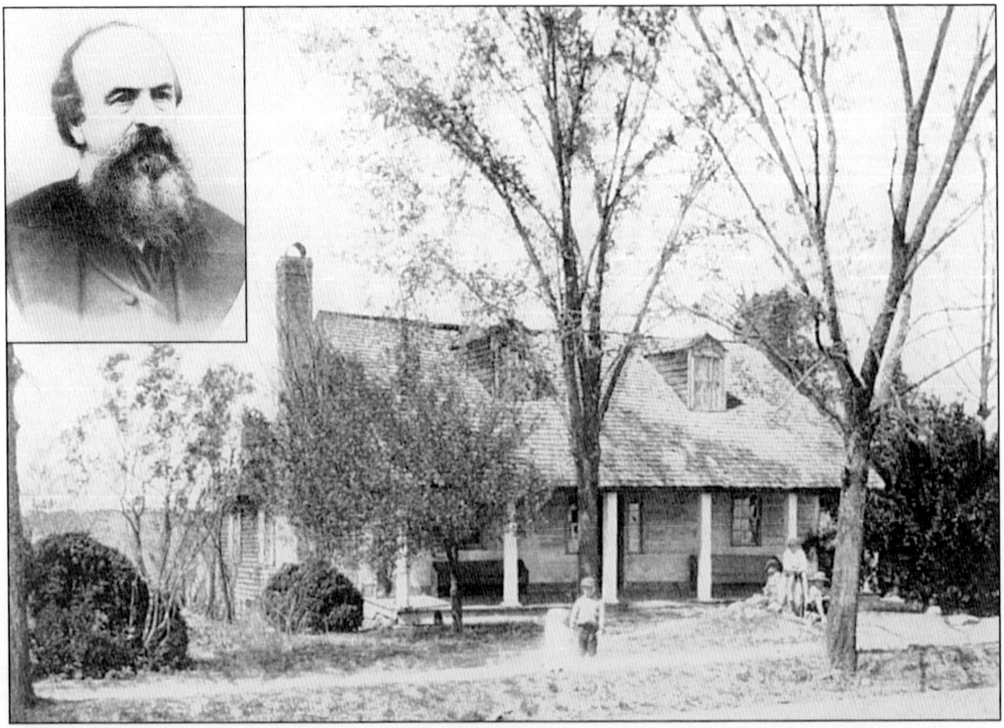

Birthplace of Edwin T. Clemmons in Clemmonsville, North Carolina. (FCL)
Inset: Edwin T. Clemmons, Founder of the Clemmons Moravian School. He was born on October 17, 1826, in Clemmonsville and died on December 20, 1896, in Salem. (FCL)

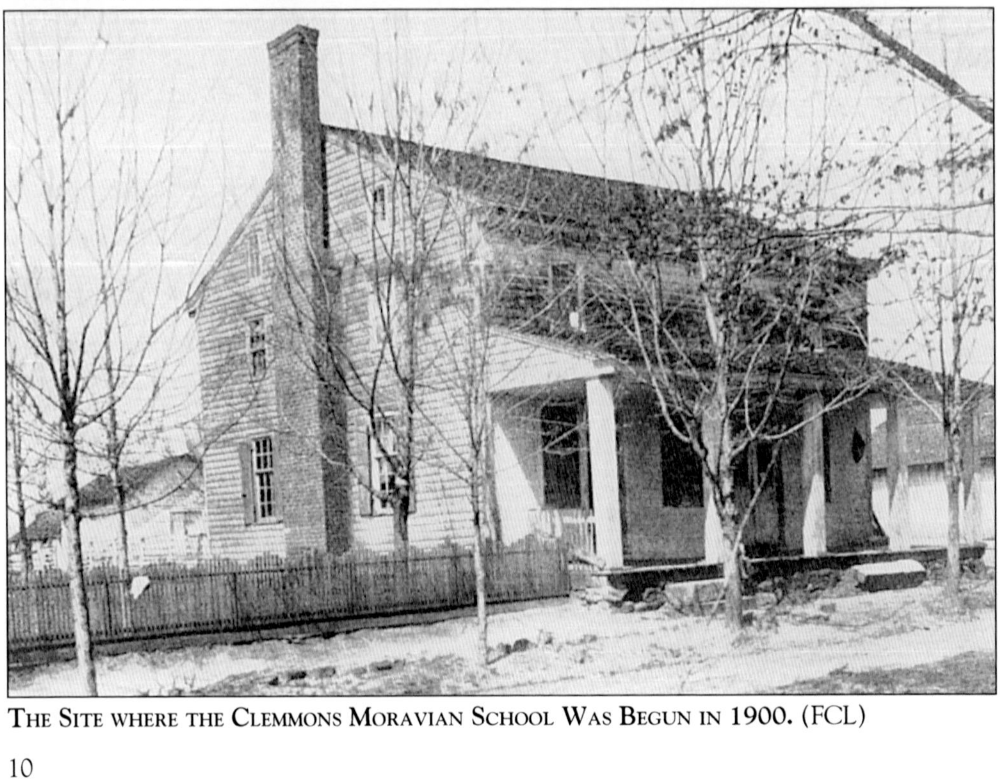

The Site where the Clemmons Moravian School Was Begun in 1900. (FCL)

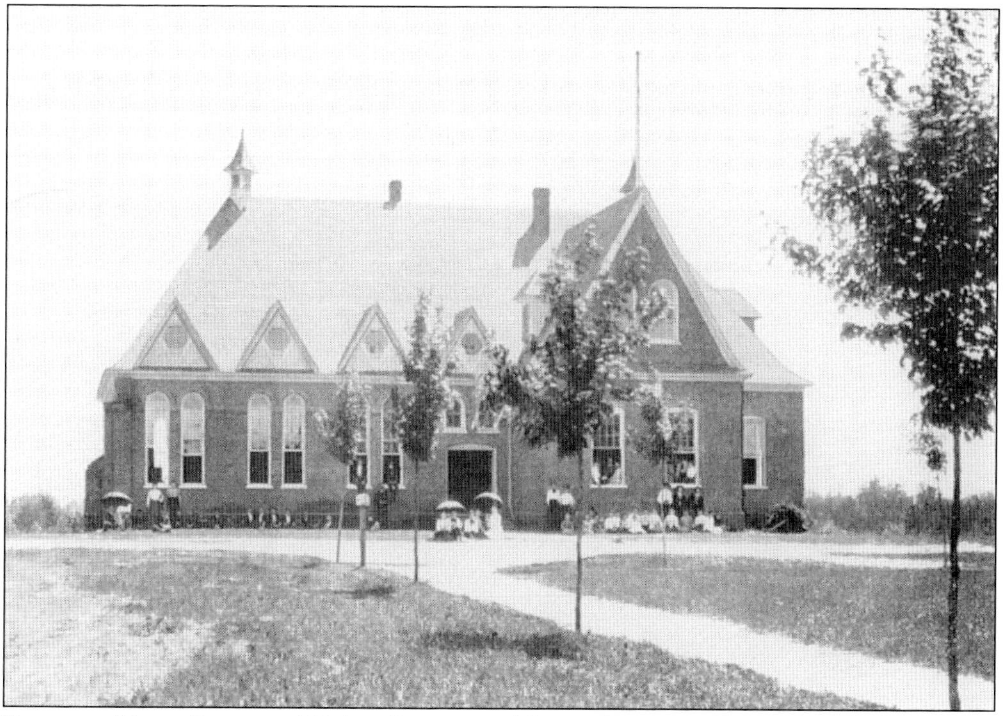

FOUNDERS HALL, BUILT IN 1901 OF BRICK AND NORTH CAROLINA PINE. The lodging for boys was on the second floor. (FCL)

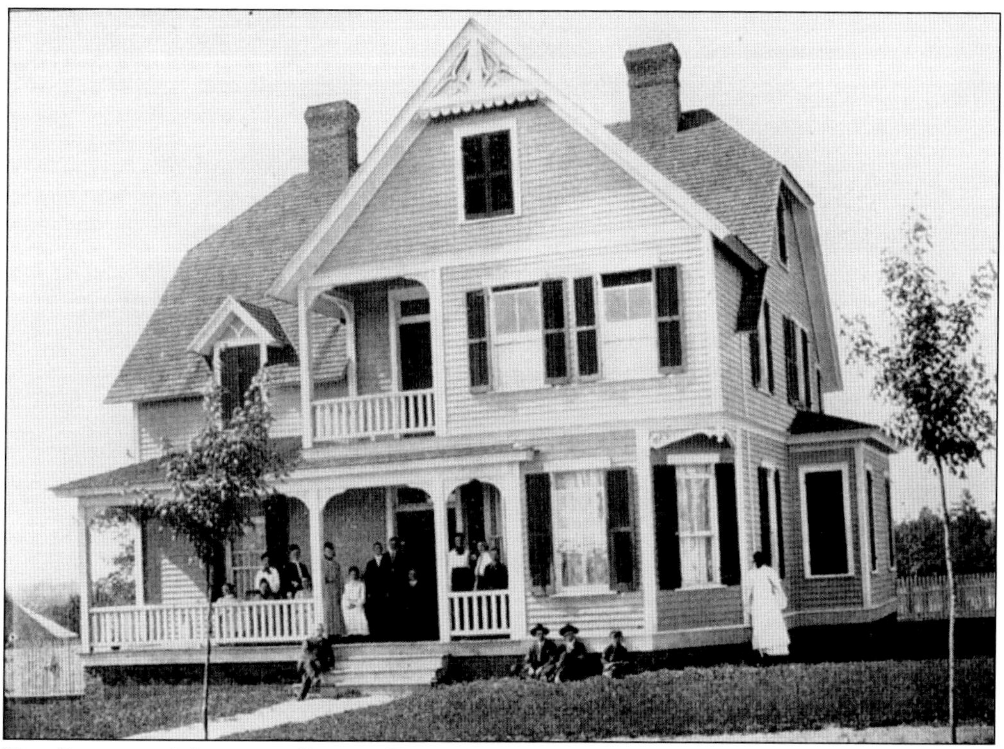

THE CLEMMONS MORAVIAN SCHOOL YOUNG LADIES' DORMITORY. (FCL)

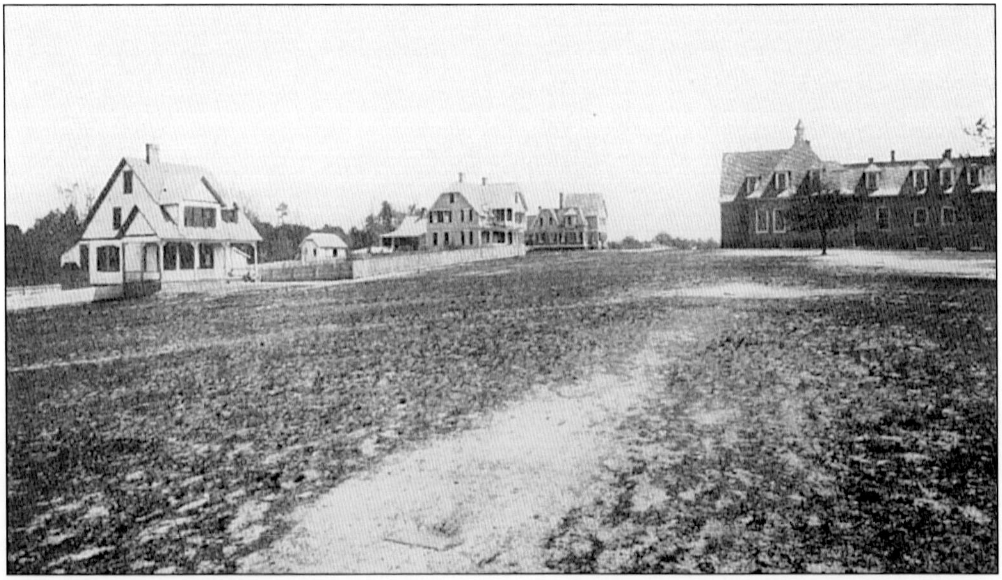

THE CAMPUS OF CLEMMONS MORAVIAN SCHOOL IN 1908, AS VIEWED FROM THE SOUTHWEST. Professor Mendenhall's home is on the left. (FCL)

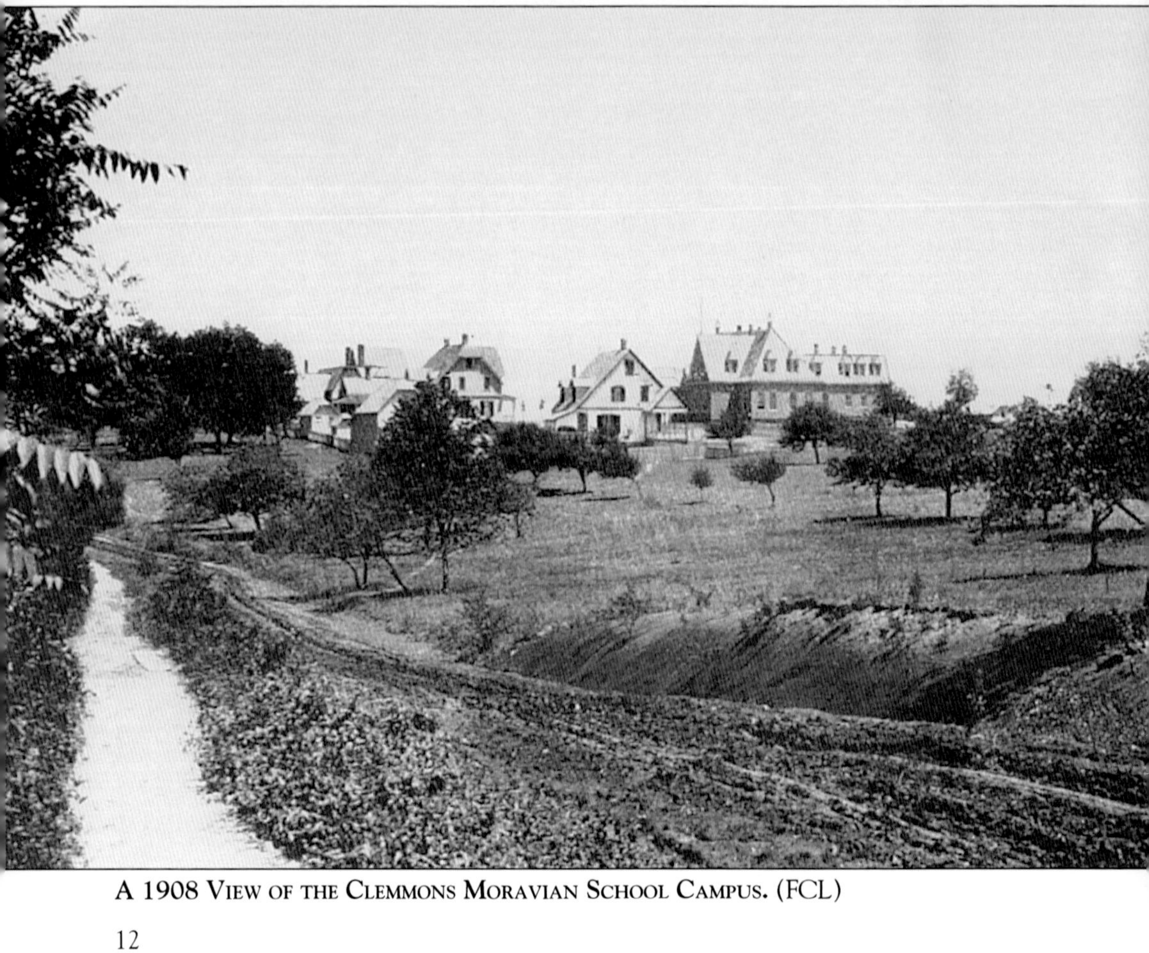

A 1908 VIEW OF THE CLEMMONS MORAVIAN SCHOOL CAMPUS. (FCL)

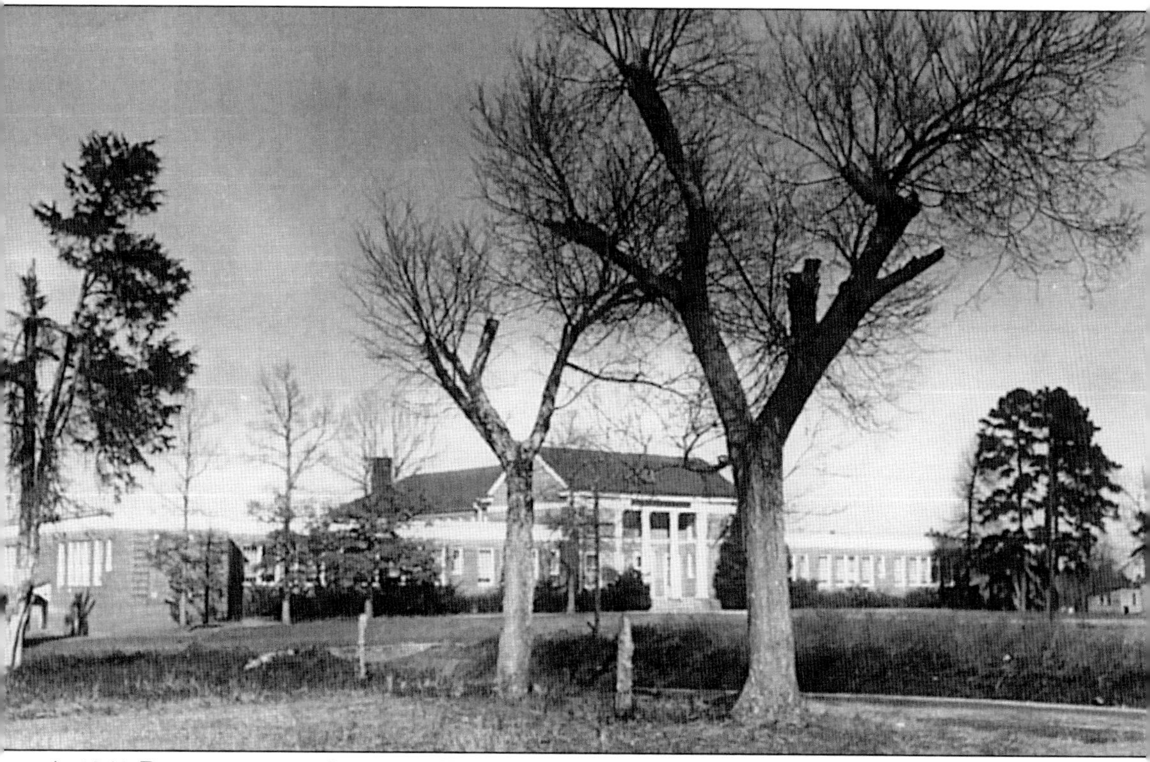

A 1941 PHOTOGRAPH OF CLEMMONS PUBLIC SCHOOL, IN CLEMMONS, NORTH CAROLINA. This building still stands, but is no longer used as a school. (FCL)

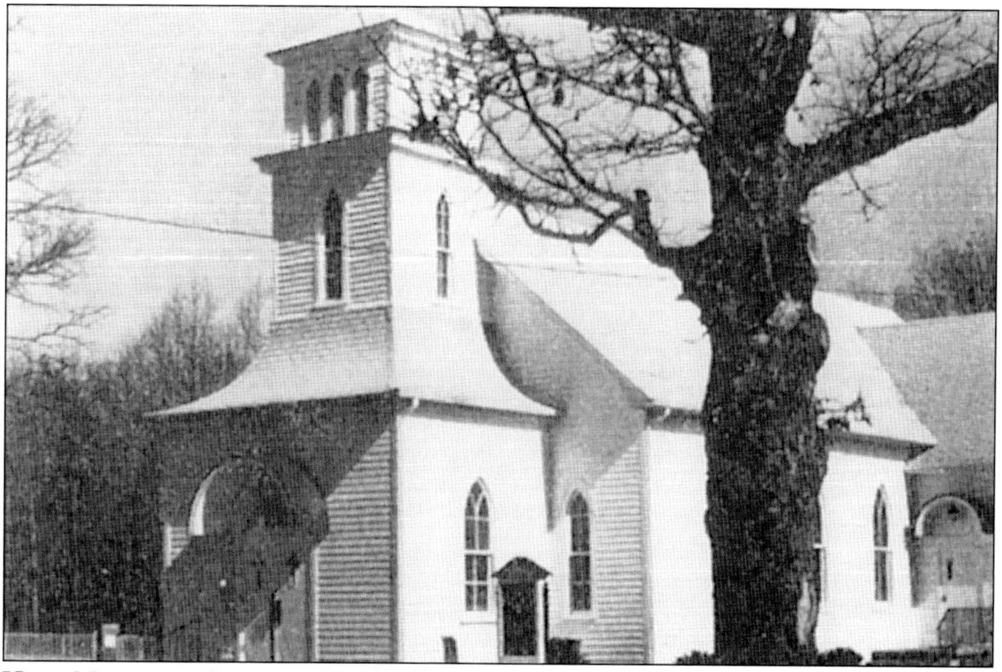

HOPE MORAVIAN CHURCH. This building was erected in 1896 and replaced the original structure. (FF)

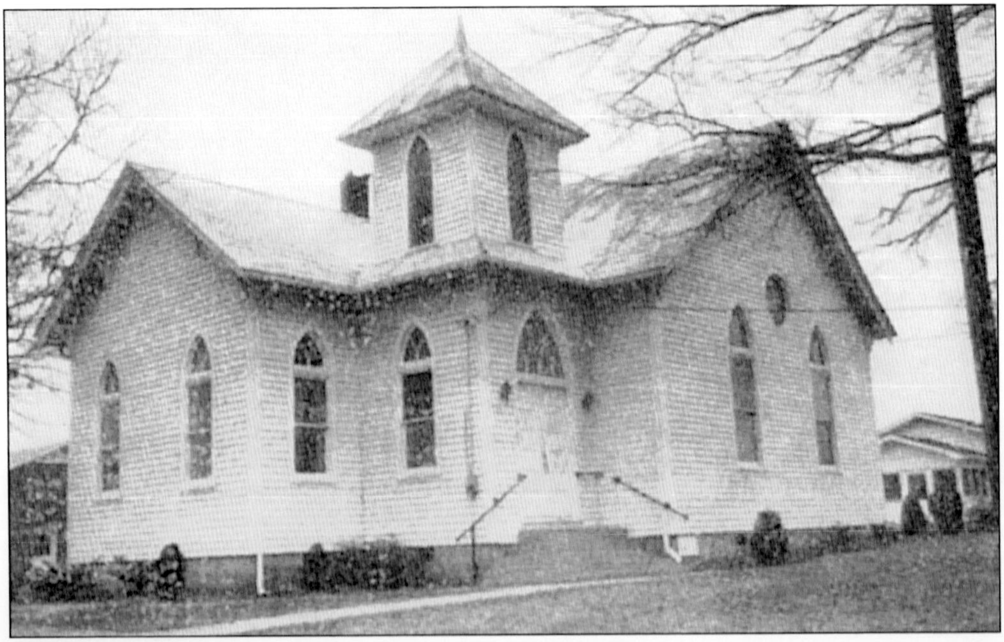

MUDDY CREEK CHURCH OF CHRIST, ERECTED IN 1924. (FF)

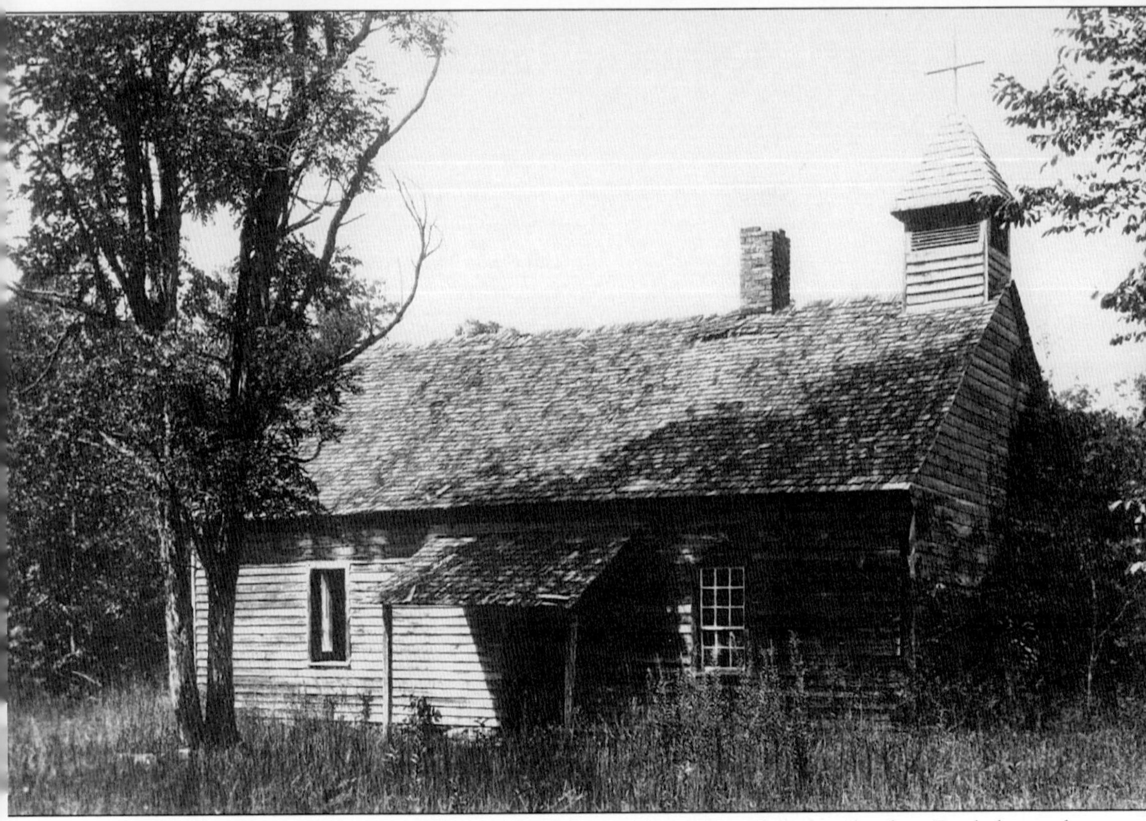

ORIGINAL HOPE MORAVIAN CHURCH, ORGANIZED IN 1780. This was the first English-speaking Moravian congregation in the Wachovia tract. (FCL)

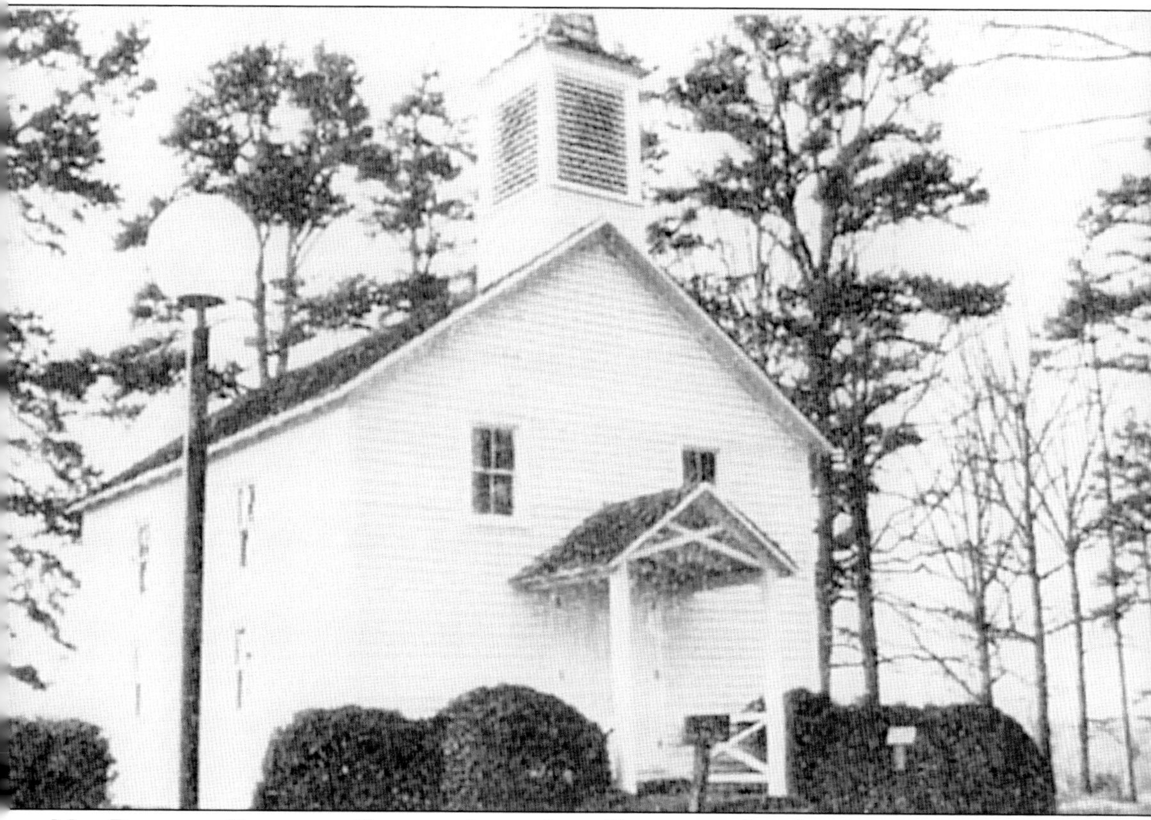

Mt. Pleasant Episcopal Church. Located in Clemmons, the church was constructed in 1809 by Henry Eccles. This is also the burial site of William Johnson, who was born on August 31, 1732, and died on September 5, 1765. Johnson's grave site predates Old Salem by one year. (FCL)

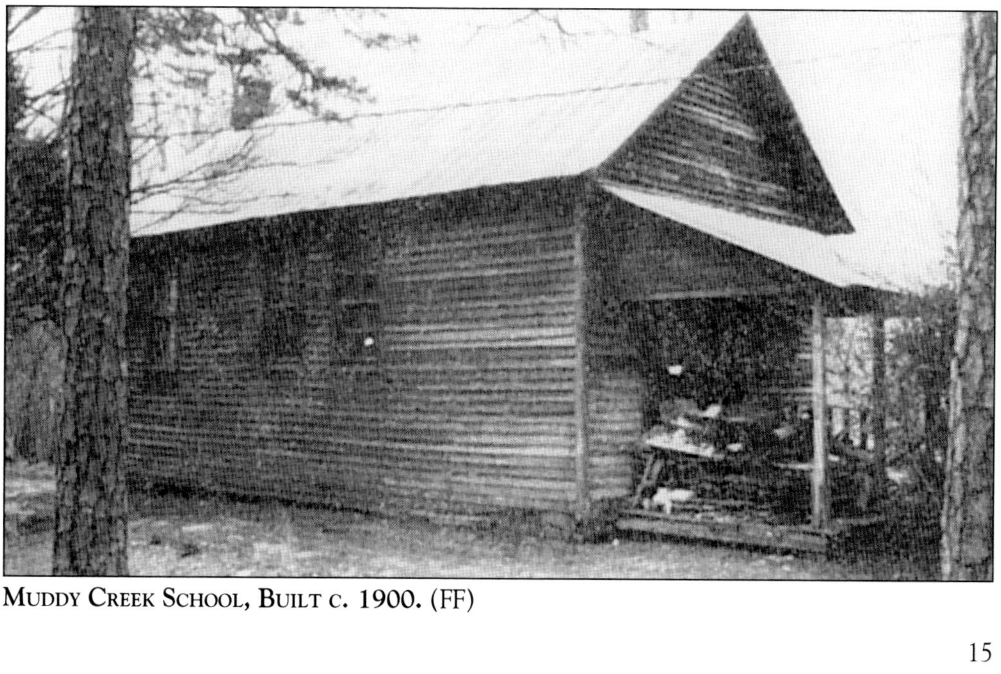

Muddy Creek School, Built c. 1900. (FF)

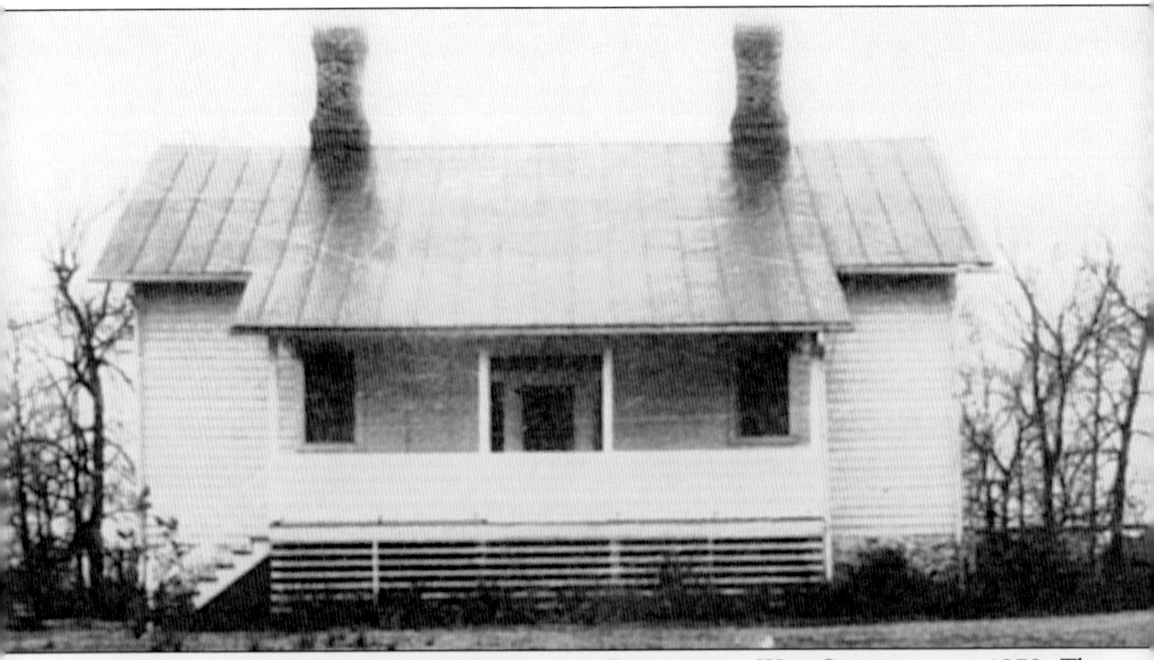

A View of Wesley Johnson's Home after Renovation Was Completed in 1972. The Johnson home was built before 1838, when he first bought property in Davie County. (FCL)

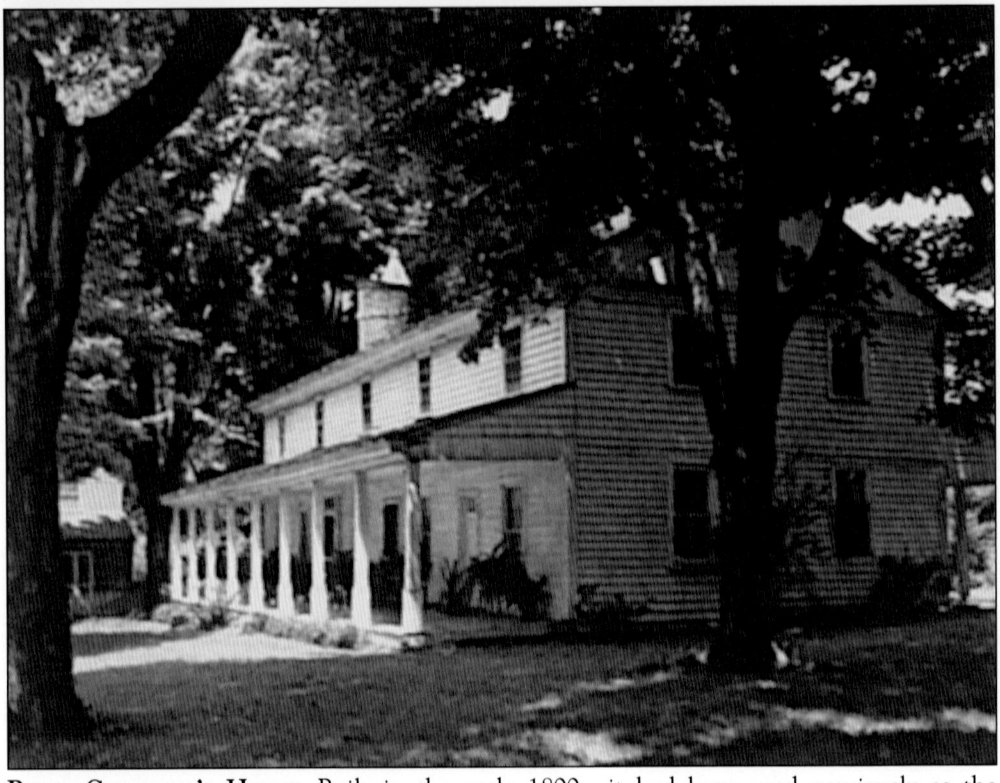

Peter Clemmons's House. Built in the early 1800s, it had been used previously as the Stagecoach House in Clemmons. (FCL)

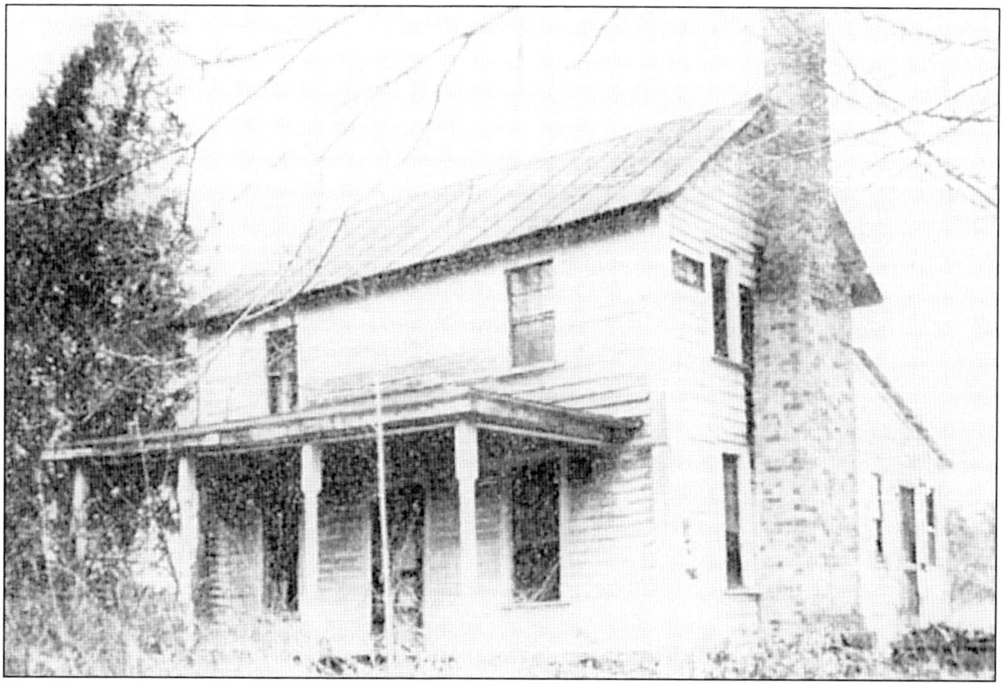

THE BRYAN JARVIS HOUSE. It was built in the late 1800s originally as a log structure. (FJM)

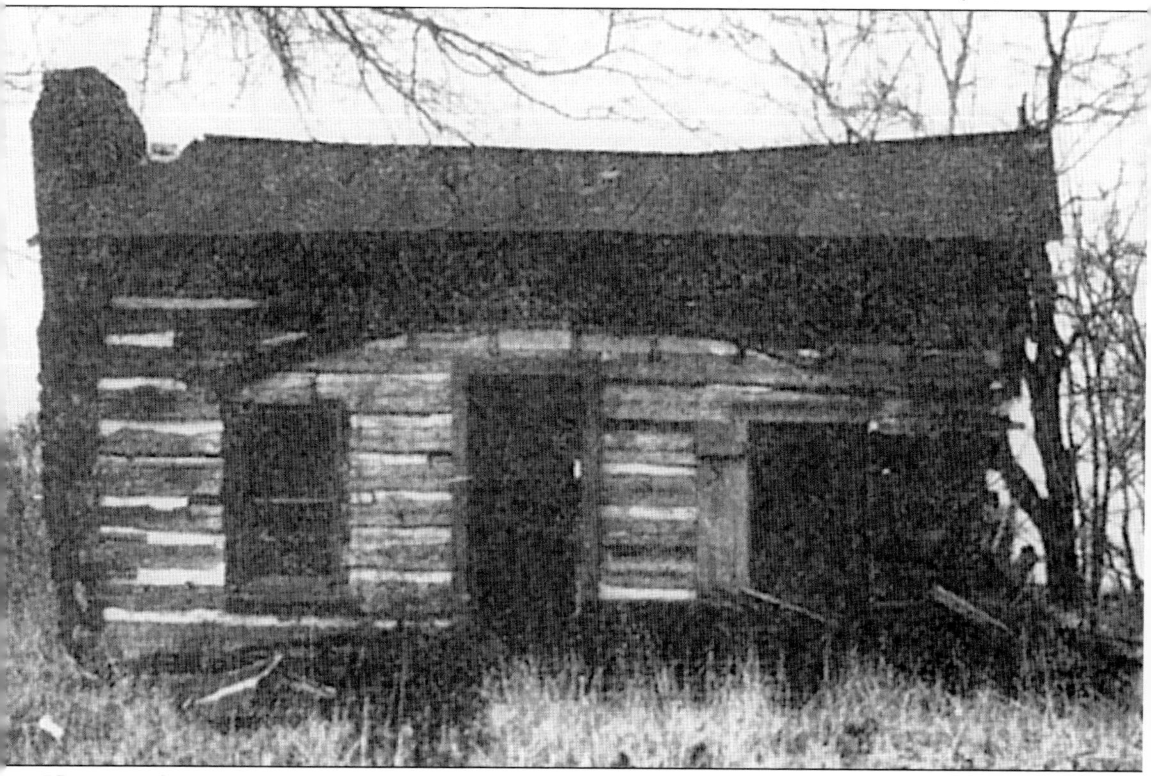

HOME OF SAM BANNER. Banner, an African American, built this log house, and upon its completion, he etched a self-portrait on a chimney stone and dated it 1855. (FF)

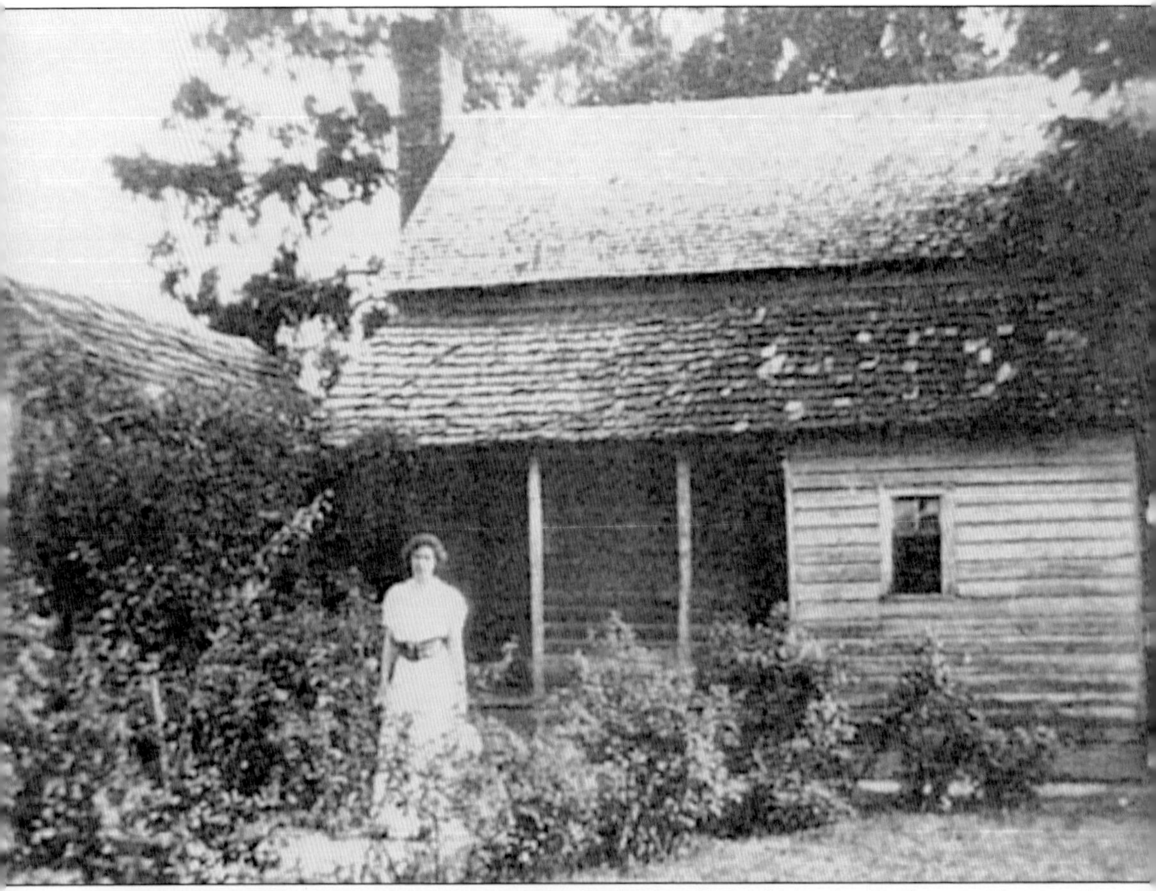

THE LEWIS MULLICAN HOUSE, C. 1900. Built in 1791, this was the home of an early English-speaking pioneer who bought land from Lord Granville and settled in what is now Clemmons. (FF)

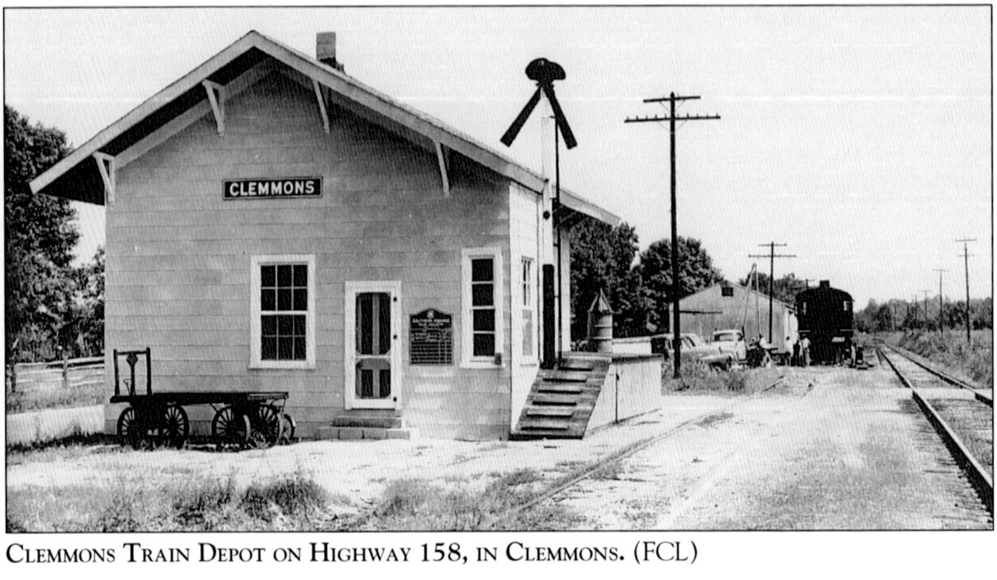

CLEMMONS TRAIN DEPOT ON HIGHWAY 158, IN CLEMMONS. (FCL)

Two

Lewisville
We'll Camp at the Shallow Ford!

Before Lewis Case Lagenauer founded Lewisville in 1860, this settlement was a mainstream of activity. Today, it is considered by some as one of the oldest settlements in Forsyth County. The Old Dutch Meeting House (1777) and Waggoner's Chapel (1781) are now known as Shiloh Lutheran Church and Concord Methodist, respectively. They continue to serve the spiritual needs of the community. The Great Wagon Road, which provided the eighteenth-century interstate immigration route from Pennsylvania, traveled through this pioneer settlement. Located west of Lewisville, the Shallow Ford crossing provided passage to General Cornwallis and his army in 1781 as they crossed the dangerous Yadkin River en route to Lewisville.

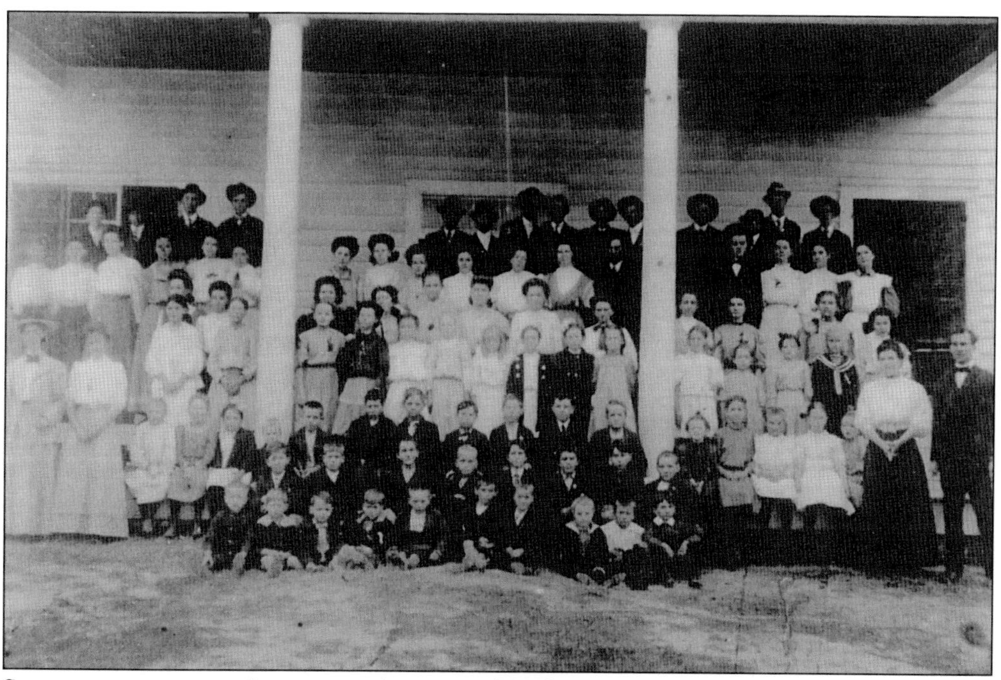

STUDENTS IN FRONT OF LEWISVILLE ACADEMY. (LHS)

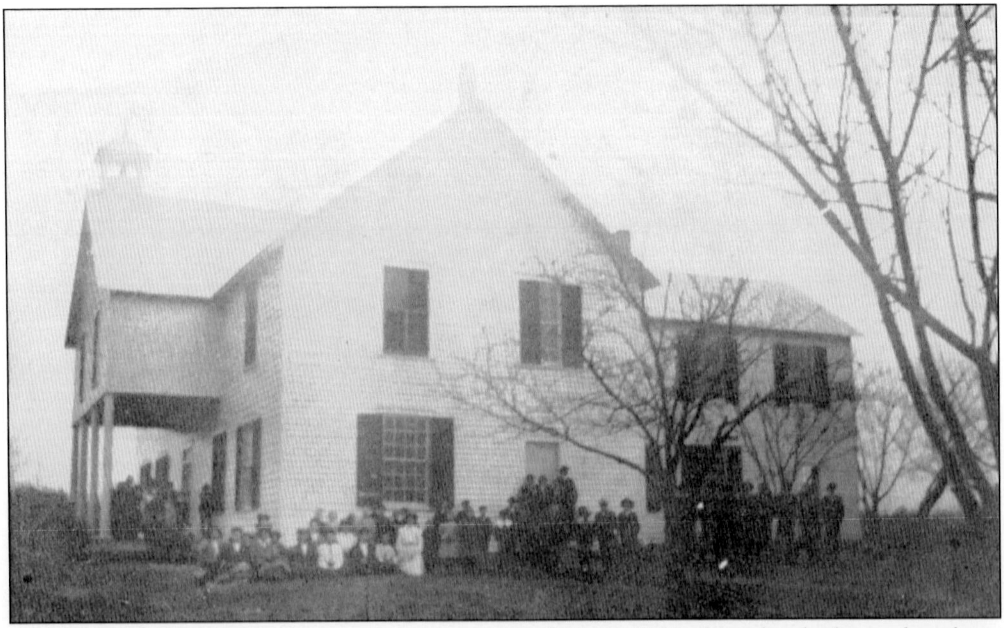

A c. 1906 Photograph of Lewisville Academy. Built in 1901, this school educated students who came from schools with only one room and one teacher in Grapevine, Black's, Warner's, and Lewisville. (LHS)

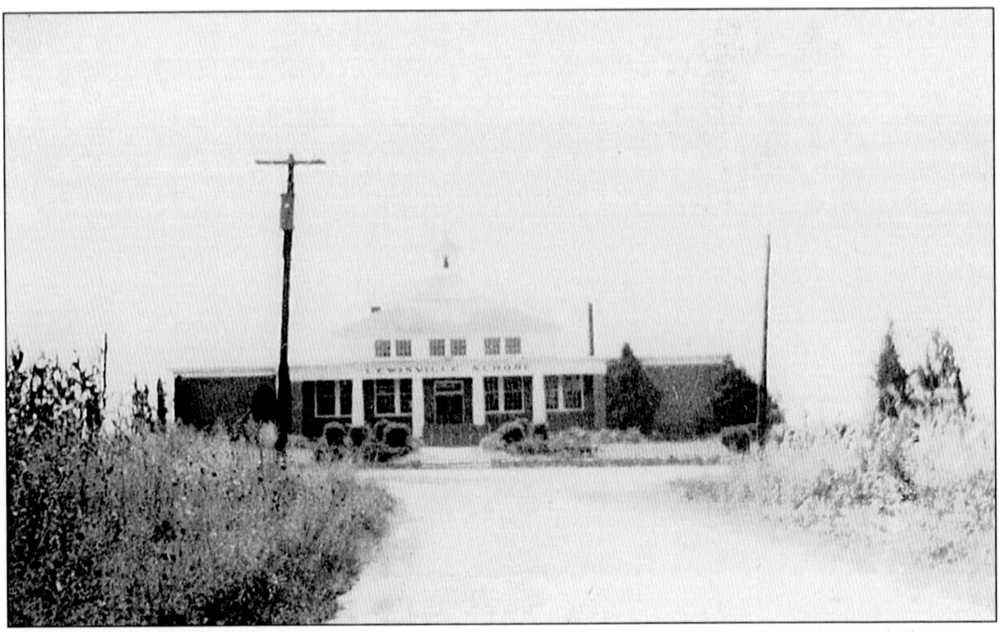

The Second Lewisville School Building, Built in 1923. The school burned down on December 2, 1945. (LHS)

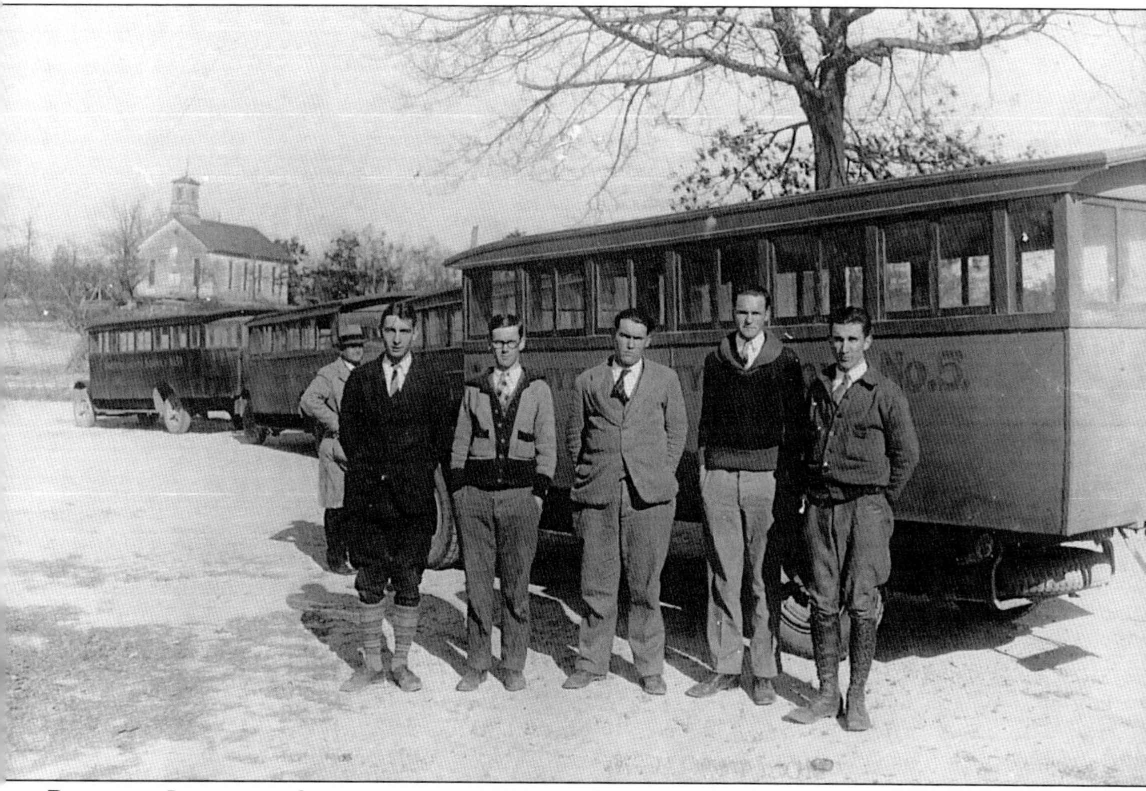

Buses for Lewisville School during 1928–1929. Principal G.D. Shore is in the overcoat (visible in the rear). The bus drivers, from left to right, are as follows: A.C. Mock, Herman Landreth, Bruce Harbin, Porter Reynolds, and Andrew Harper. Lewisville Baptist Church is in background. (LHS)

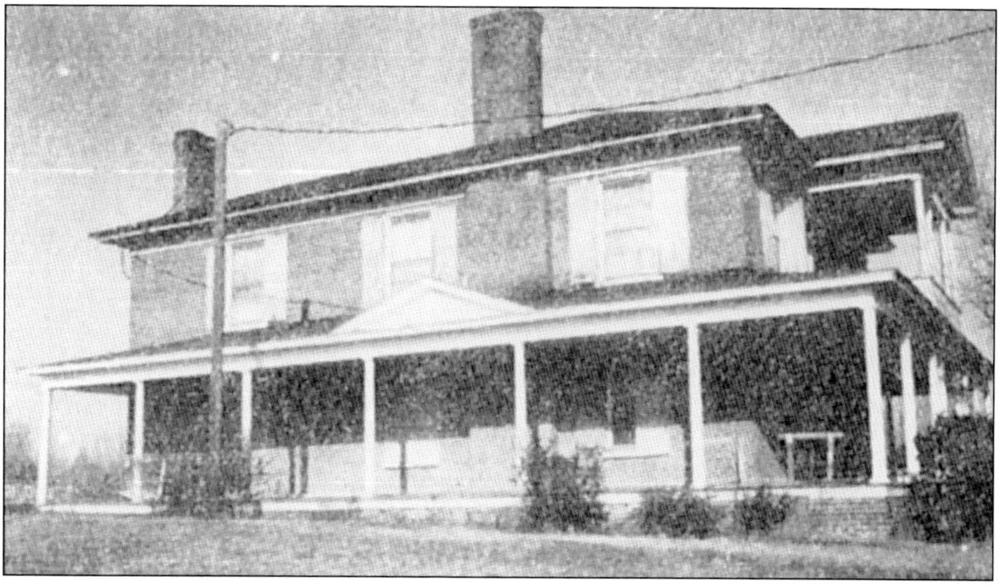

The 1860 Home Built by Lewis Case Lagenauer, Founder of Lewisville. It still stands majestically in the center of Lewisville. (LHS)

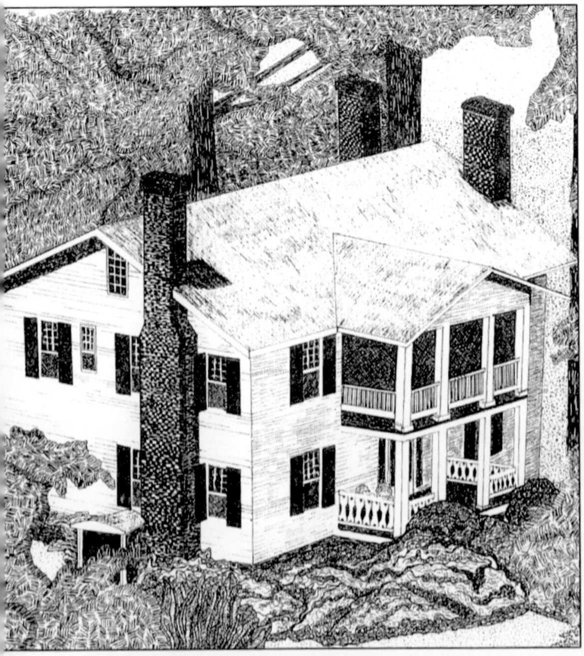

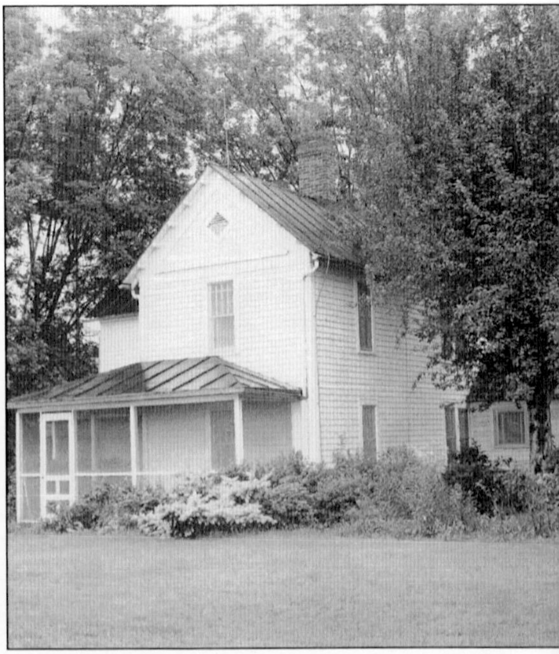

Left: **HILLTOP HOUSE.** Located west of the town of Lewisville, the Hilltop House is situated at the intersection of Conrad and Grapevine Roads. This house was built during 1856–1857 by Augustus Eugene Conrad on land he inherited from his grandfather, "River John" Conrad. This land also witnessed the launch of Gen. George Stoneman's North Carolina raid. (LHS)
Right: **THE LAMB ARCHIBALD REYNOLDS HOUSE, BUILT IN 1885.** This house is still a beautiful structure in Lewisville. (LHS)

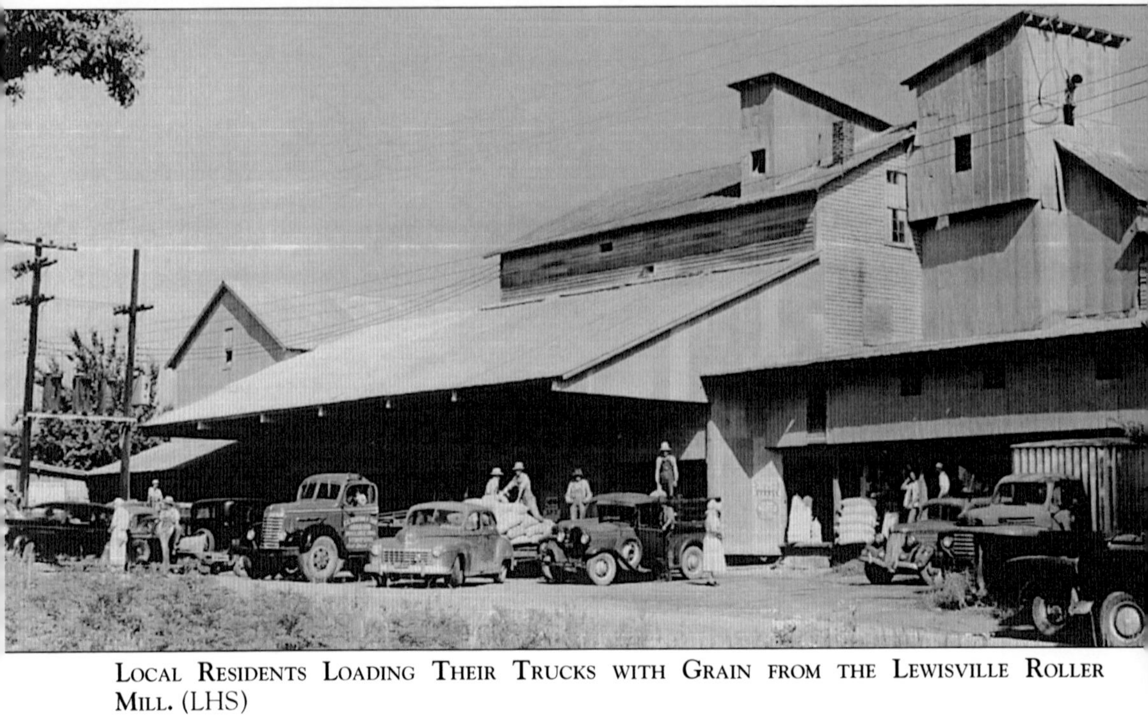

LOCAL RESIDENTS LOADING THEIR TRUCKS WITH GRAIN FROM THE LEWISVILLE ROLLER MILL. (LHS)

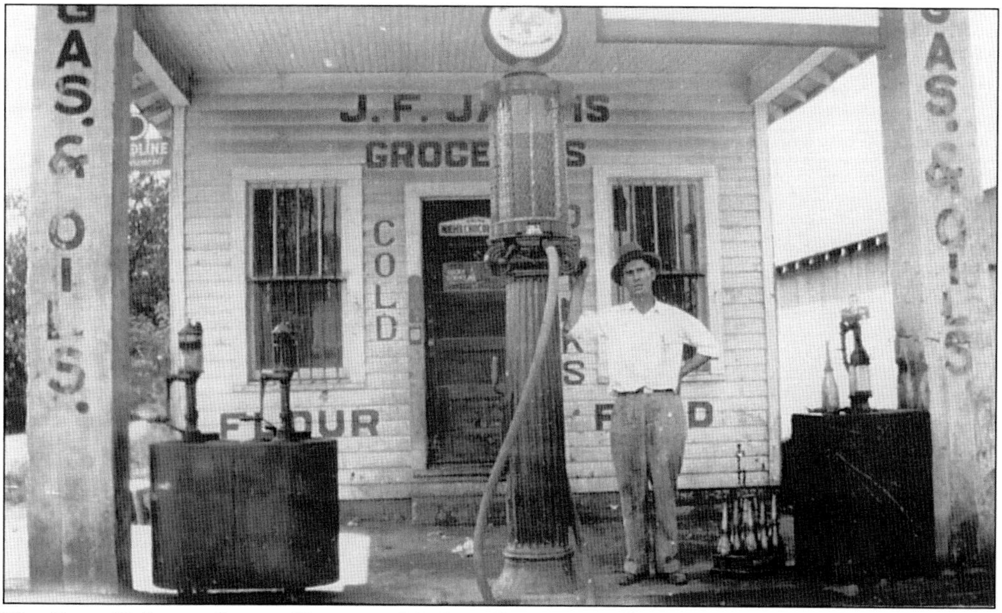

THE JOHN F. JARVIS STORE, BUILT IN 1912 ON LEWISVILLE-CLEMMONS ROAD. A warm pot-belly stove and a game of checkers were always guaranteed. (FJM)

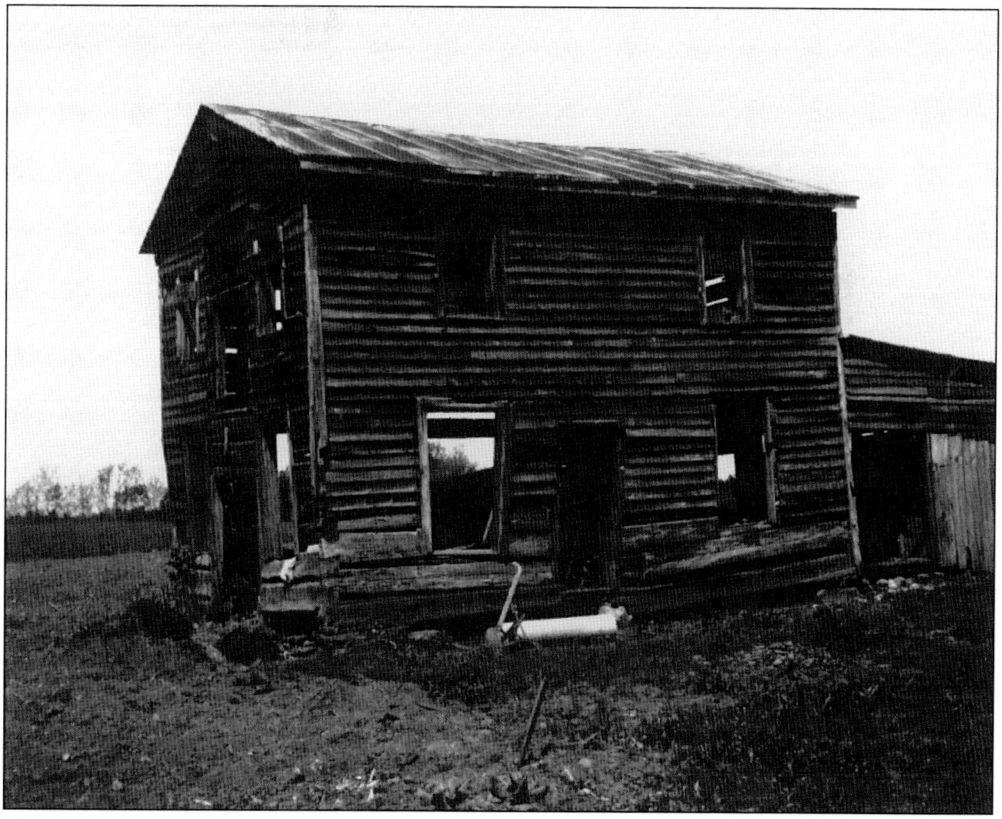

HOME OF TENNISON JARVIS AND MARY JANE BOYER JARVIS. This house was built in 1850 on Lewisville-Clemmons Road and torn down in 1958. (FJM)

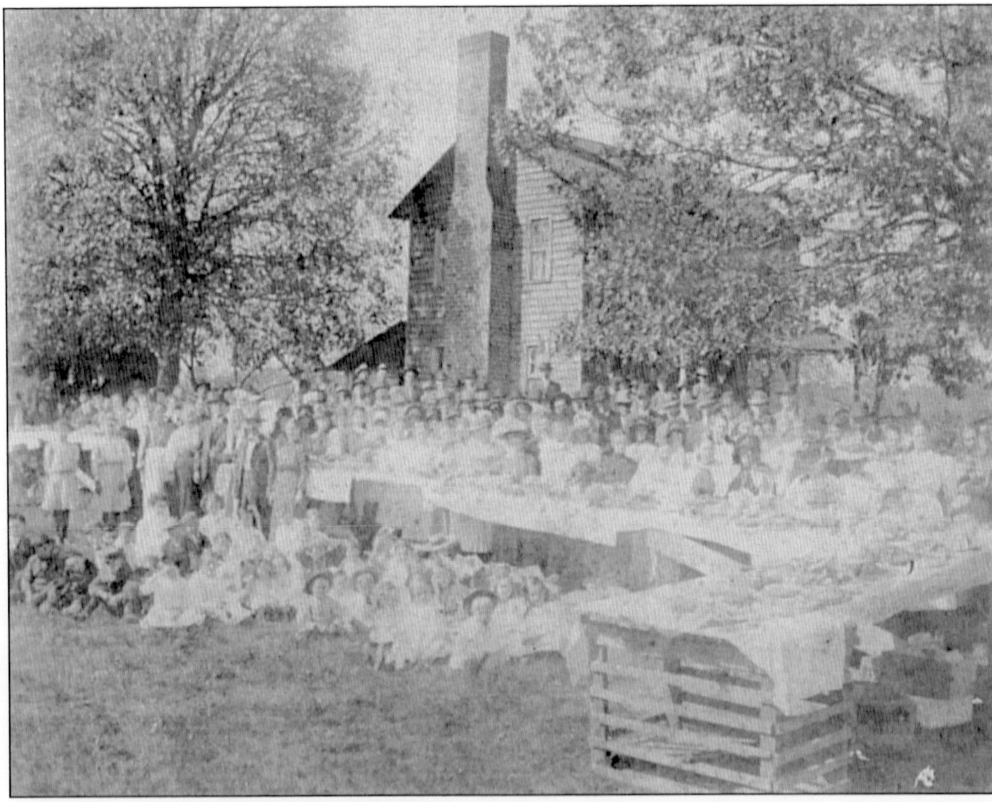

THE JARVIS FAMILY REUNION IN 1900 AT THE JAMES EDWARD JARVIS HOME. This home was once located on Lewisville-Clemmons Road. (FJM)

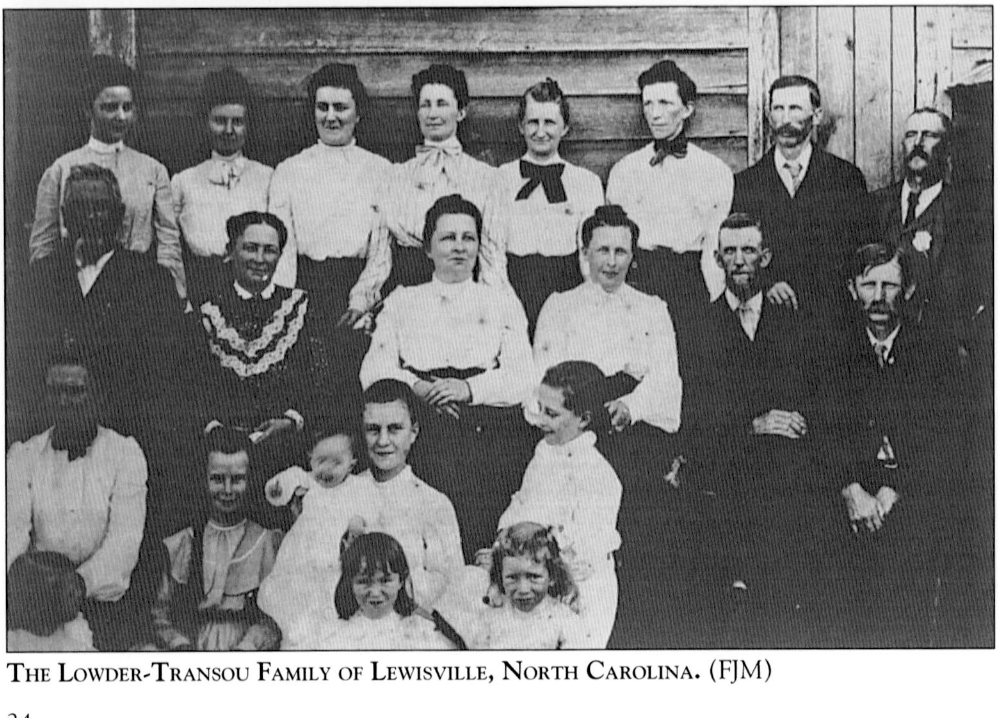

THE LOWDER-TRANSOU FAMILY OF LEWISVILLE, NORTH CAROLINA. (FJM)

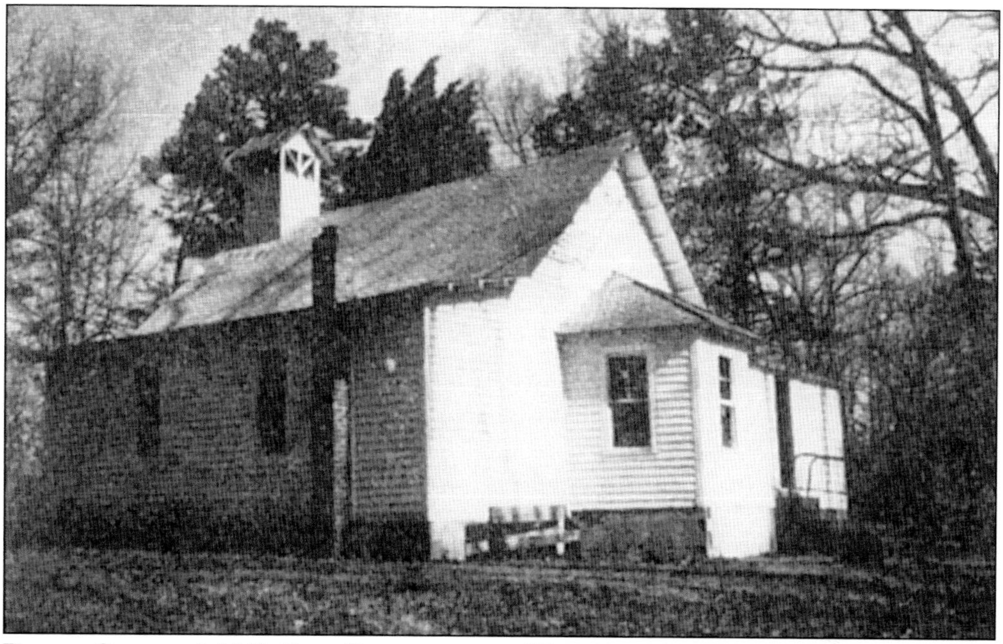

DOUBLE SPRINGS A.M.E. ZION CHURCH IN THE WEST BEND VICINITY. Tradition says it was organized by slaves from nearby Williams Plantation. (FF)

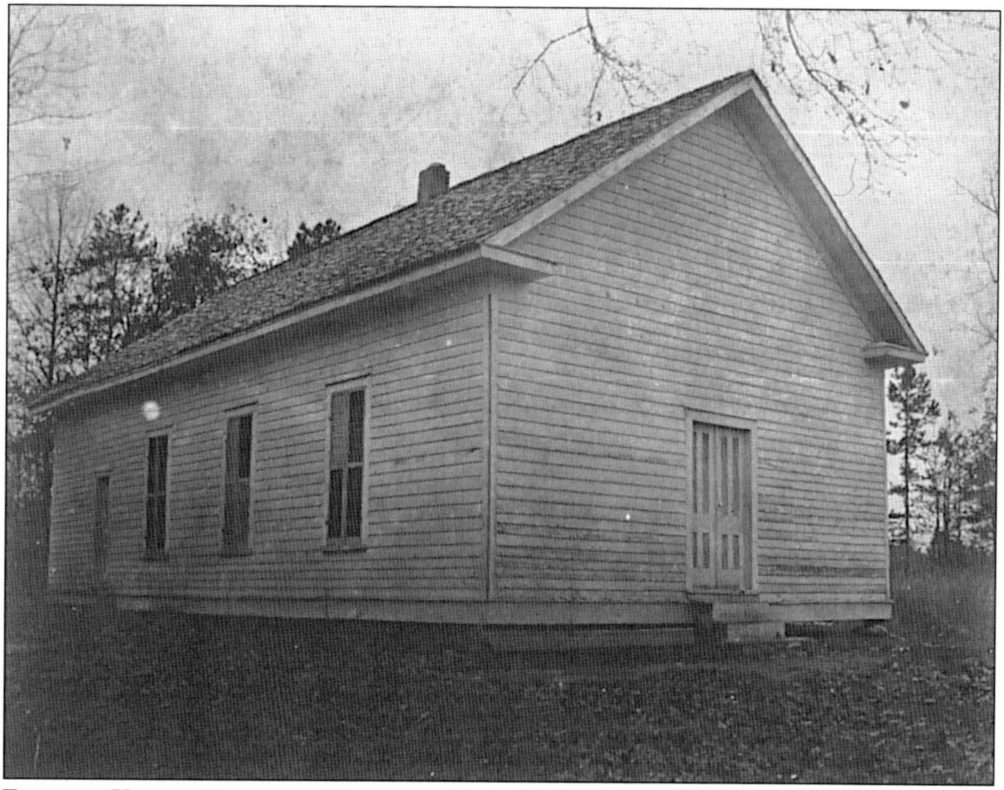

EARLIEST KNOWN PHOTO OF HARMONY GROVE METHODIST CHURCH, BUILT IN 1887 ON LEWISVILLE-CLEMMONS ROAD. A new church has recently been built in its place. (FJM)

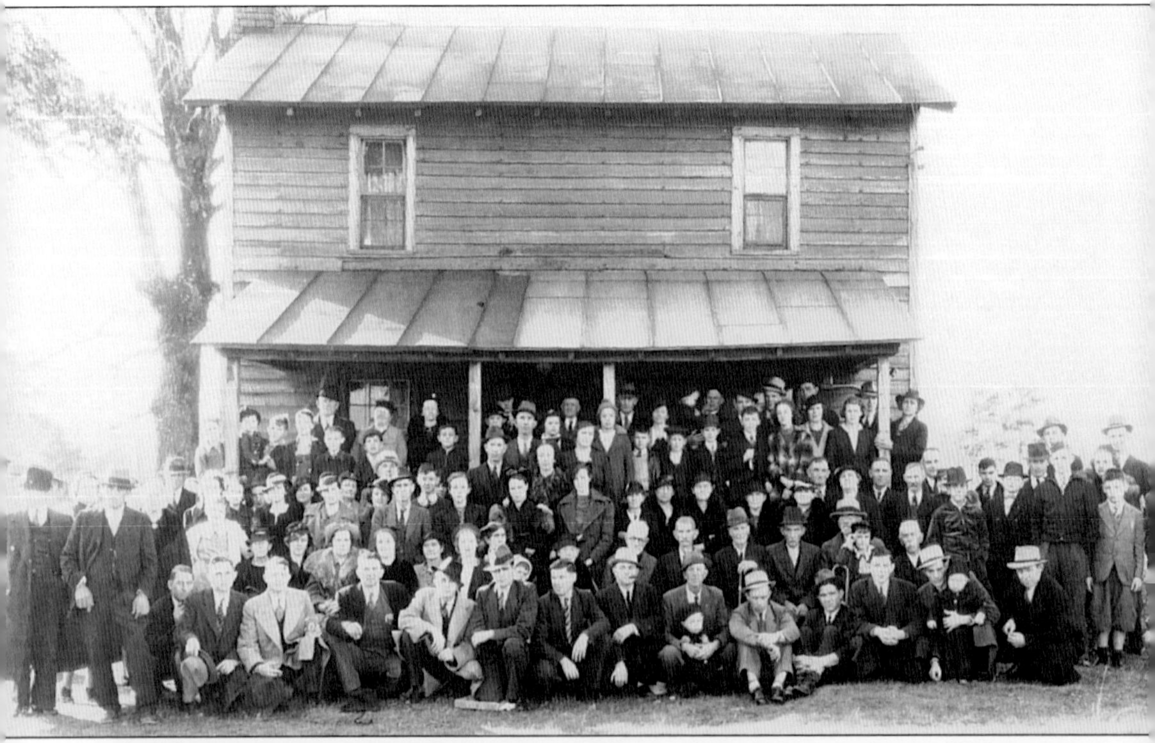

THE HARPER-JARVIS FAMILY REUNION, C. 1935, AT JAMES EDWARD JARVIS HOMEPLACE IN LEWISVILLE. (FJM)

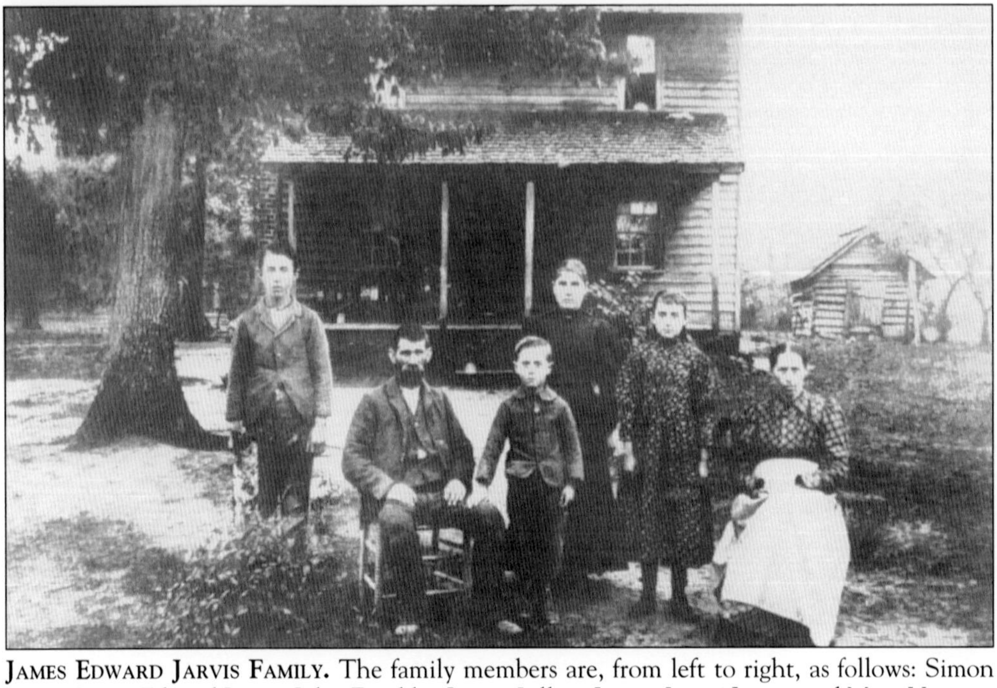

JAMES EDWARD JARVIS FAMILY. The family members are, from left to right, as follows: Simon Jarvis, James Edward Jarvis, John Franklin Jarvis, Lillian Jarvis, Laura Jarvis, and Mary Victoria Harper Jarvis. (FJM)

Three

Pfafftown

Methodism and Campellism

Quietly nestled in the Yadkin Valley on the western edge of the historic Wachovia tract is a little community called Pfafftown. This settlement was founded over 200 years ago by Peter Pfaff of Kaiserlauten. Upon his arrival to America in 1749, he settled his family in Pennsylvania. Then, with his Moravian brethren, Peter relocated to North Carolina, which was the "new land" of the Wachovia tract. Pfaff remained at his Friedberg farm until 1786, and then moved his family to the community that soon became known as Pfafftown. Some prominent family names of this small community were Flynt, Transou, Hauser, Pfaff, Goslen, and Miller.

There were several other religious founders in Pfafftown. Doub's Methodist Church, founded by Rev. John Doub (1743–1814) and his spouse, Mary Eve Spainhower Doub (1755–1835), is located in what was referred to as Doub's Chapel community. Another pioneer evangelist, Virgil Angelo Wilson (1834–1905), came to this small community in the 1860s. He founded the present-day Pfafftown Christian Church, which is located on Transou Road.

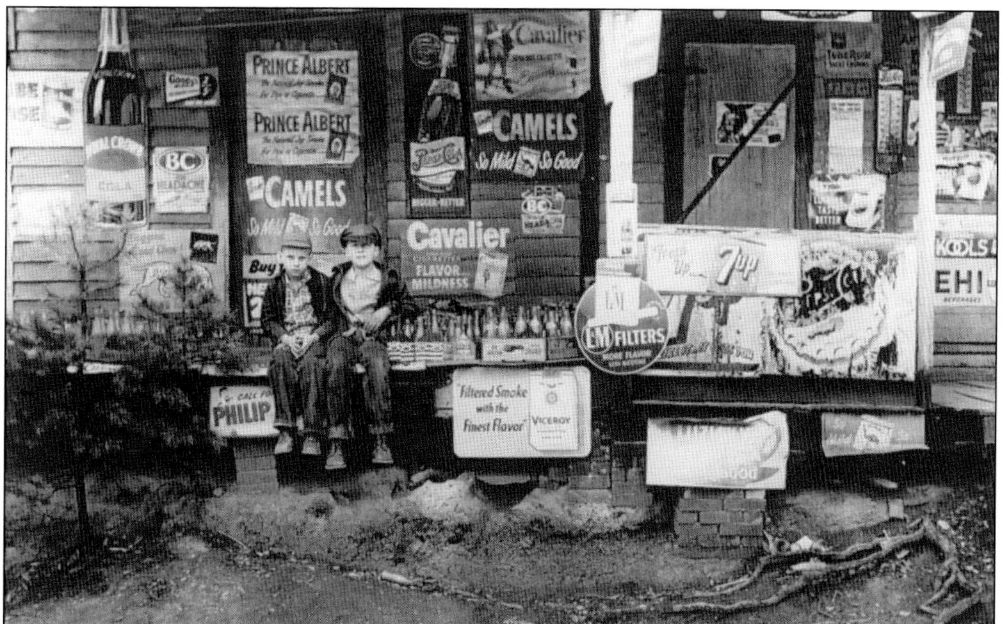

E.G. DAVIS STORE ON OLD 421-YADKINVILLE HIGHWAY. The store is still standing, but is no longer in use. (FCL)

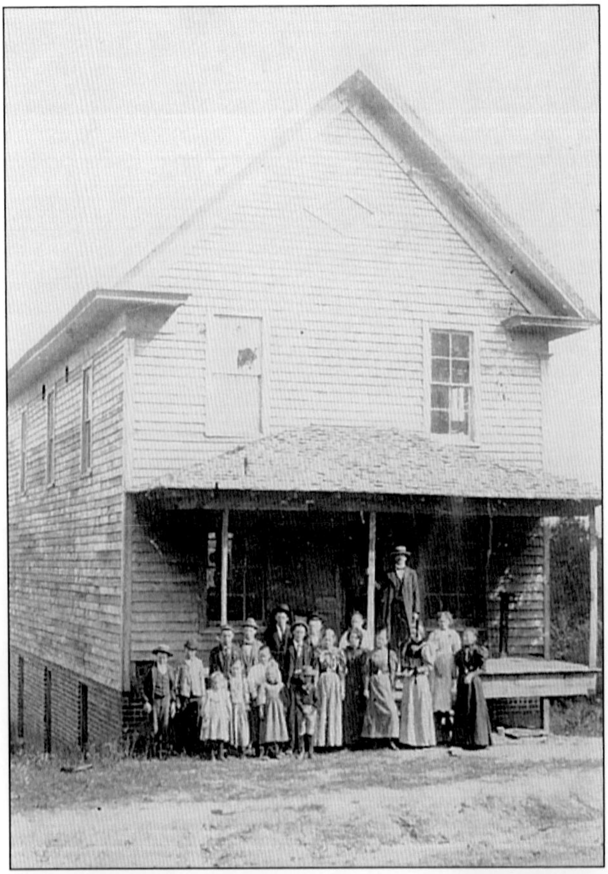

THE LABOR EXCHANGE SCHOOL, BUILT ON TRANSOU ROAD AND ORGANIZED IN 1900. The school's purpose was to provide a satisfactory exchange of labor and the products of labor within the community. It is presently being used by the Boy Scouts.

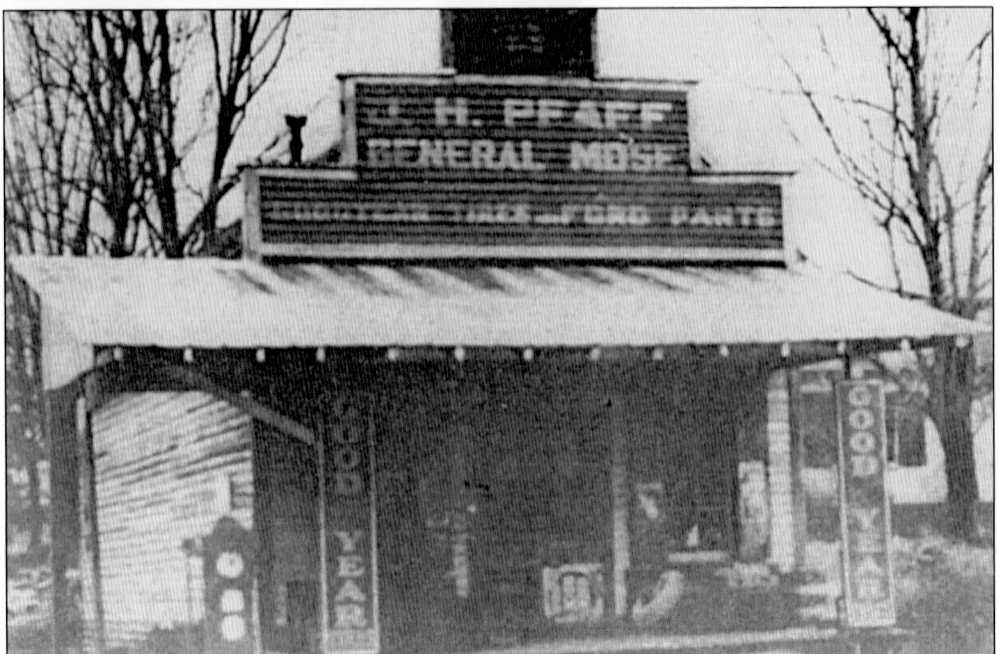

THE PFAFFTOWN CROSSROADS STORE. John Henry Pfaff was its longtime proprietor. (SIW)

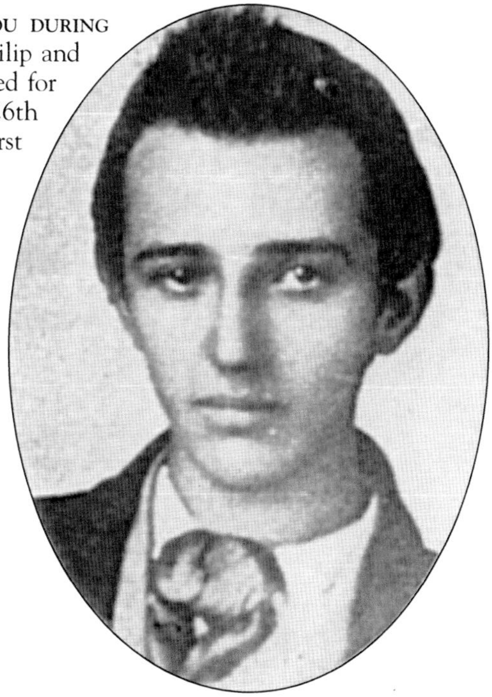

A Photograph of Julius Abraham Transou during His Early Years. He was born *c.* 1830 to Philip and Mary Stoltz Transou. At age 30, he volunteered for Confederate service and enrolled in N.C. 26th Regiment in March 1862. He was also the first recruit of the Salem band of musicians. (SIW)

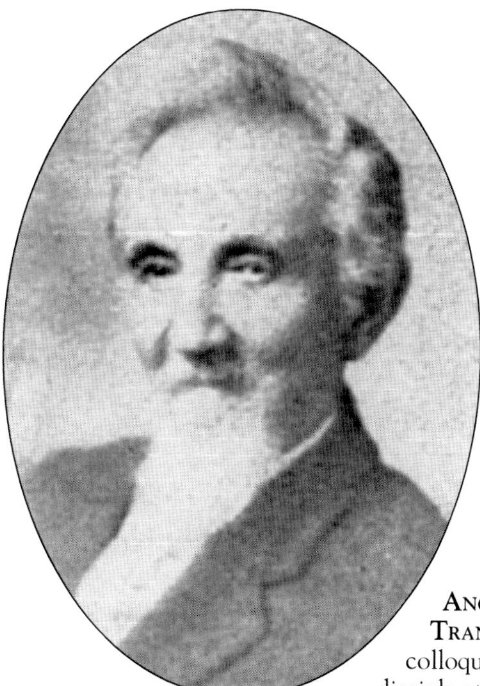

Another Photograph of Julius Abraham Transou, during His Late Years. He was known colloquially as "Uncle Ule." He was also the first resident disciple at Pfafftown. (SIW)

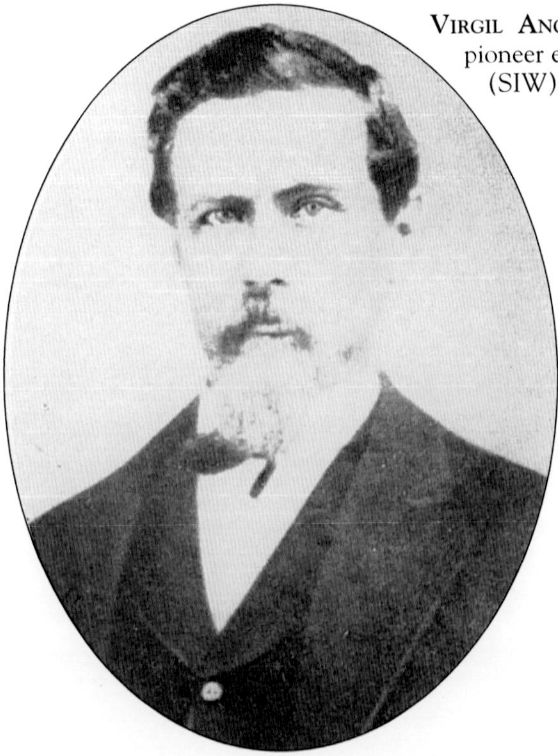

Virgil Angelo Wilson (1834–1905). He was a pioneer evangelist at Pfafftown Christian Church. (SIW)

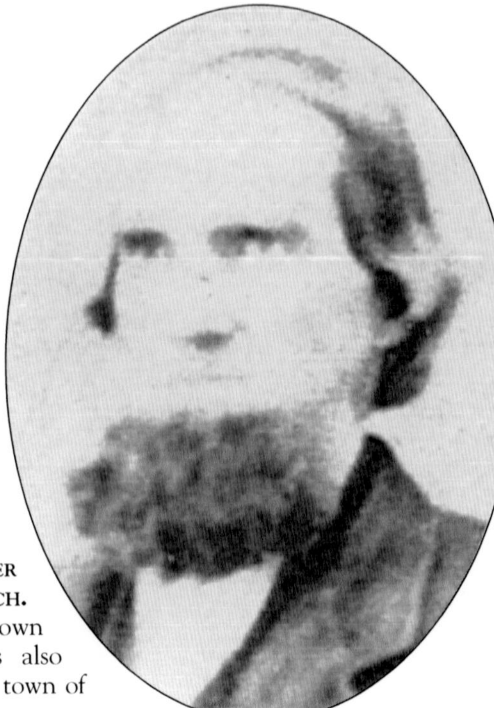

Solomon Augustine Miller, Pioneer Deacon of Pfafftown Christian Church. In addition to being active in the Pfafftown community, Solomon and his son Julius also strongly participated in shaping the railroad town of nearby Rural Hall. (SIW)

JOHN A. STYERS, PIONEER DEACON OF PFAFFTOWN CHRISTIAN CHURCH. (SIW)

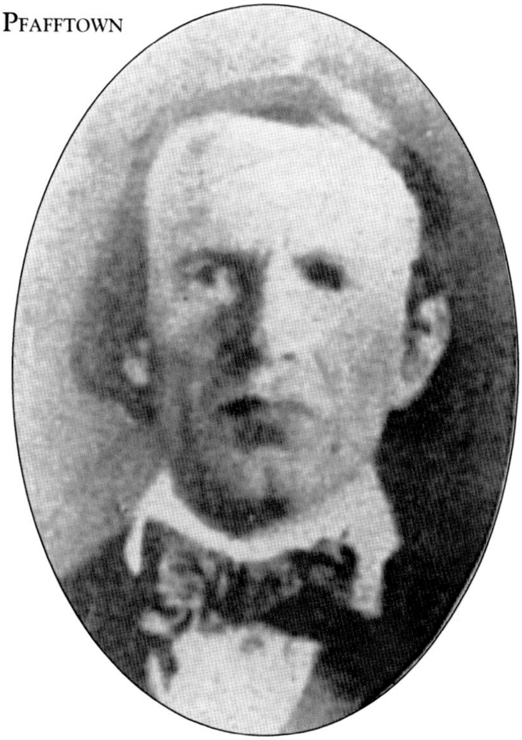

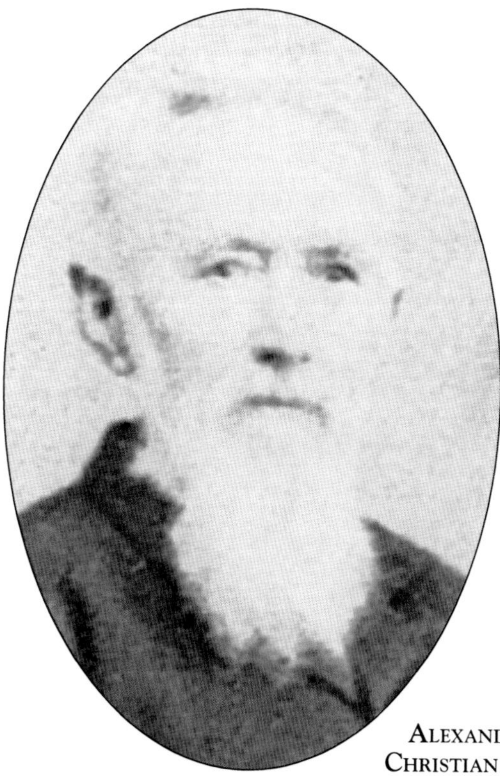

ALEXANDER TRANSOU, PIONEER DEACON OF PFAFFTOWN CHRISTIAN CHURCH. (SIW)

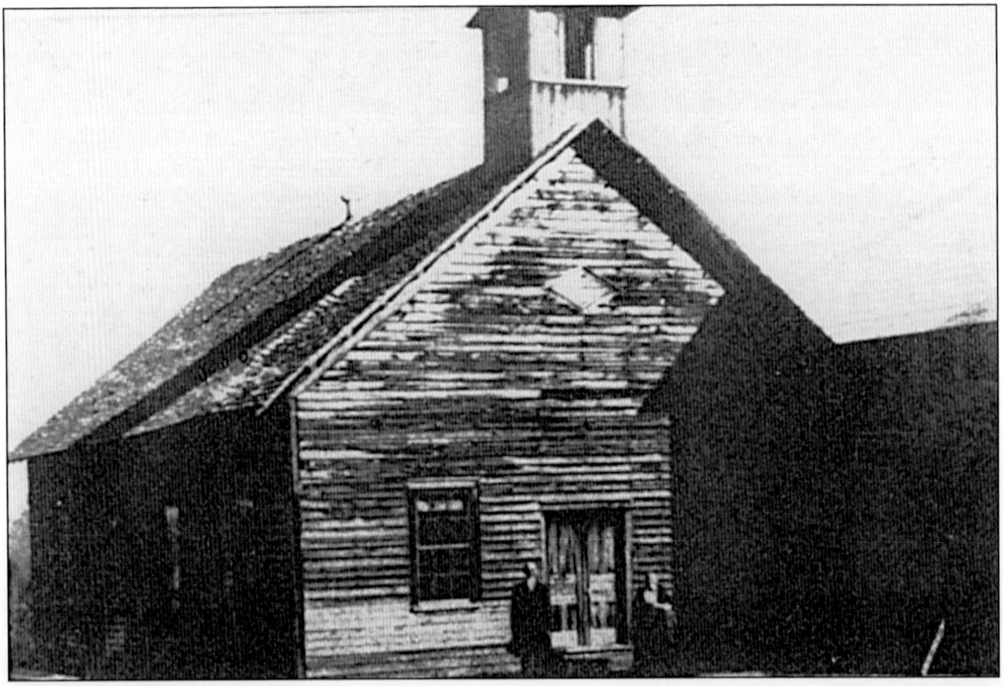

ORIGINAL PFAFFTOWN CHRISTIAN CHURCH, AS SEEN IN 1870. Pictured are Julius Abraham Transou and Mrs. Virgil Angelo Wilson. (SIW)

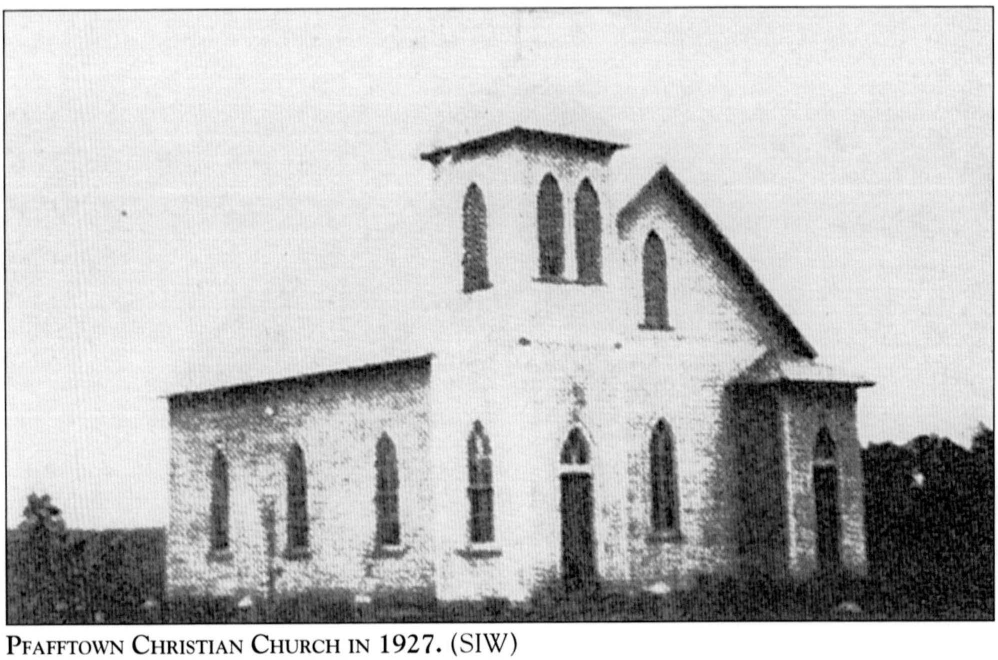

PFAFFTOWN CHRISTIAN CHURCH IN 1927. (SIW)

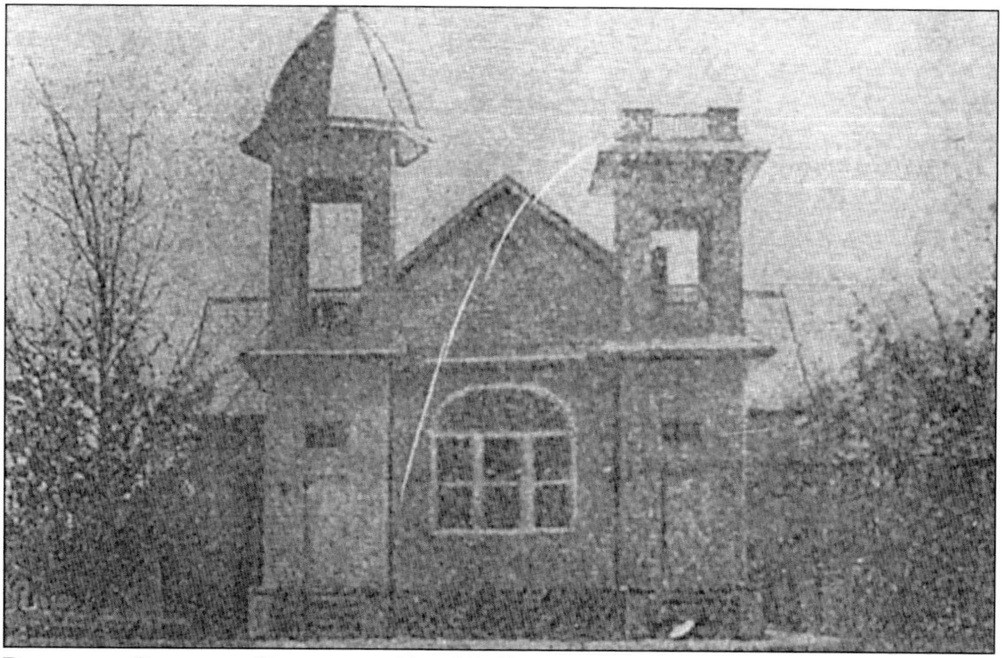

PFAFFTOWN CHRISTIAN CHURCH IN 1939. (SIW)

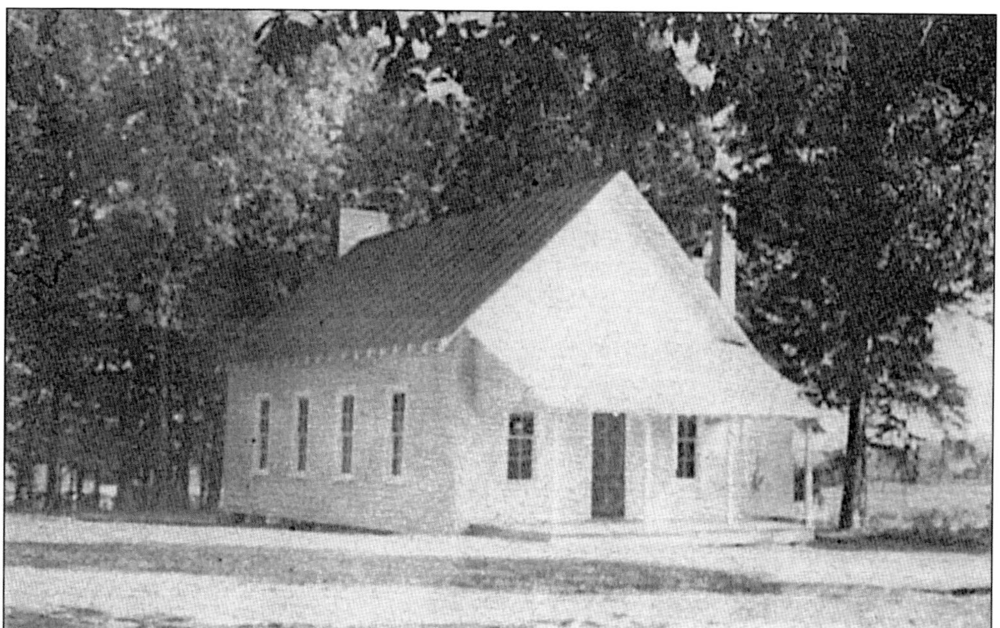

PFAFFTOWN CHRISTIAN CHURCH FELLOWSHIP HALL. (SIW)

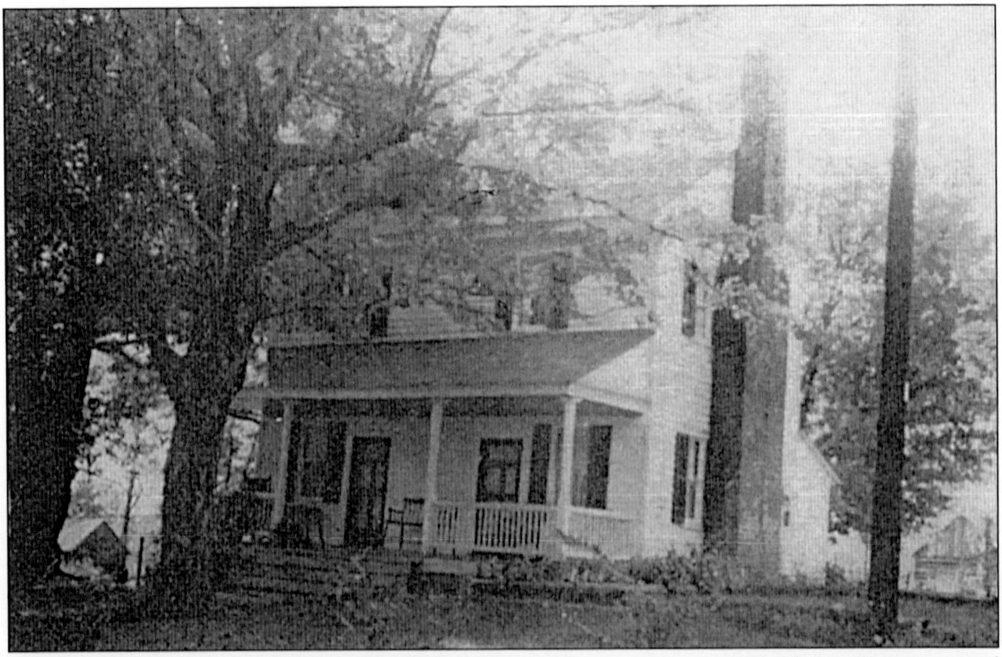

Former Residence of Alexander Transou. He was the son of Philip Transou and Mary Stoltz Transou. When the Pfafftown post office opened in 1888, it was placed in his store. (SIW)

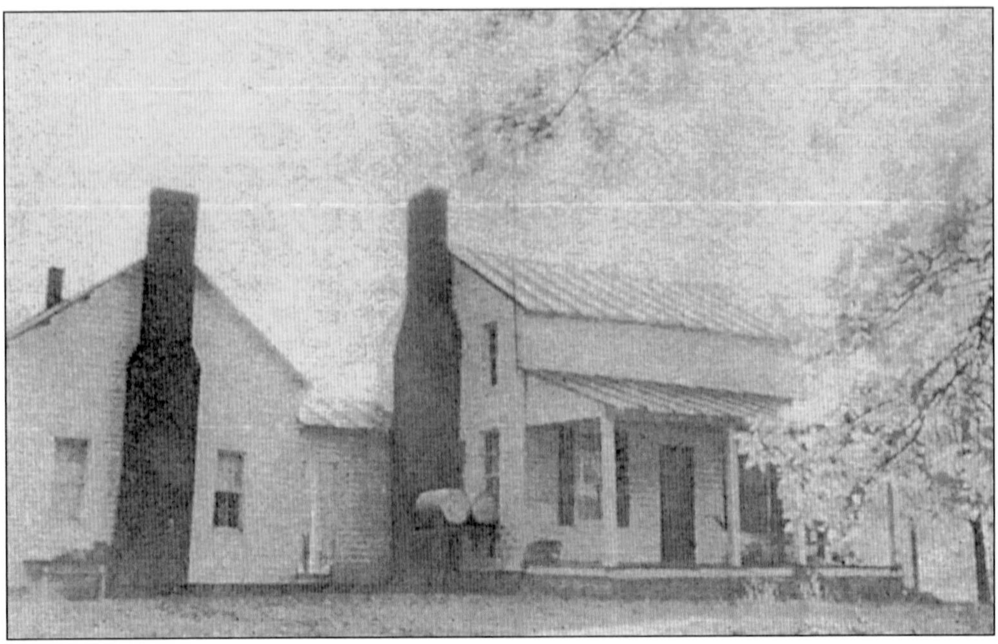

Former Residence of Solomon Augustine Miller. (SIW)

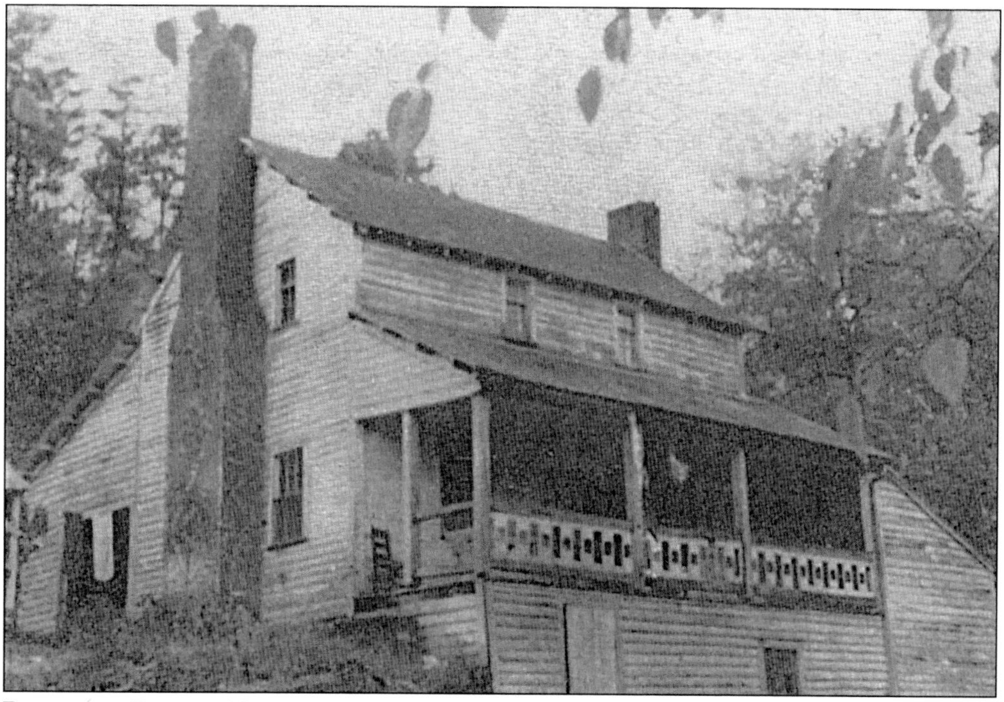

Pfafftown Pioneer Home of Jesse Styers and Mary K. Pfaff, Who Owned the Mill on Muddy Creek. He provided the heart-pine lumber in 1869 for the initial construction of the Pfafftown Christian Church. (SIW)

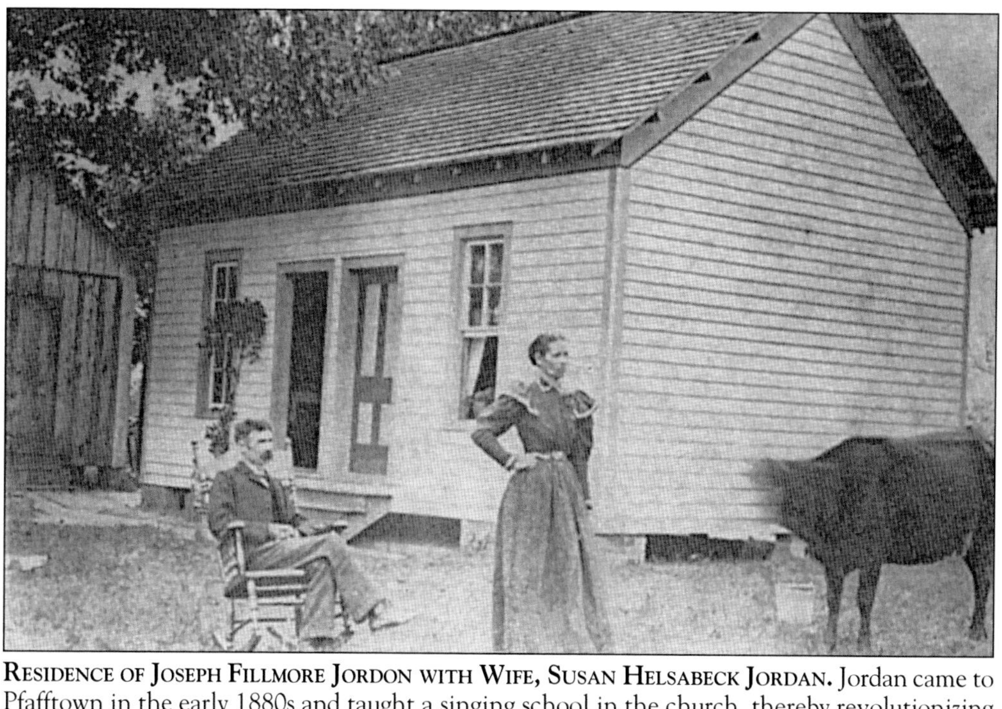

Residence of Joseph Fillmore Jordon with Wife, Susan Helsabeck Jordan. Jordan came to Pfafftown in the early 1880s and taught a singing school in the church, thereby revolutionizing the method of sight-singing by the congregation. (SIW)

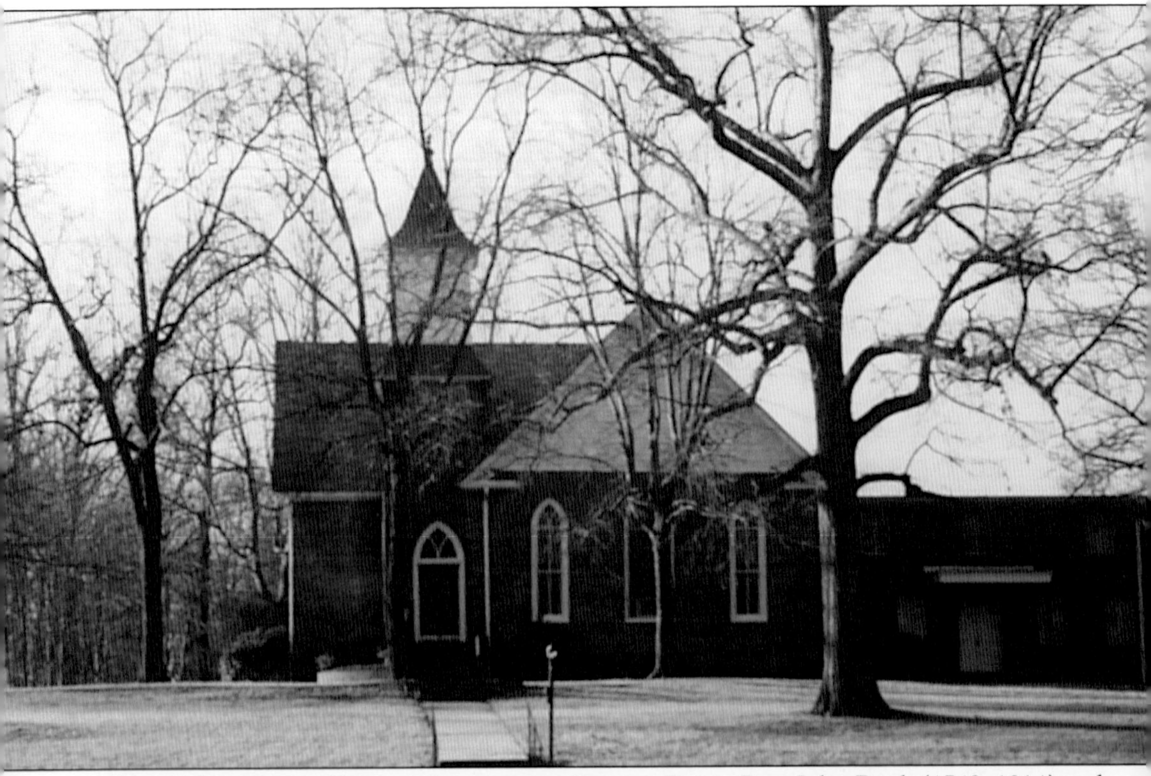

DOUB'S METHODIST CHURCH, LOCATED ON SEWARD ROAD. Rev. John Doub (1743–1814) and Mary Eve Spainhower Doub (1755–1835) founded this church. Born in Germany and baptized Johannes Daub, John immigrated to America in 1773. (CHC)

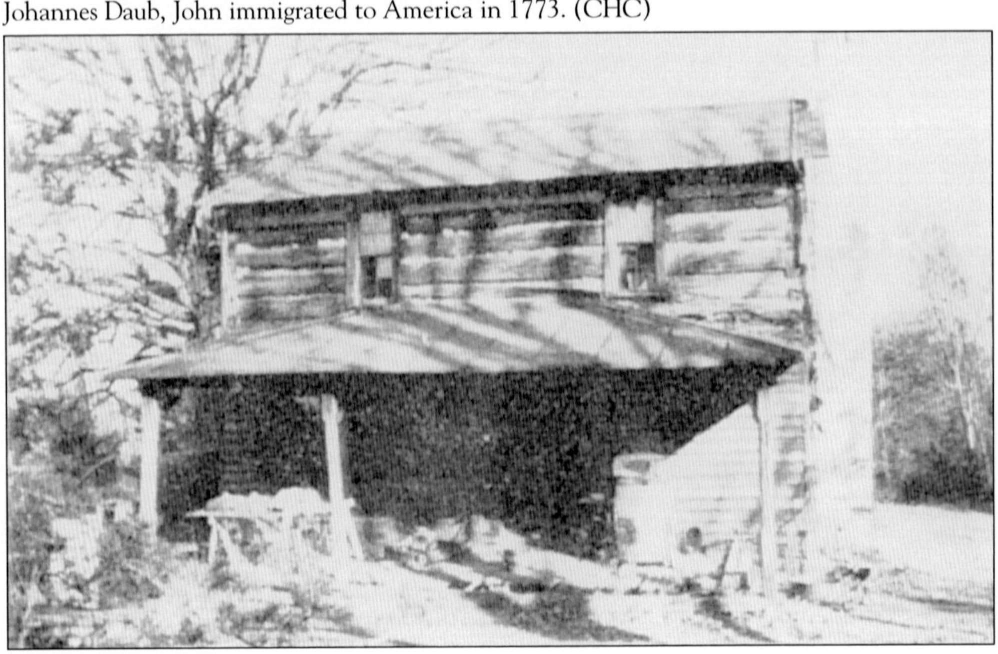

A HOUSE BUILT BY WILLIAM HENRY CONRAD, AN AFRICAN-AMERICAN CARPENTER, IN THE LATE 1800S. The home is located in the Dozier vicinity. (FF)

Four

Rural Hall

Landmark of Colonial Times

Rural Hall's heritage runs deep. Settled in the late 1700s by Lutherans and Methodists, Rural Hall was given its name in 1875, when the first post office was established in Anthony Bitting's homeplace, named "The Hall." This town embraces the idea of community. Pioneers traveled from Maryland and Pennsylvania via the Great Wagon Road to come to Rural Hall. Craftsmen, clergymen, and agriculturists settled their families in the Beaverdam Creek area. Names of the earliest settlers in Rural Hall were Shore (c. 1759), Flynt (c. 1781), Moore (c. 1770s), Shouse (c. 1800s), Mueller (now spelled Miller), Zimmerman (late 1700s), Bitting (late 1700s), Keiger (1778), Bostic, Kiser, Styers, and Stultz. After the completion of the railroad in 1888, two schools opened. Following the opening of the private Hooksville School on Thacker Road, the Rural Hall Colored School (Rosewall School) opened on Pine Street to serve the needs of the African-American community. Many of Rural Hall's descendants still live in the Rural Hall area and attend the churches organized 200 years ago.

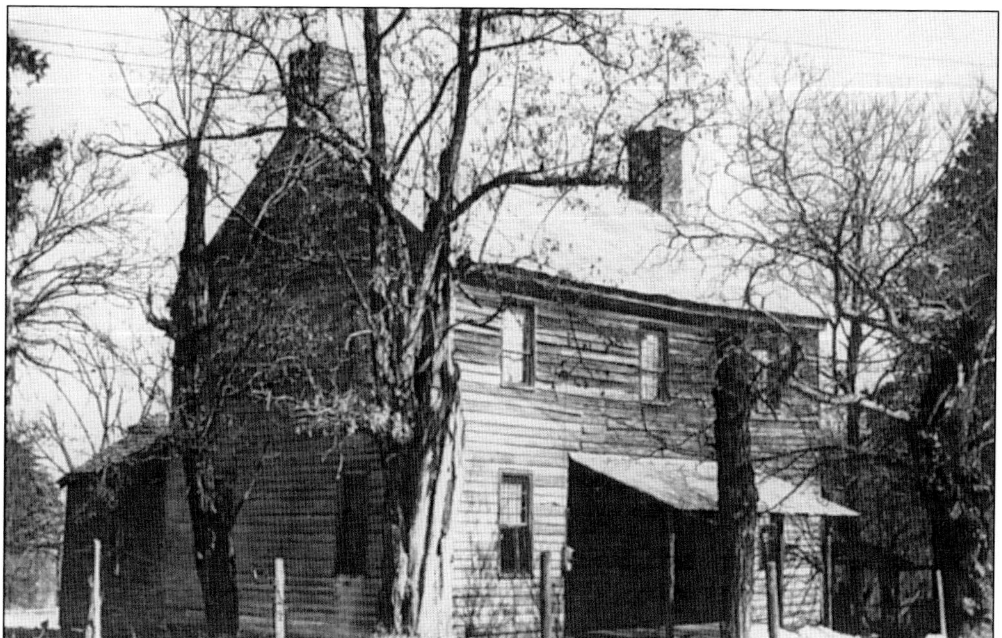

BITTING PLANTATION. The large home was erected by Anthony Bitting *c.* 1835 in the center of his plantation, which once embraced hundreds of acres, covering what is now the town of Rural Hall. The main hall stretched from the front to the back of the house and was wide enough to drive a wagon through. Hence "the Hall" became a popular name for this home and a community gathering place. (FCL)

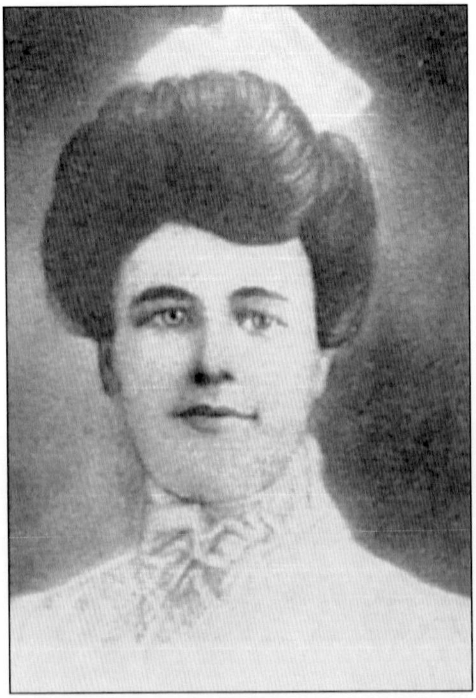

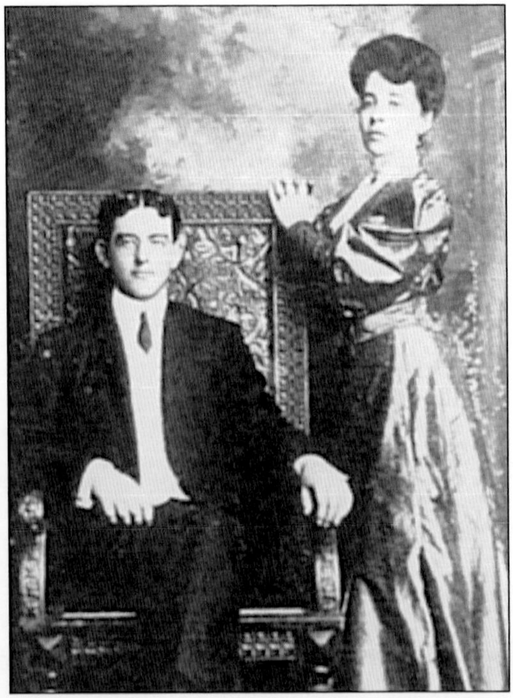

Left: **KATE CLARK (MRS. E.E.) SHORE IN 1904.** E.E. Shore founded the Commercial and Farmers Bank in 1906. (HRH)
Right: **WEDDING PICTURE OF MR. AND MRS. E.A. HELSABECK IN 1905.** Mr. Helsabeck operated the Rural Hall Grocery Store and made deliveries in a horse-drawn wagon. (HRH)

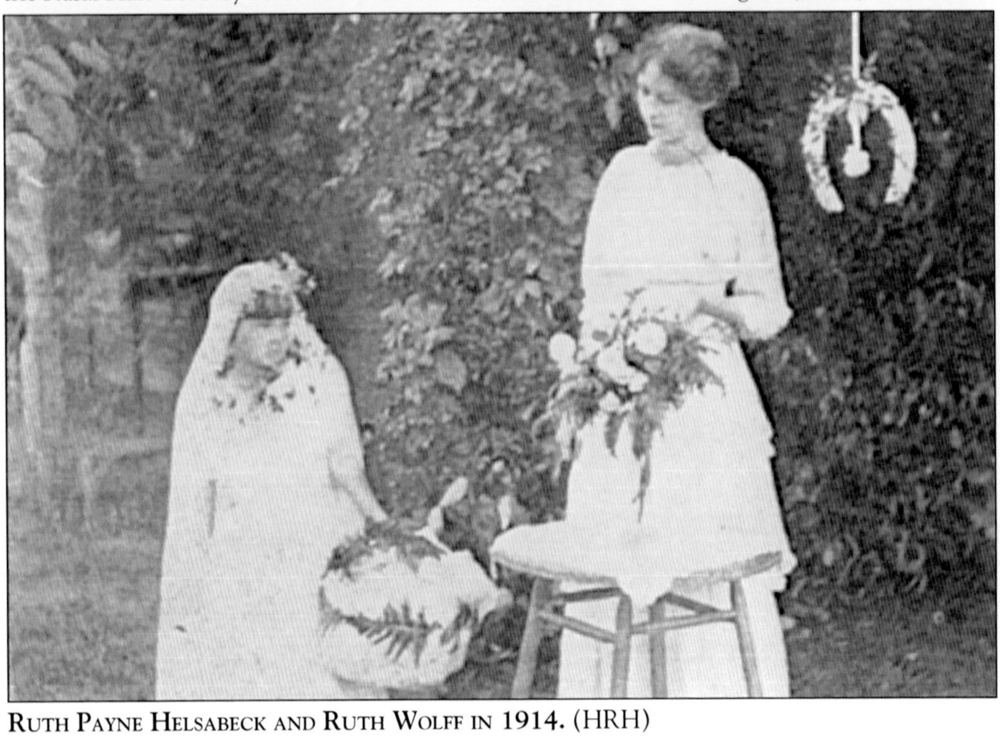

RUTH PAYNE HELSABECK AND RUTH WOLFF IN 1914. (HRH)

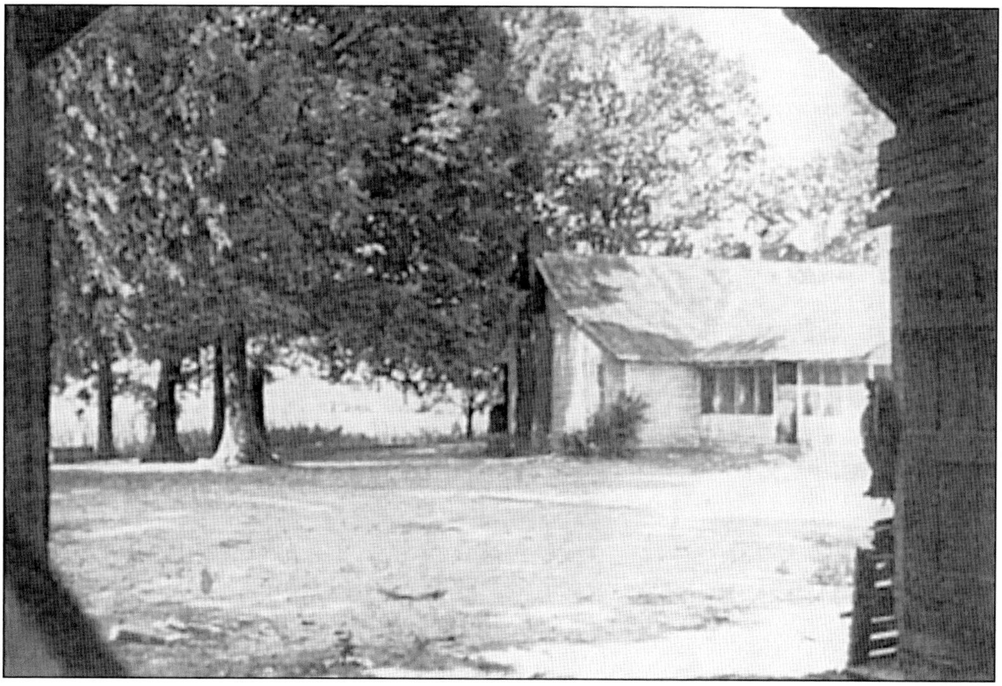

Julius A. Kiger Homeplace. (HRH)

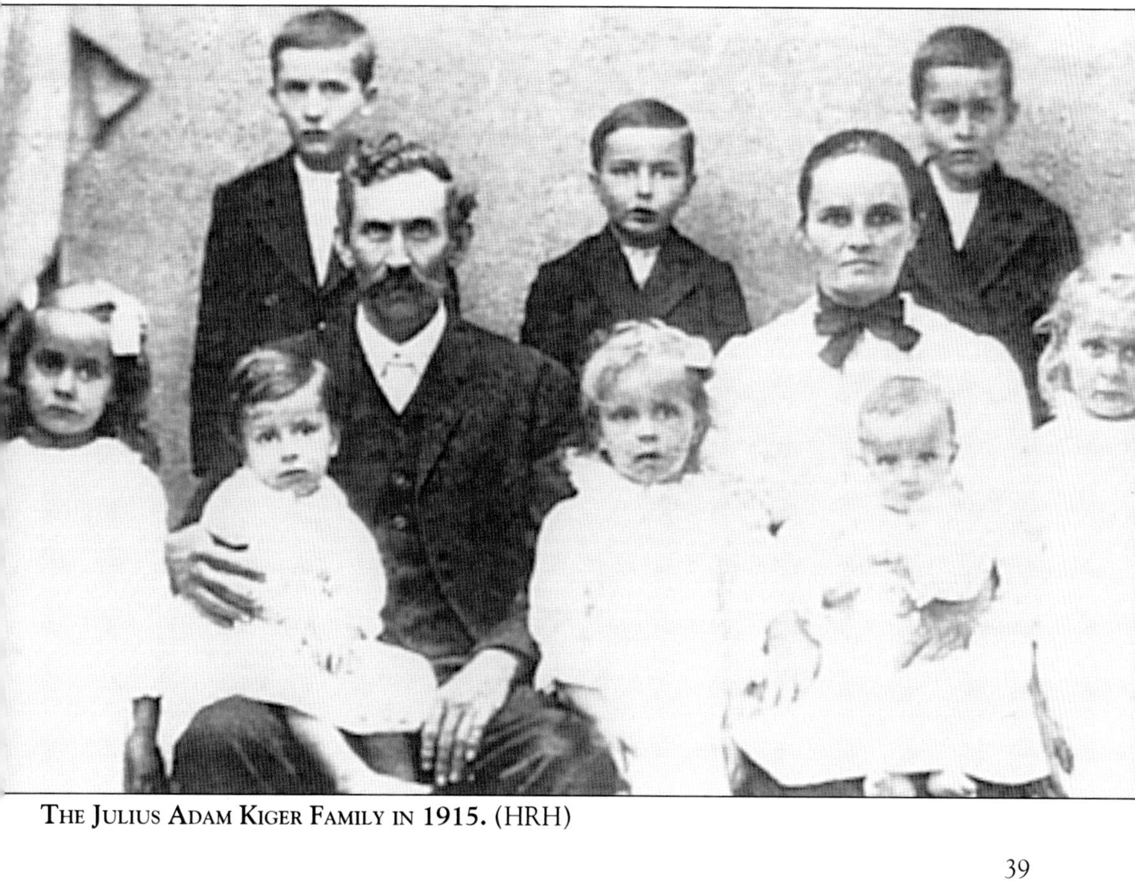

The Julius Adam Kiger Family in 1915. (HRH)

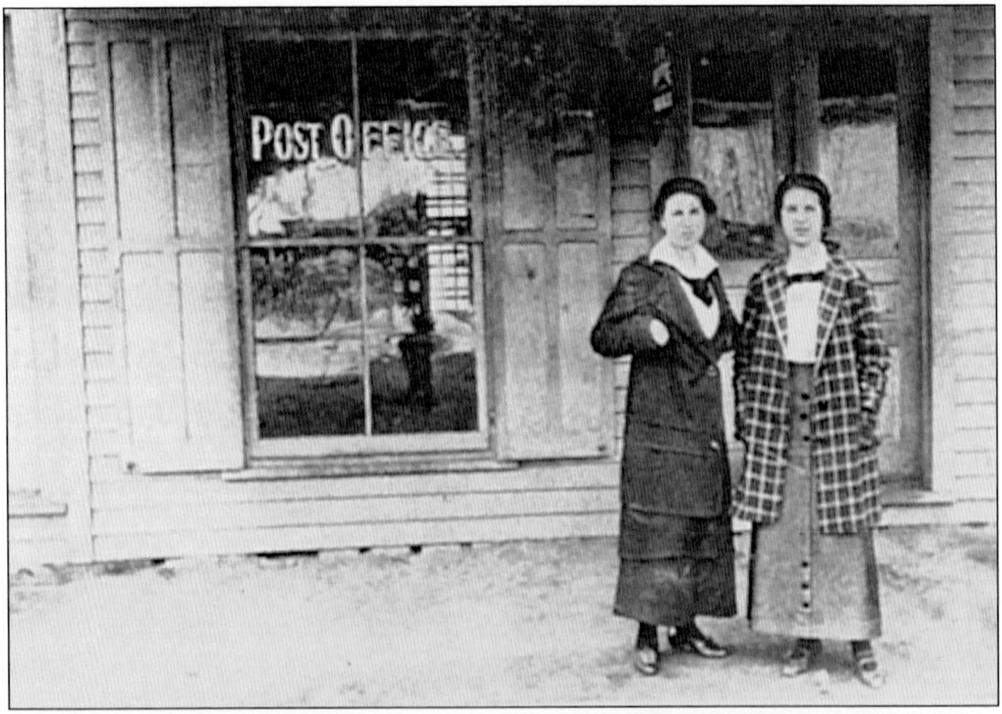

Mrs. Venora Z. Kizer. She was the first appointed postmistress in the first post office building. Standing to the left of Mrs. Kizer is her sister, Stella Zimmerman Scott. (HRH)

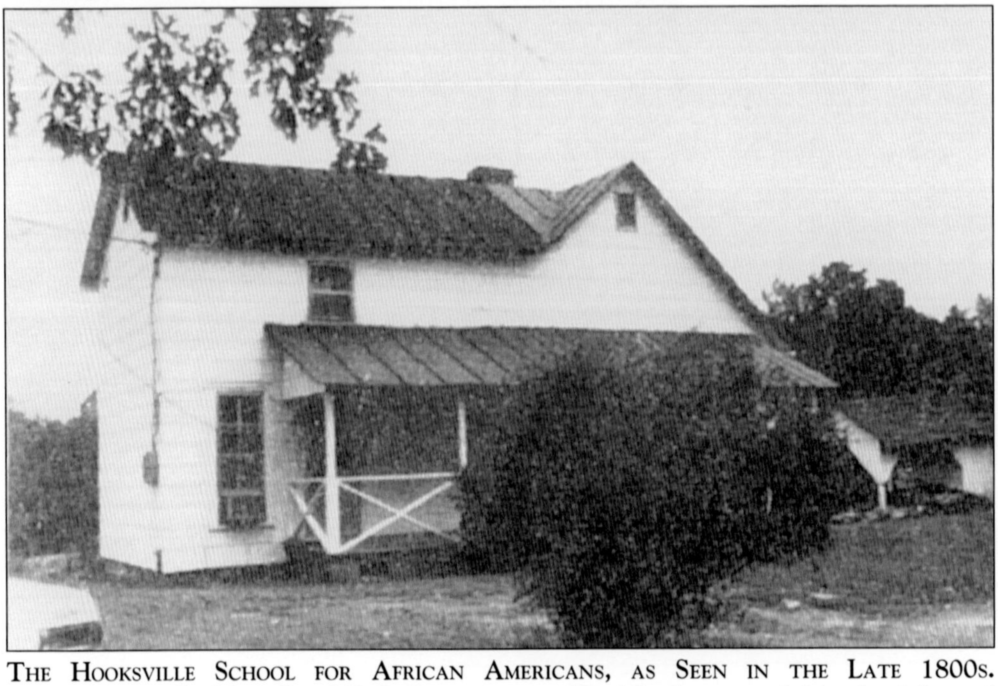

The Hooksville School for African Americans, as Seen in the Late 1800s. The children walked from Rural Hall, Germanton, and Red Bank to attend this school, located in the vicinity of Rural Hall. It is believed that school was held only four months out of the year. (FF)

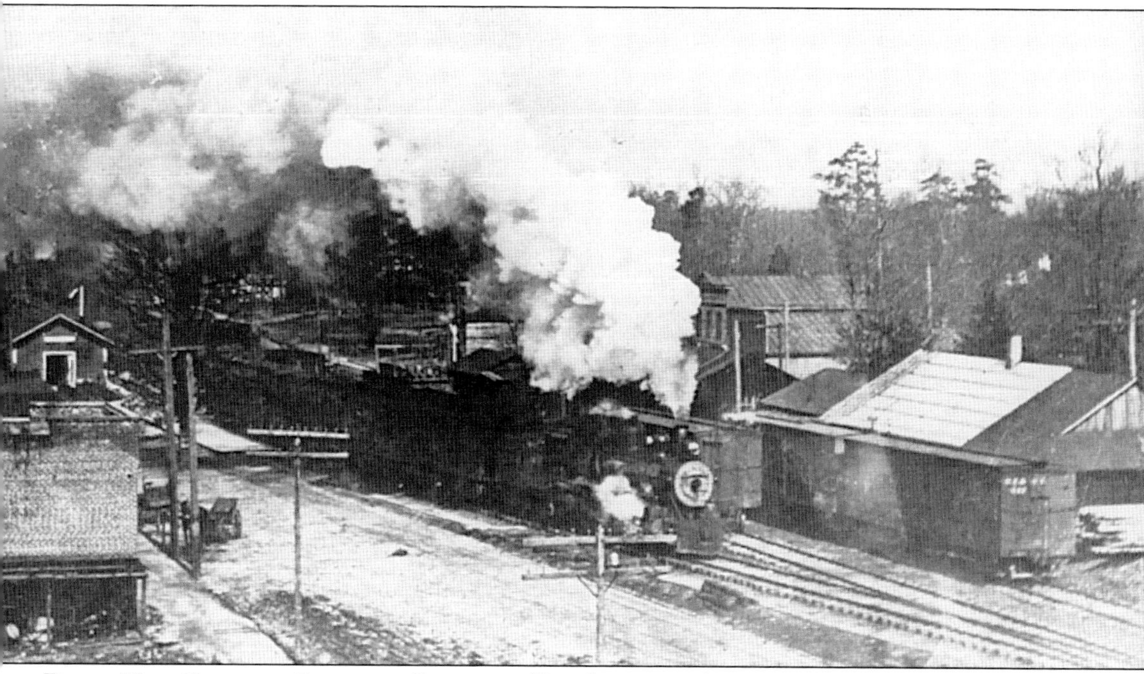

Rural Hall Railroad Stations: Southern (Left) and the Atlantic and Yadkin (Right). The first train came through on June 20, 1888. Later the Atlantic and Yadkin each built its own depot and celebrated their openings April 16–17, 1890. (HRH)

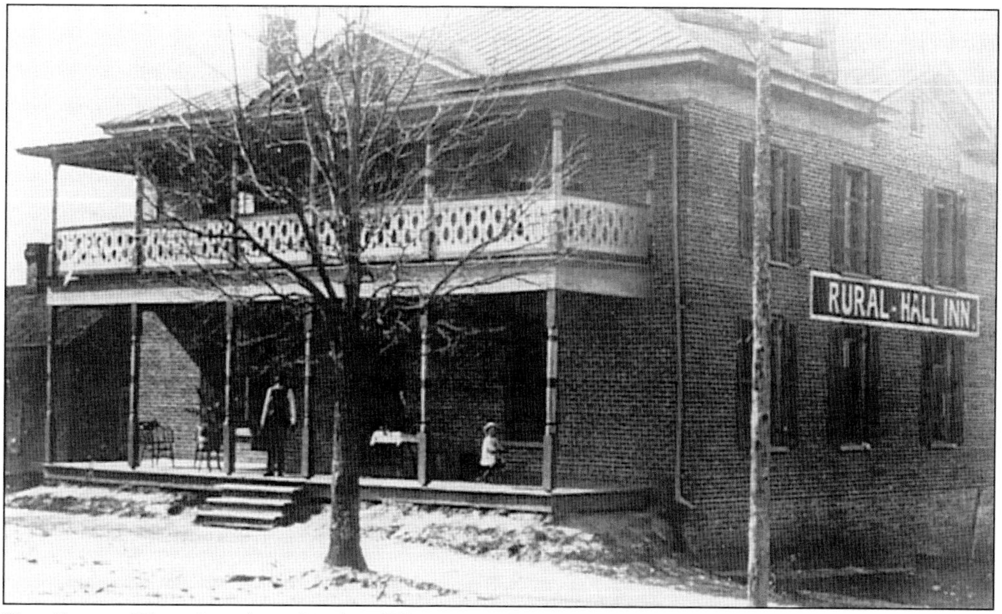

The Rural Hall Inn (c. 1900), a Welcomed Sight to Travelers. It was convenient to the train depot, and a room and a hot meal were only $2 per day. (HRH)

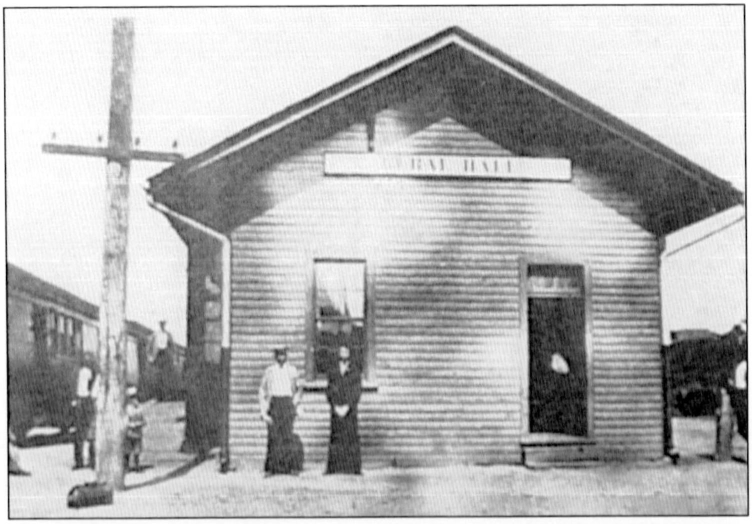

RURAL HALL STATION HOUSE. (HRH)

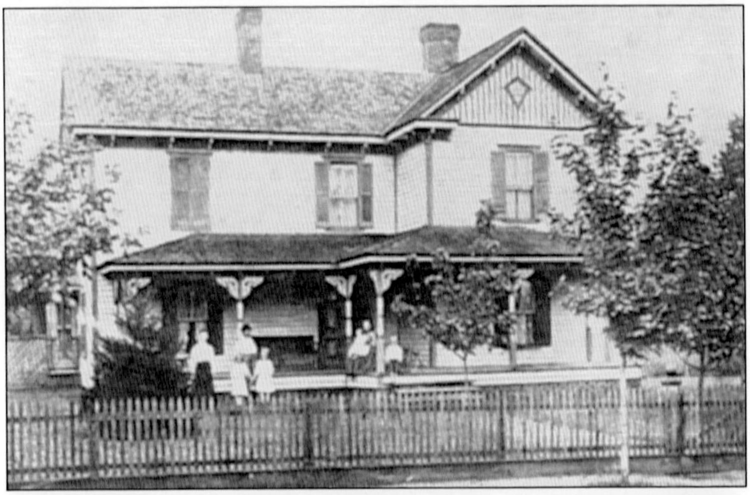

THE PETTYCORD HOME BUILT IN 1871 BY BEN BITTING. The owners, the S.L. Vest family, are on the porch. (HRH)

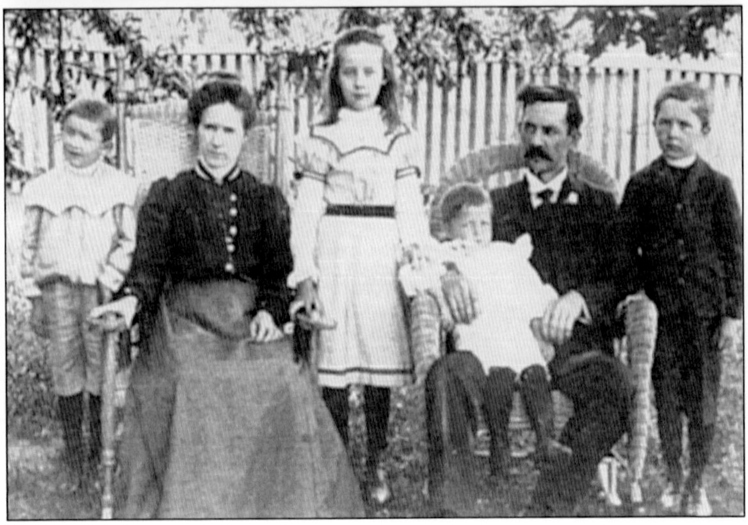

THE ANTHONY L. PAYNE FAMILY, c. 1900. Mrs. Elizabeth Bitting Payne was instrumental in getting the railroad to come through Rural Hall. (HRH)

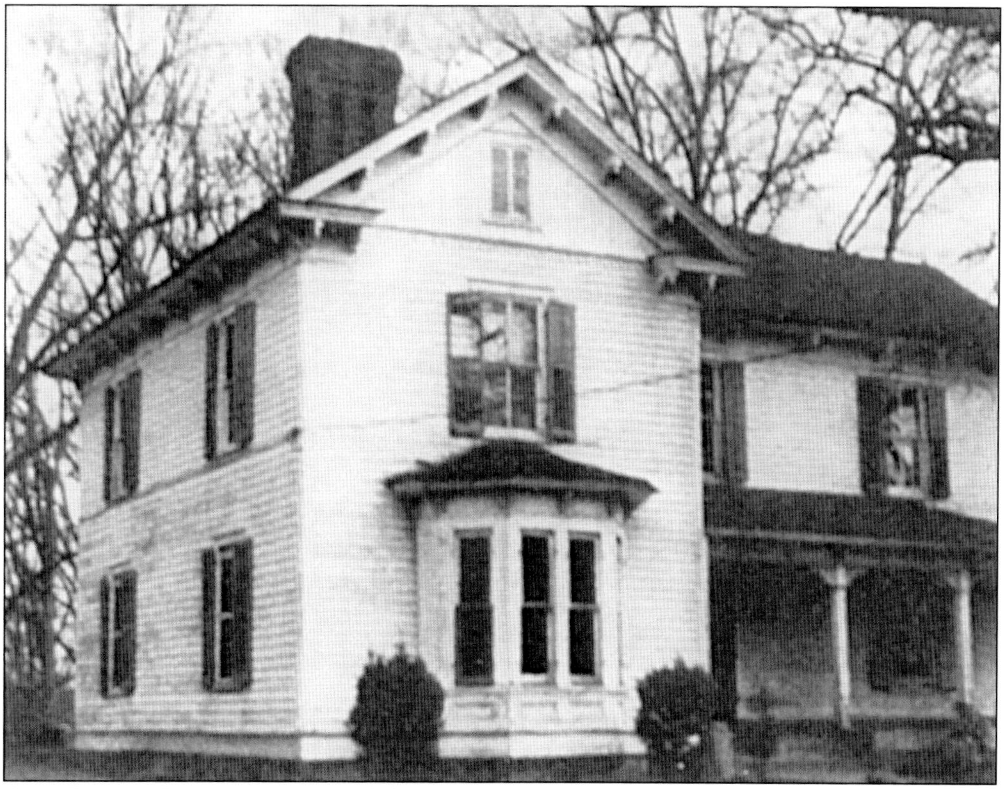

A.L. Payne Home, c. 1880. While the railroad was being built, Mrs. Payne provided a makeshift "commissary" behind her house. (HRH)

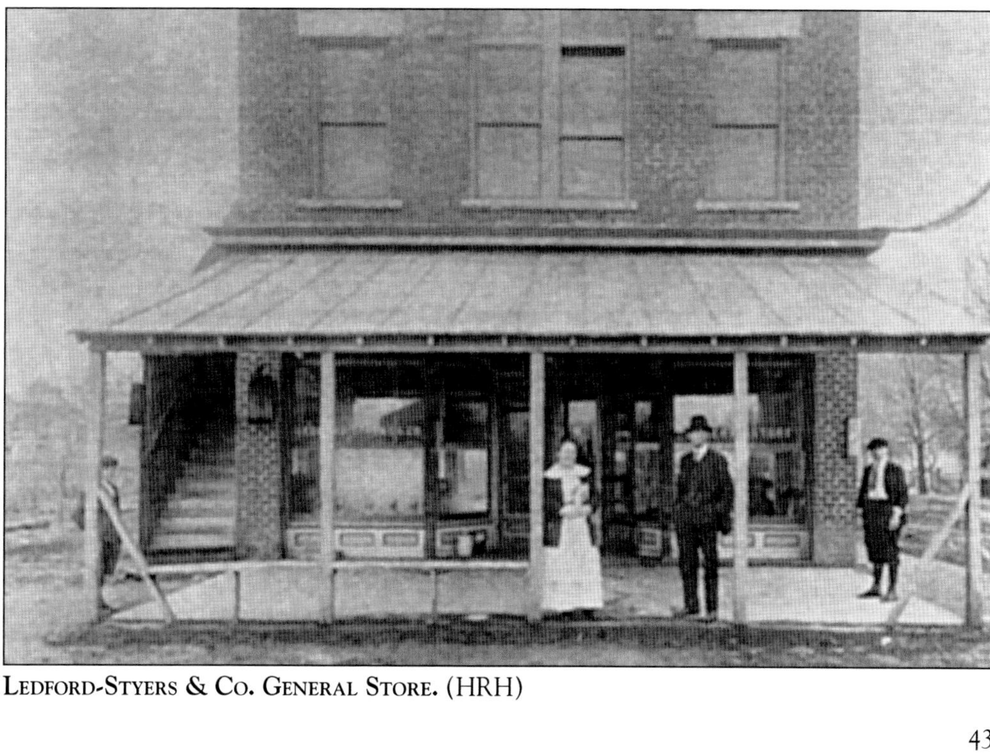

Ledford-Styers & Co. General Store. (HRH)

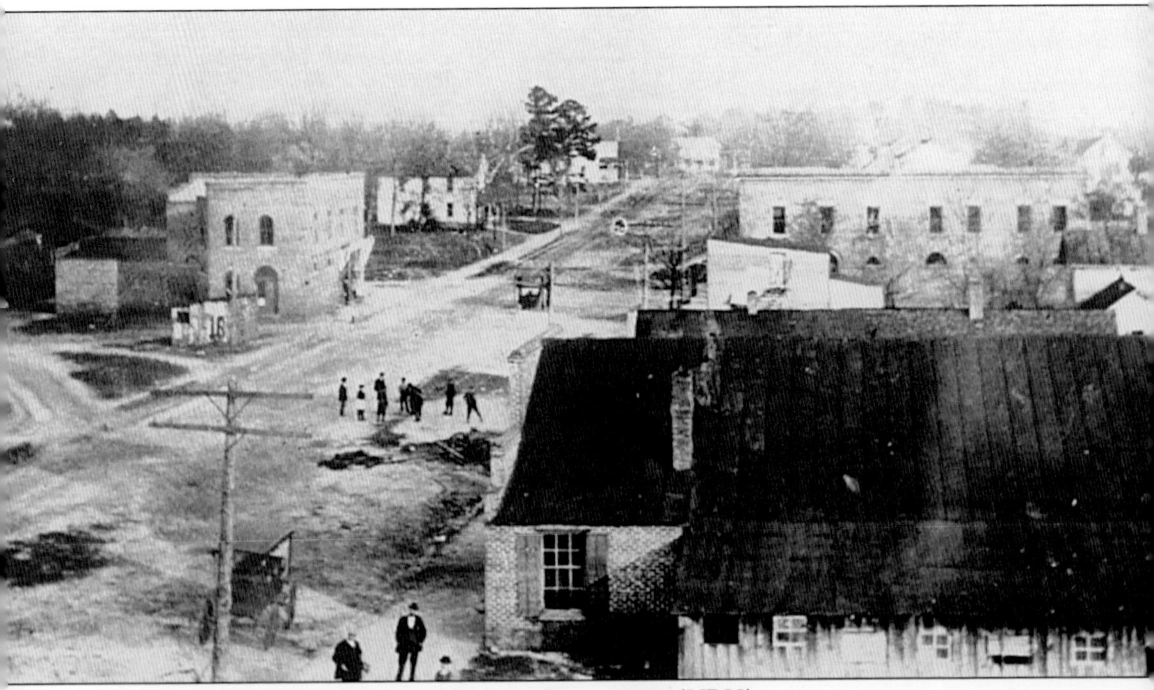

BUSINESSES ON MAIN STREET IN RURAL HALL, 1907. (HRH)

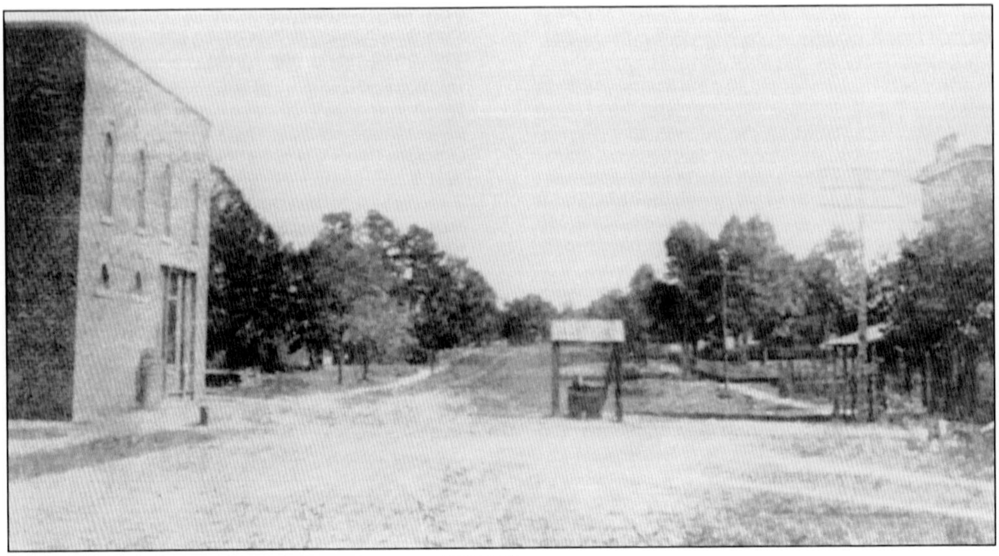

A WELL IN THE MIDDLE OF MAIN STREET. (HRH)

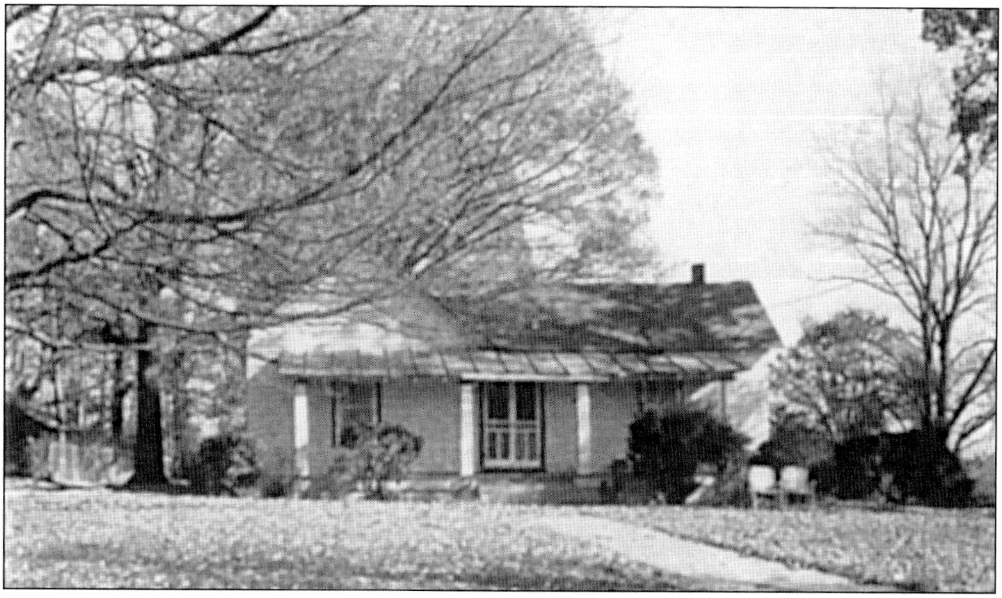

THE D.M. WRIGHT HOME, BUILT IN 1865 AND ALSO THE BIRTHPLACE OF FRED HAUSER. Hauser served as the county commissioner in Forsyth County. (HRH)

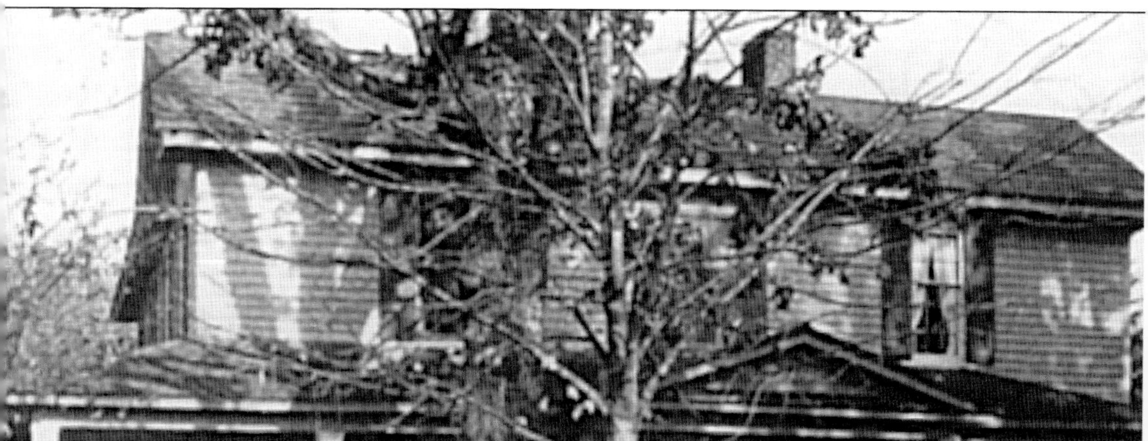

W.F. WALL HOME, AS SEEN PRIOR TO 1900. (HRH)

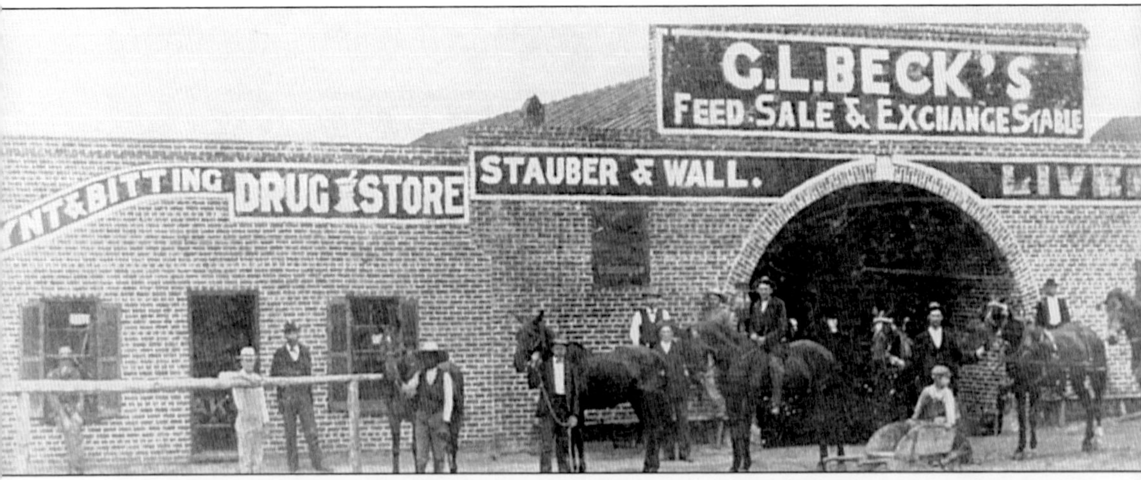

The Gathering Place. Standing in front of Flynt and Bitting Drugstore are Calvin Butner, Frank Butner, Dr. S.S. Flynt, and Vasco Eldridge. In front of the livery and Beck's store are Tom Gunn (holding the horse), J.C. Lawrence (standing on a bench), G.L. Beck, W.E. Stauber (on a horse), W.F. Wall (holding two horses), Dallas Kirby (in the wheelbarrow), Z.B. Bitting (standing on a bench), and C.T. Wall (on horseback). (HRH)

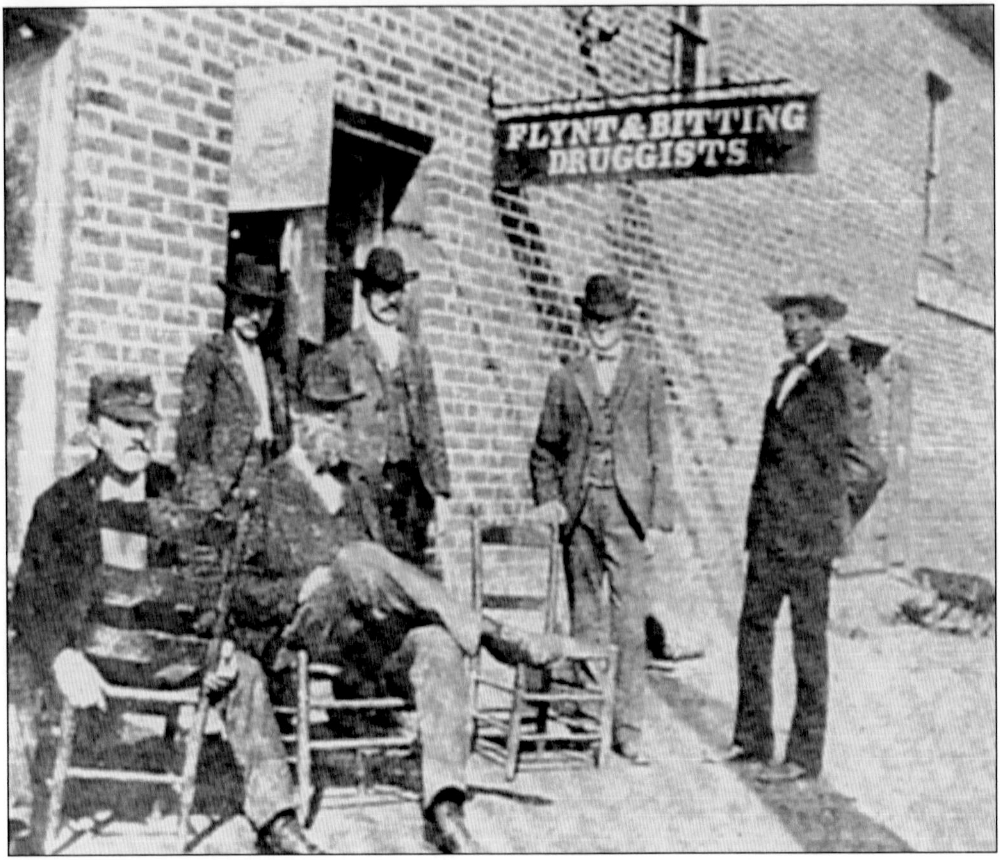

Drugstore Visitors. From left to right are as follows: (seated) Squire Vest and Dr. S.S. Flynt; (standing) P.A. Griffin, Ben Bitting, Claude Kiser, and Zeb Bitting. (HRH)

Five

Tobaccoville
Land of the Leaf

At one time, Tobaccoville was a little community boasting of a post office, a stage, and churches for all religions. In the 1870s, the stage route from Winston to Mt. Airy passed by C.R. Orrender's general store and plug tobacco factory. Upon the establishment of the post office and stage stop, Orrender's store became their headquarters. Because his plug tobacco was a favorite for the stagecoach passengers, he chose the name Tobaccoville for the little town that sat amidst hundreds of acres of tobacco. When the trains replaced the stagecoach in the late 1800s, the general stores again offered special treats to entice the train passengers. Orren Pfaff offered music from his fiddle, Robert Petree offered homemade ice cream, and Leon Butner made oyster stew.

Though being home to the one the largest tobacco manufacturing plants in the country, Tobaccoville still remains a small town proud of its history. On Friday mornings, the women of the Tobaccoville Historical Society meet at the Town Hall, and on Sundays, one can still hear the sweet sounds from the church choirs.

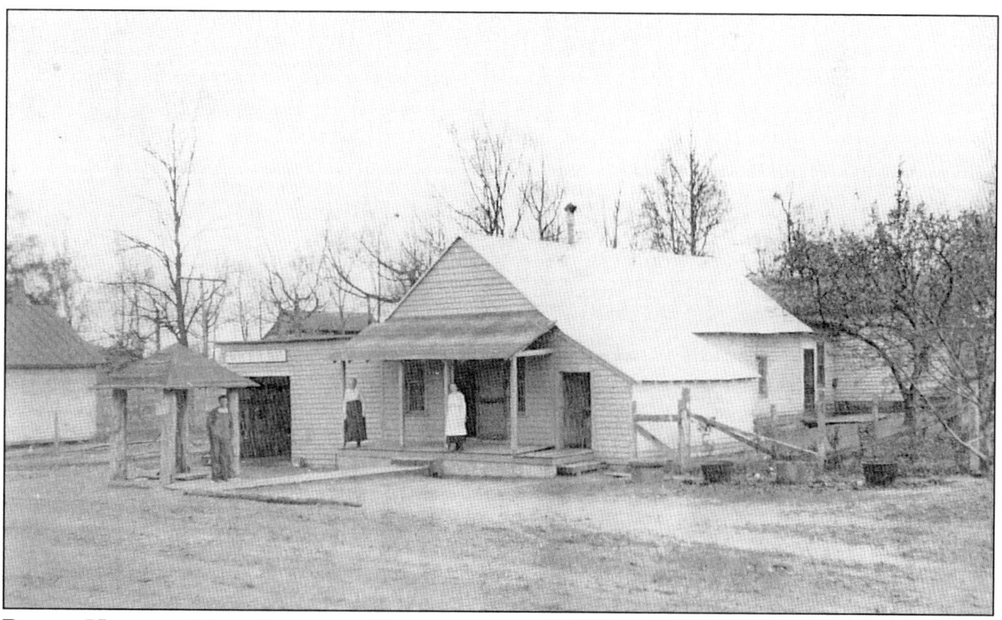

PETREE HOME ON MAIN STREET IN TOBACCOVILLE. (THS)

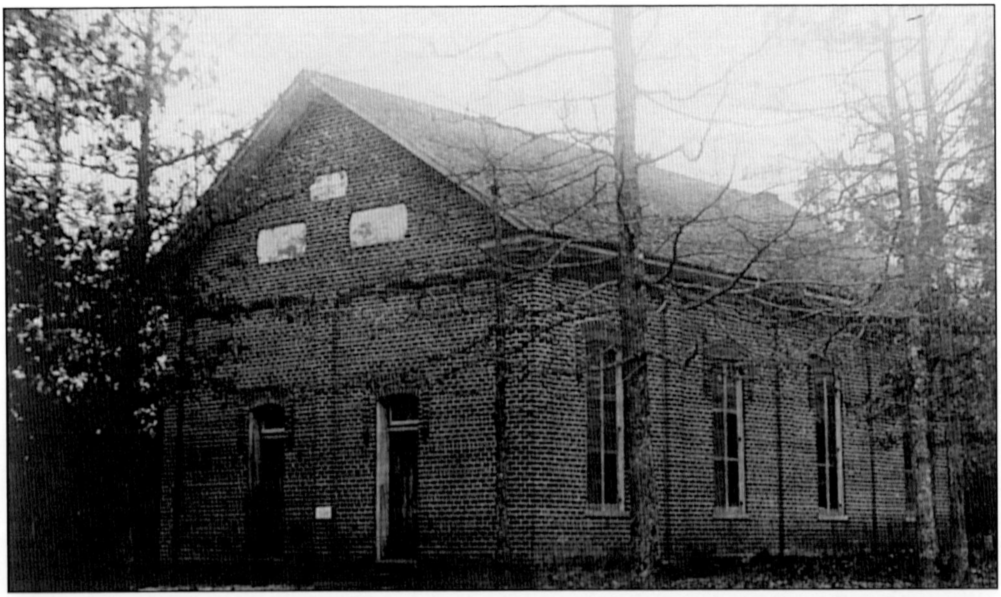

Macedonia Baptist Church. Founded in 1882, the church is located on Doral Street in Tobaccoville. (THS)

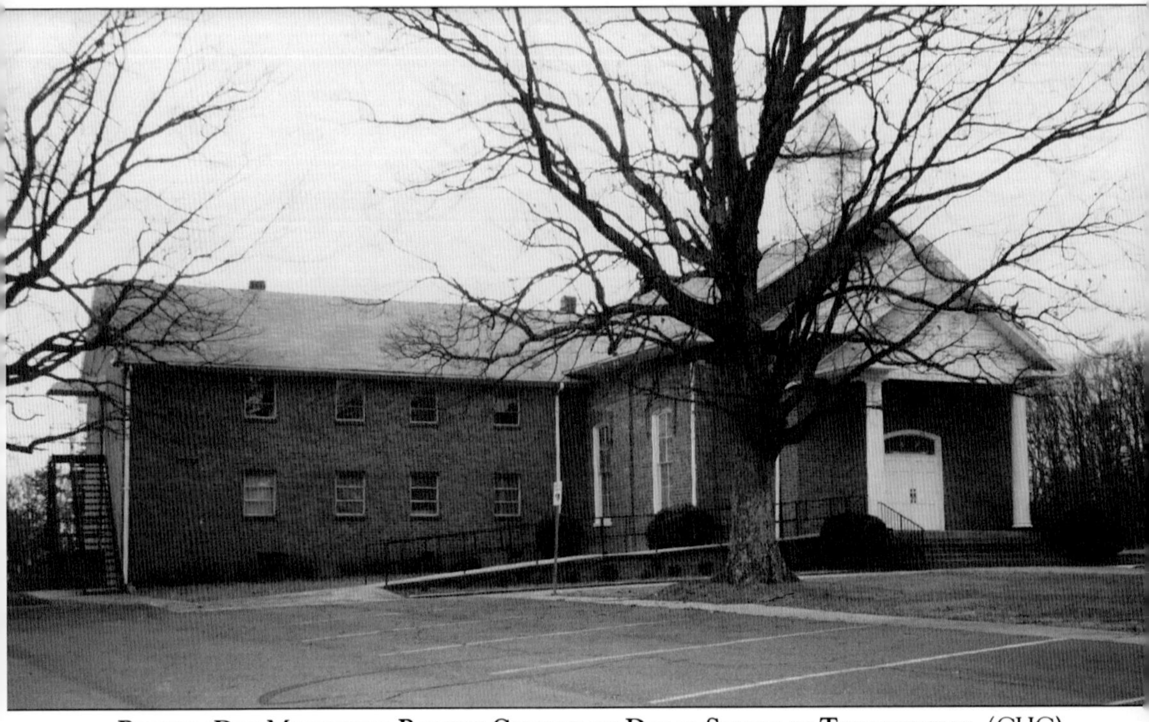

Present-Day Macedonia Baptist Church on Doral Street in Tobaccoville. (CHC)

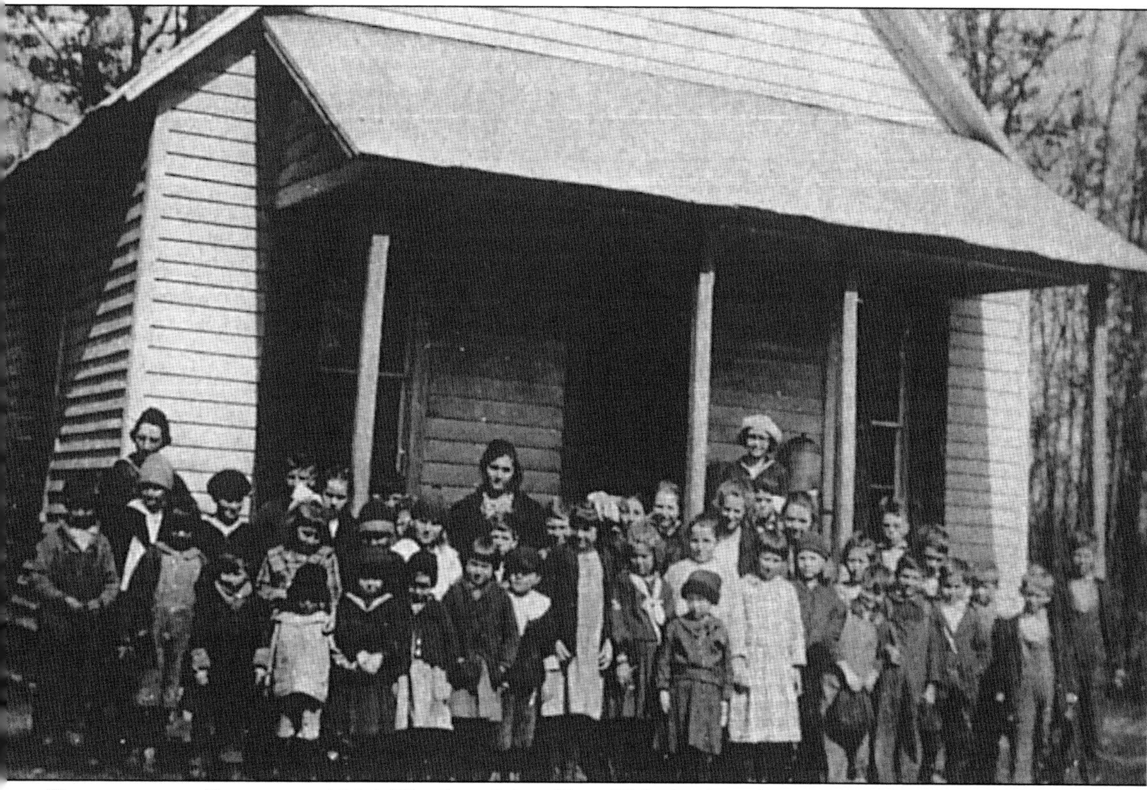

Tobaccoville School in 1920. Teachers Miss Clara Helsabeck and Mrs. Ina Talley are shown here. (THS)

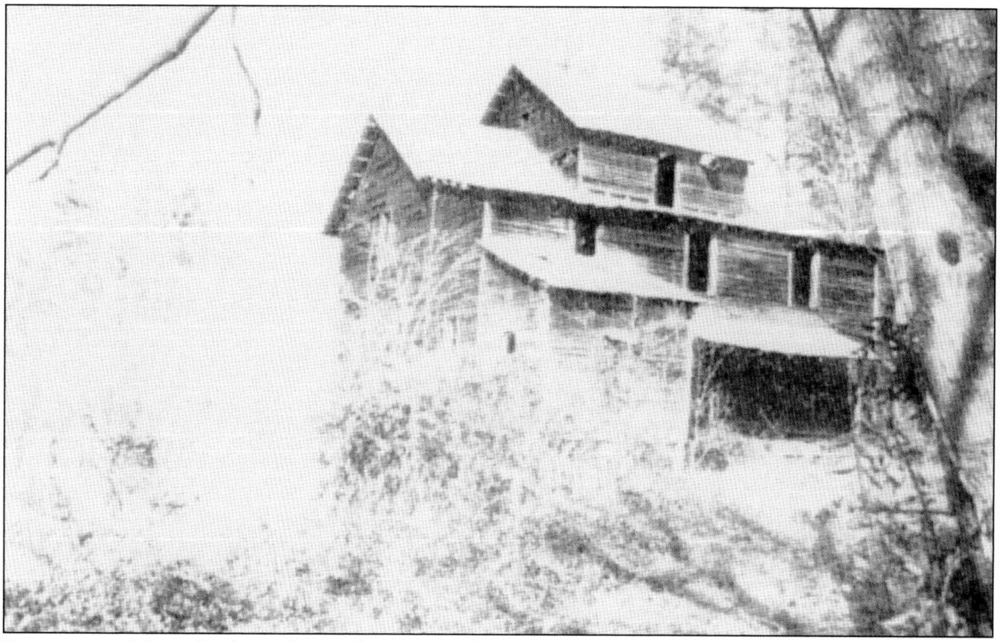

Spainhour Mill. Built in the mid nineteenth century, Spainhour Mill was destroyed by fire in September 1979. (FF)

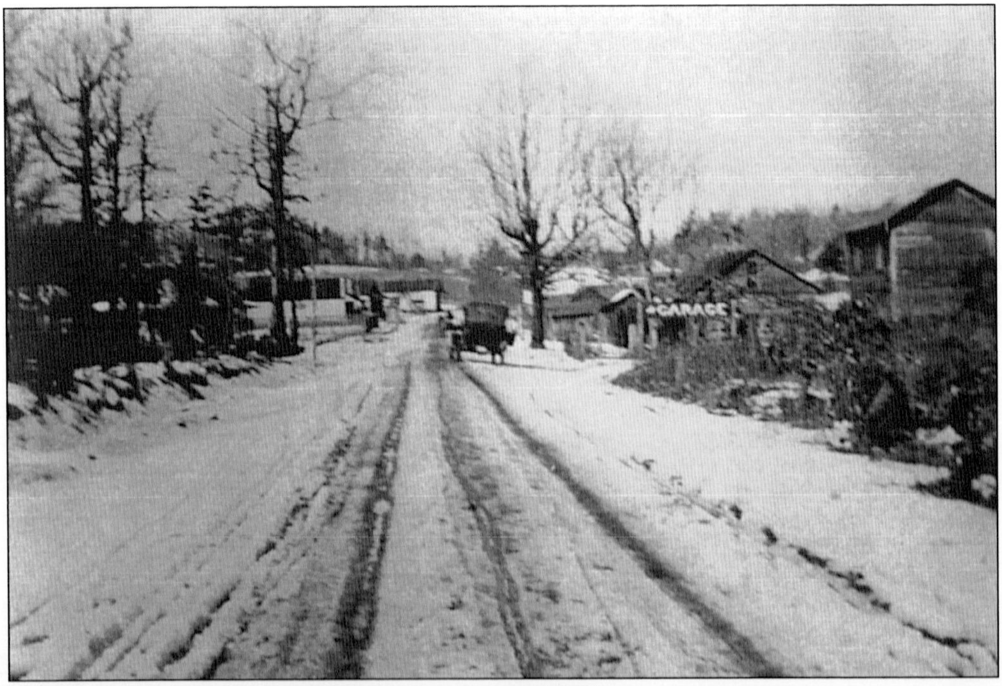

A 1920 View of Main Street in Tobaccoville. (FCL)

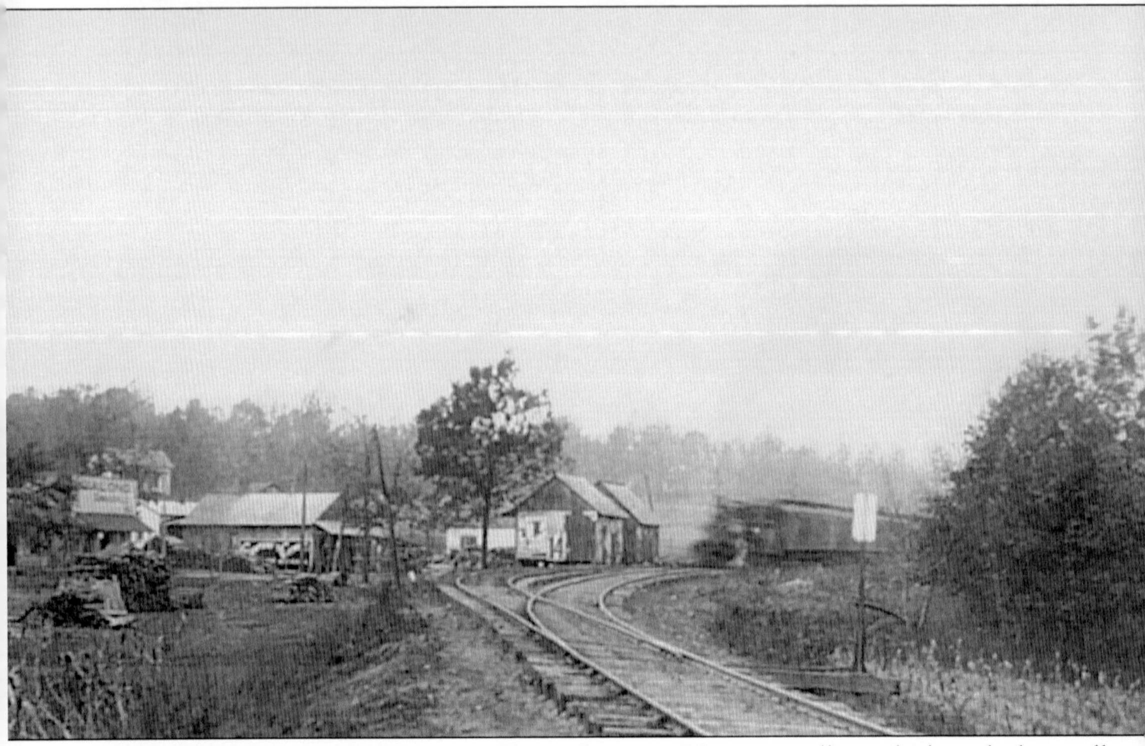

Early Days of the Tobaccoville Train Station. The train still travels through the small town. (THS)

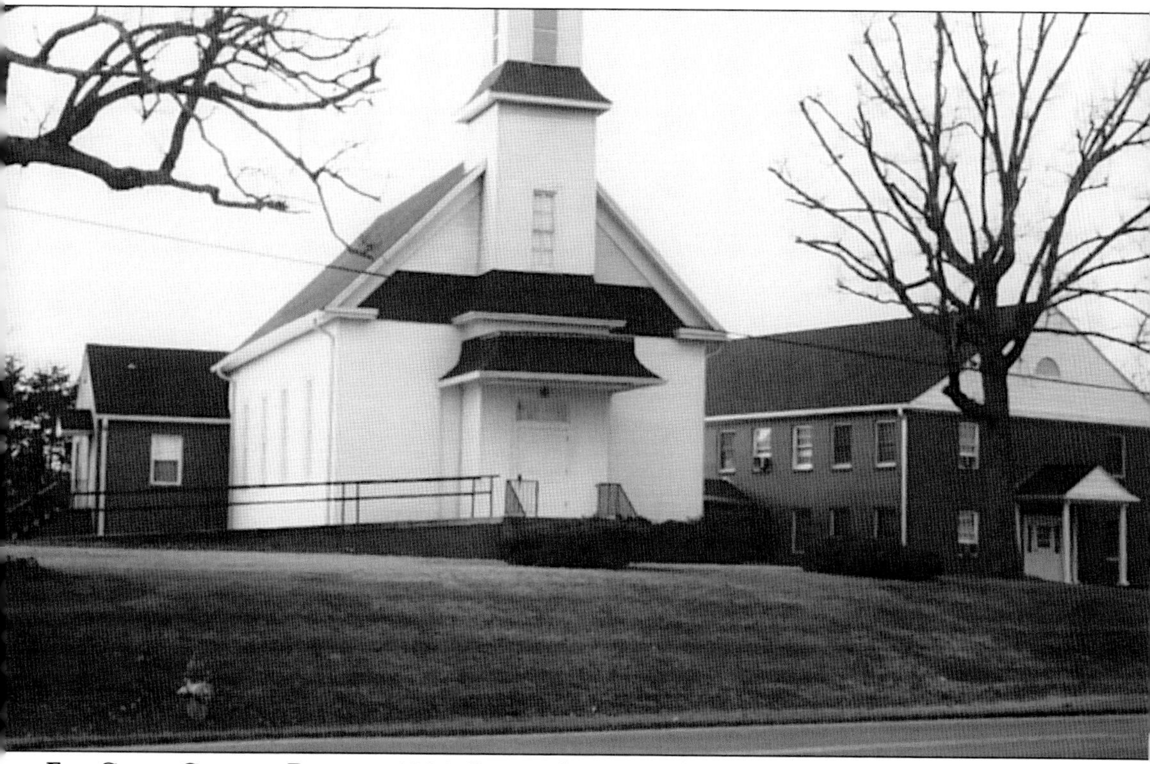

Elm Grove Church, Built in 1894. Due to changes in district lines, Elm grove Church is now part of Pfafftown. (CHC)

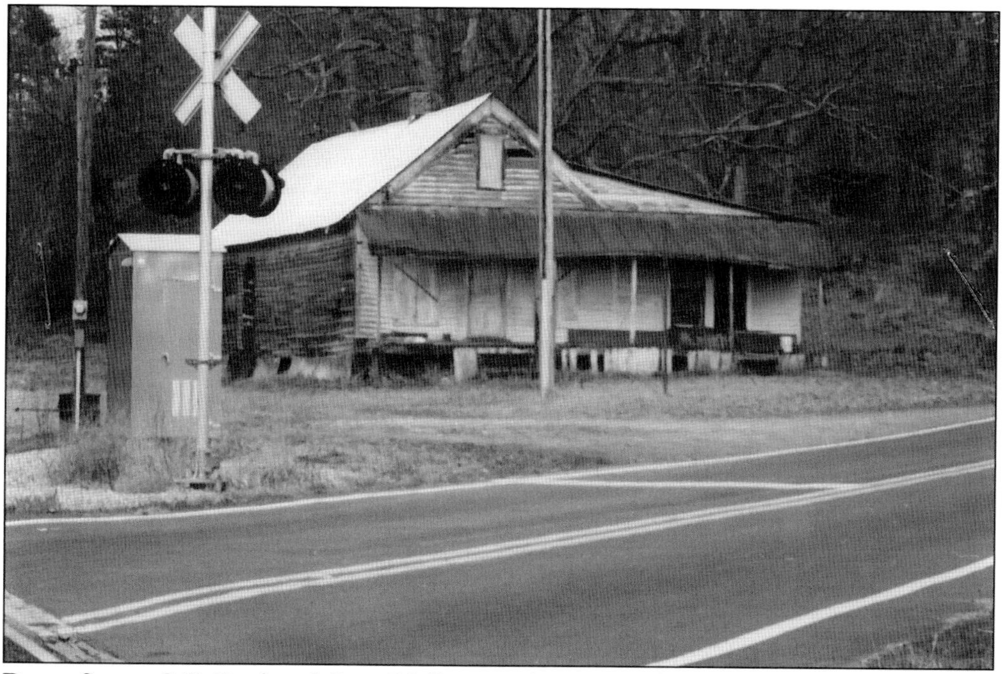

Depot Store. S.G. Doub and Oren Pfaff operated a store at this location next to the railroad tracks. (CHC)

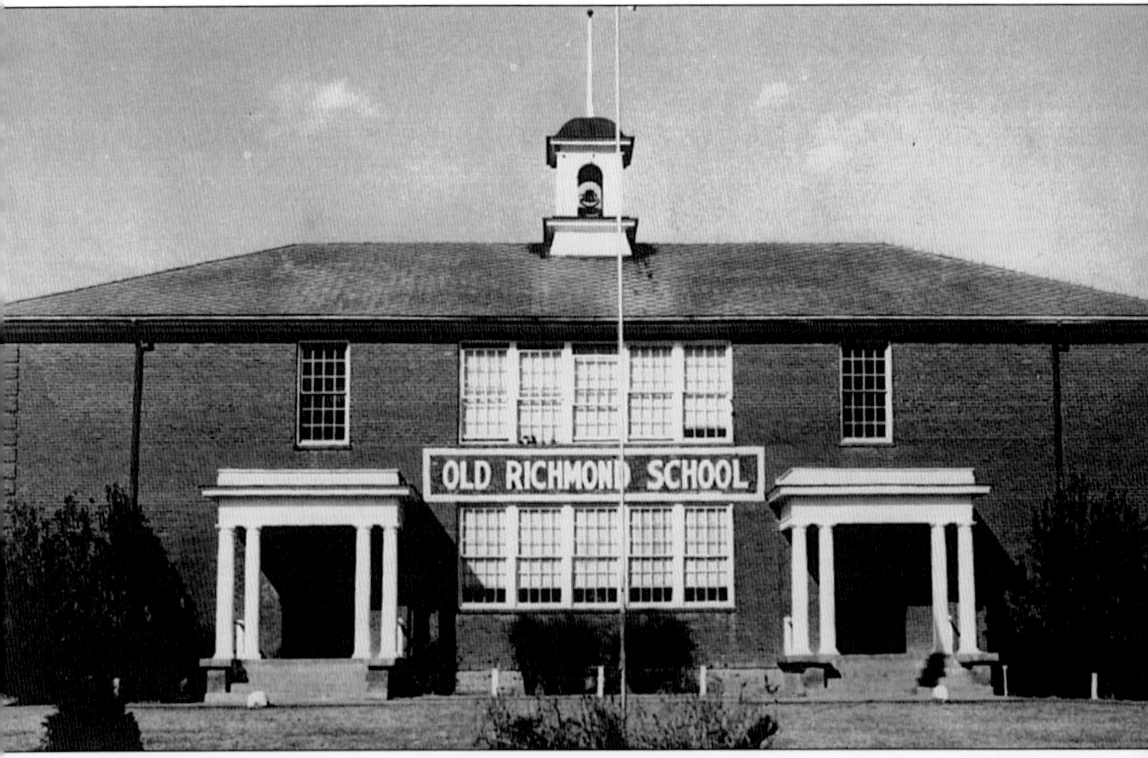

GONE BUT NOT FORGOTTEN. Rossie S. Shore was assigned as the principal of the Old Richmond High School, which was completed in 1922. There had only been 427 graduates by 1955, when the school was changed to serve the elementary-age children. (THS)

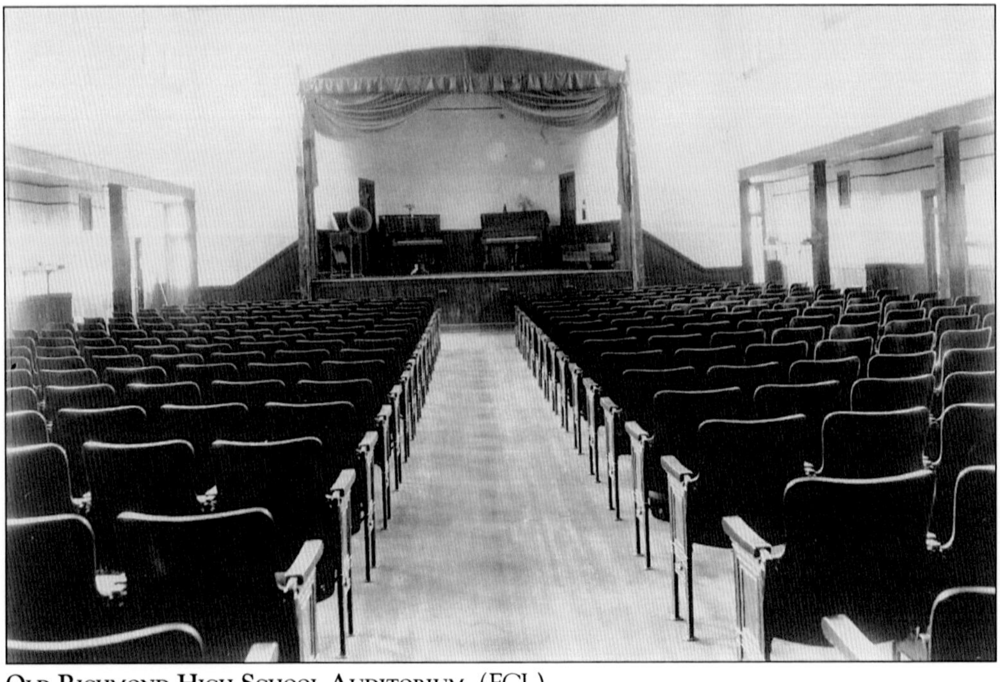

OLD RICHMOND HIGH SCHOOL AUDITORIUM. (FCL)

Six

Kernersville
No Time to Sit Still

Kernersville was first settled about 1760 by Caleb Story, an Irishman. Local folklore states he bought the original tract of 400 acres for 4 gallons of rum. Eventually, he sold the land to William Dobson, who opened a thriving tavern at the crossroads. Gottlieb Shober of Salem then purchased the land, and in 1818, sold it to Joseph Kerner. From that point, the settlement was known as Kernersville.

Under the supporting hands of strong leaders, Kernersville began to grow from a frontier community into a thriving township. By 1850, there was a Methodist and Moravian church, a small school, a new hotel, a mercantile shop, coachmakers, and a wheelwright. In 1857, John Fredrick gave a parcel of land to build Kernersville Academy, a private school, which operated until 1909. In 1884, the first public school, called the "free school," opened and Rev. J.W. Pinnix served as its principal. A public school for blacks also opened and was directed by Mr. Rush. By 1888, the population had doubled from 500 to 1,000, and Kernersville was on the map.

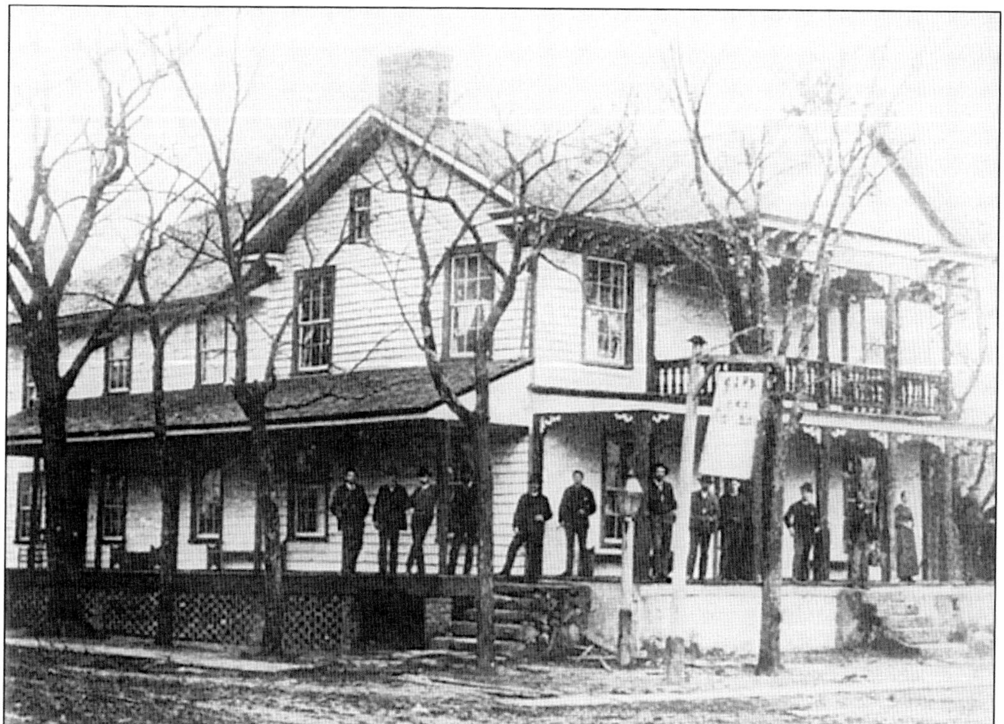

DOBSON'S TAVERN AT THE CROSSROADS. Built by William Dobson, this tavern has been documented as the first stopover place between the Moravian settlement of Salem, North Carolina, and Bethlehem, Pennsylvania. (JK)

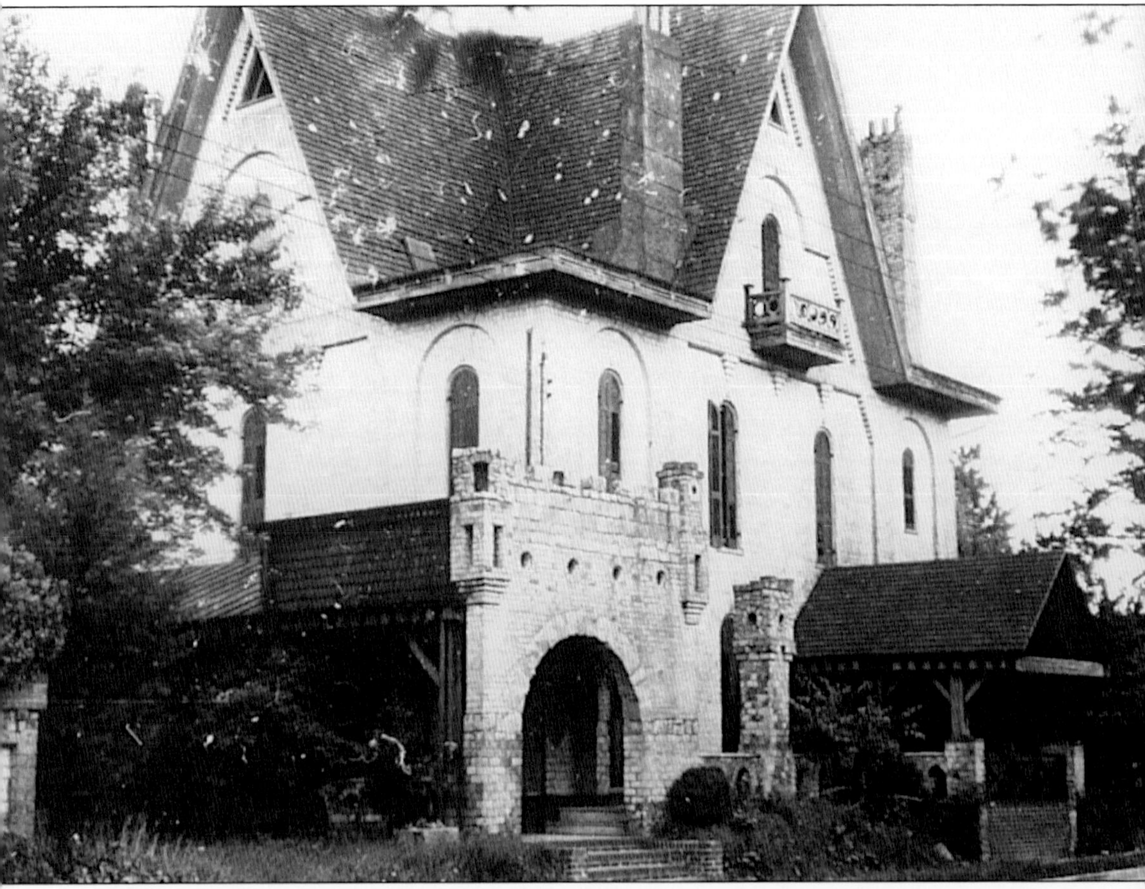

KERNER'S FOLLY. Built in 1878, Jule Kilmer Korner's home came to be known as "Kerner's Folly." This home was later enlarged in 1886. (FCL)

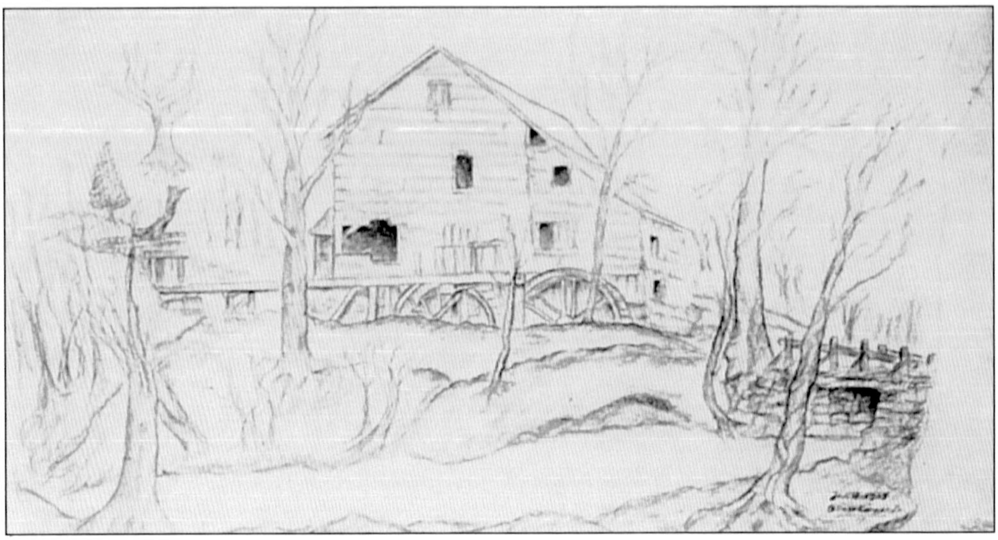

"THE BIG MILL," AS SKETCHED BY JULE K. KORNER, C. 1905. The mill was built in 1876 by Dr. Elias Kerner. (JOK)

JUDITH GARDNER (1807–1853), WIFE OF PHILIP KORNER. (KB)

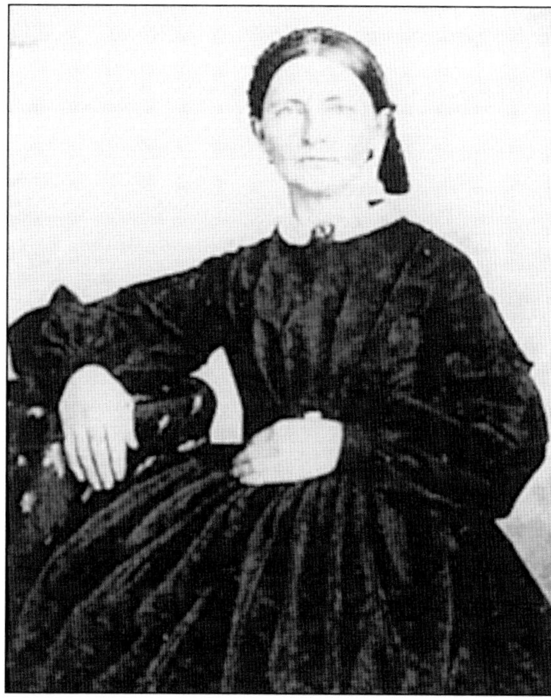

PHILIP KORNER (1805–1875) AND HIS NINE-YEAR-OLD SON, JULE, IN A PHOTOGRAPH TAKEN c. 1860. (KB)

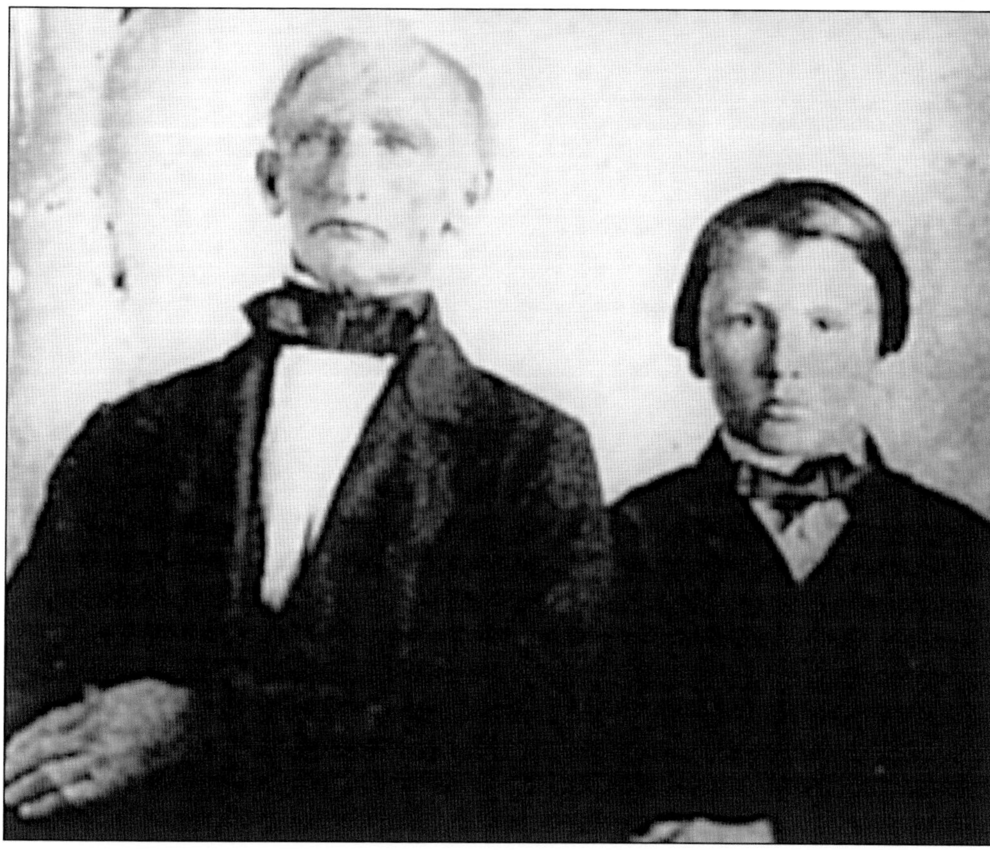

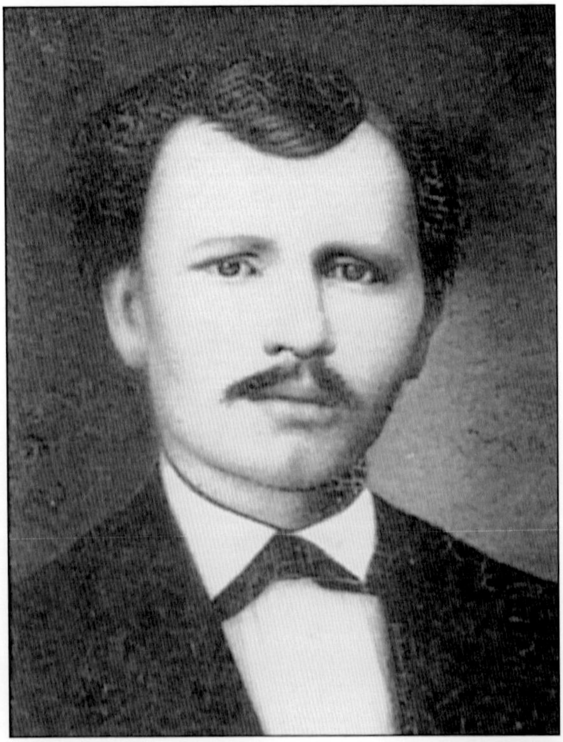

SELF-PORTRAIT BY JULE KILMER KORNER AT AGE 23 (1874). (KB)

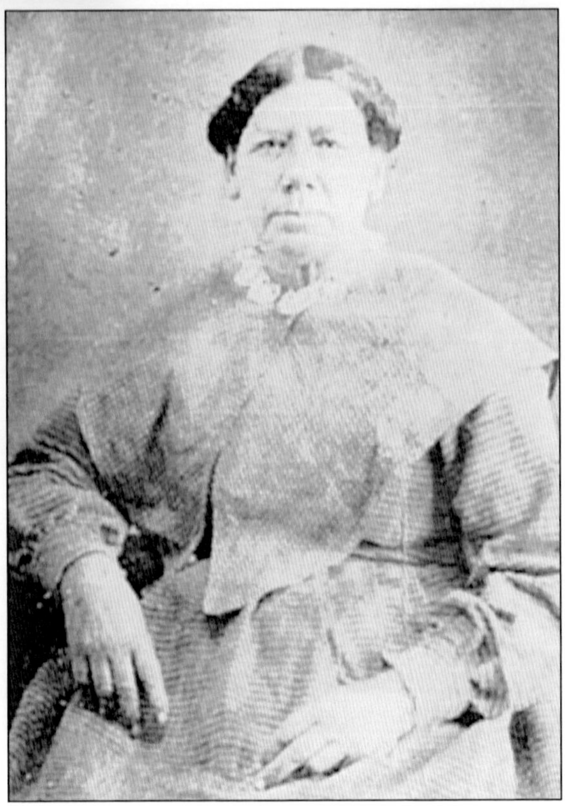

CLARA KORNER (1820–1896), COMMONLY KNOWN AS "AUNT DEALY." Outraged by his family members and the community's objection to bury the family's former slave in the Moravian church's cemetery, Jule Korner purchased the plot of land just outside the cemetery. He buried Aunt Dealy facing west instead of east, built a brick enclosure, and gave her his family name, changing its spelling to "Korner." (KB)

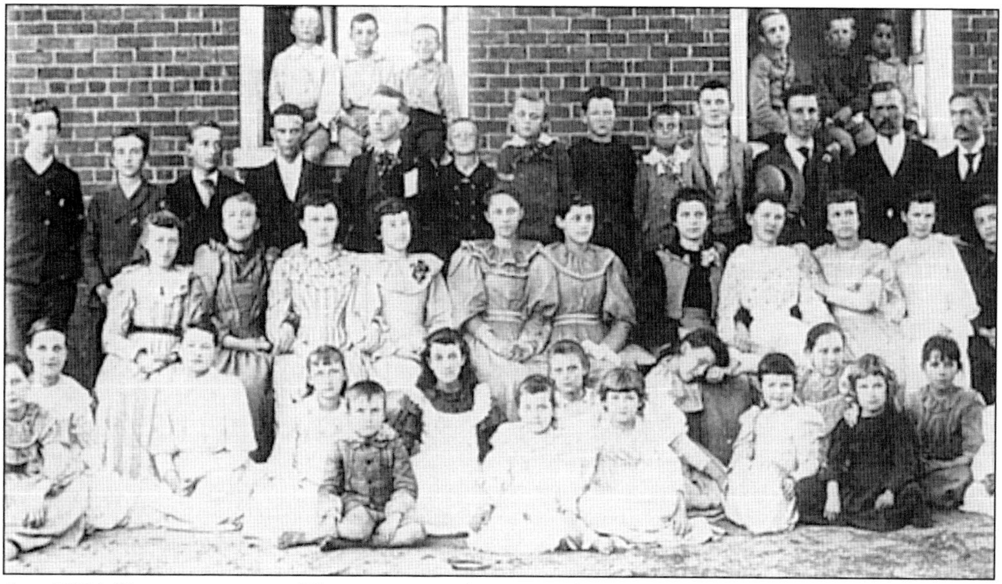

AN 1894 PHOTOGRAPH OF KERNERSVILLE ACADEMY (1857–1909). From left to right are as follows: (front row) unidentified, Emma Vogler, Eura Ragland, Annie Kerner, Baxter Crews, Mozelle Beard, Mable Leak, Mattie Leak, Jessie Leak, Maude Bodenhamer, Ina Davis, Mary Hastings, Annie Leak, Carrie Pinnix, and Edythe Kerner; (middle row) Nina Brookbank, Mary Lindsay, Sue Lindsay, Mina Pepper, Ida Sapp, Carrie Beard, Meta Kerner, Betha Fulp, Agnes Stockton, Madye Leak, and Rosa Griffith; (back row) Robin Fetter, John Greenfield, Frank Leak, Charlie Sapp, Kerr Pepper, Charlie Huff, Clyde Lowrey, unidentified, Cary Ragland, Lester Lowrey, unidentified, James F. Dicks (teacher), Reverend E.J. Poe (M.E. Church teacher), and De Moir (teacher); (first window) unidentified, Elmer Leak, and unidentified; (second window) Frank Kerner, Hugh Leak, and Clifton Leak.

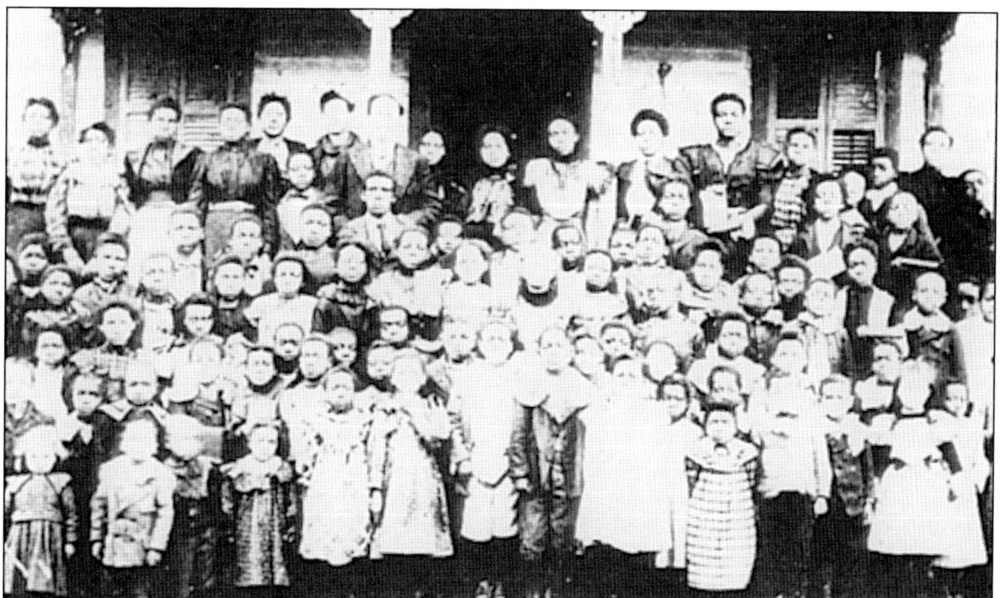

SCHOOL FOR AFRICAN AMERICANS, 1898. Mr. Thomas Matthews was the principal, and Mrs. Cornelia Johnson was the assistant. The names of the children are unknown. (KB)

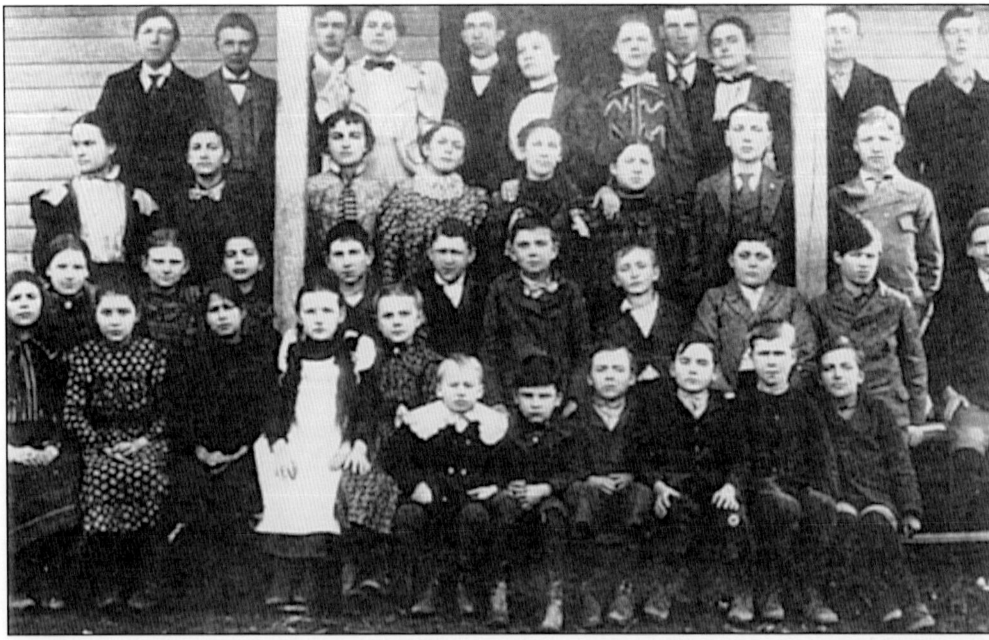

Students of Pine Grove School. In this 1899 photograph of Pine Grove School are, from left to right, as follows: (first row) Levia Vance, Amelia Morgan, May Highfield, Cora McCuiston, Alma Hunter, Marvin Vance, Cletus Morgan, Emory Dillon, Henry Ingram, Gaither Warren, and Arnold Dwiggins; (second row) Gertrude Vance, Flossie Crews, Fanny Hunter, Lewis Motsinger, Elias Landreth, Loften Dwiggins, Arrelius Nelson, David Barrow, Proscoe Vance, and Homer Vance; (third row) Gertrude Stegall, Caroline Morgan, Allie Dwiggins, Bertha Barrow, Addie Dwiggins, Lucy Vance, Charles E. Hunter, and Edgar Vance; (fourth row) Wesley Landreth, Oscar Vance, Thomas Warren, Minnie Barrow, M. Vance Fulp (teacher), Carrie Crews, Rosa McCuiston, Addison Stegall, Blancoe Dwiggins, Lorenza Dillown, and Henry Sapp. (KB)

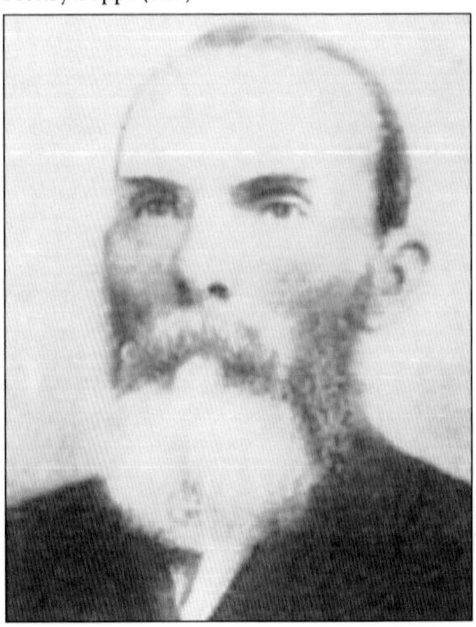

Rev. J.W. Pinnix, Principal of the First Public School of Kernersville, 1884. (KB)

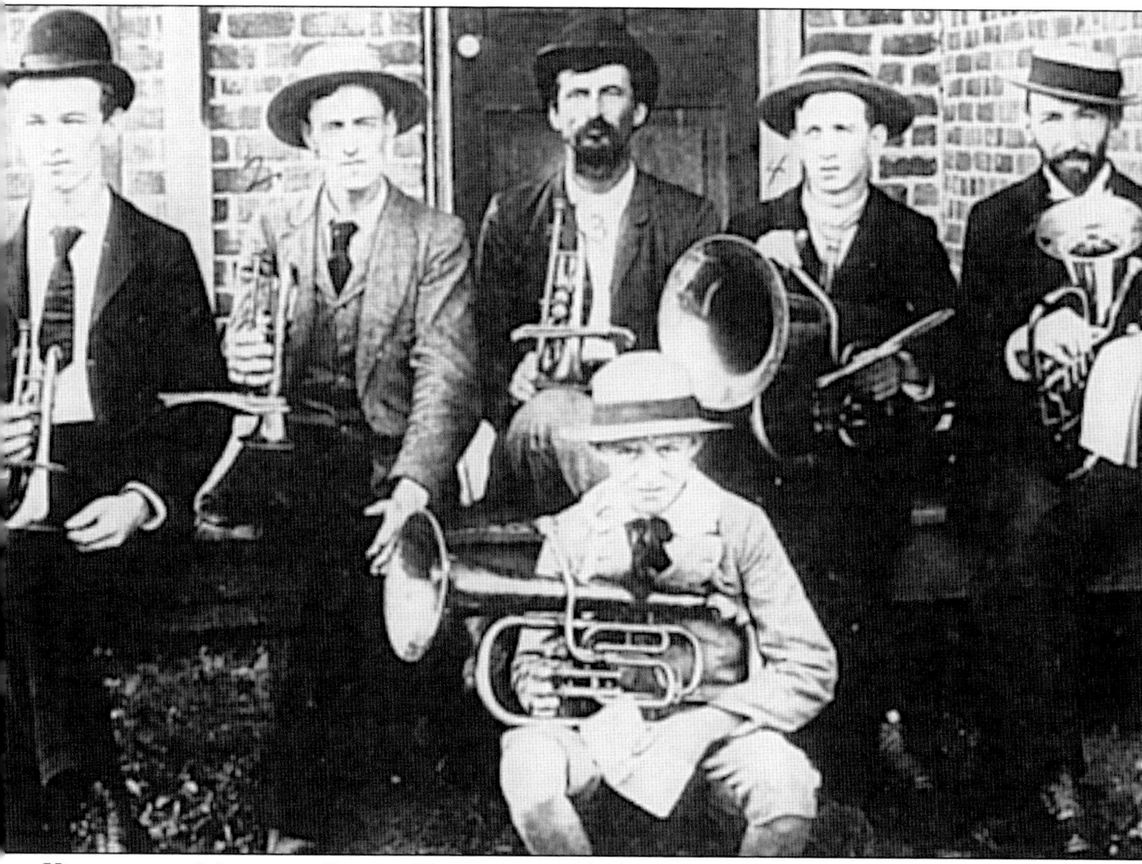

KERNERSVILLE MORAVIAN CHURCH BAND, 1890. The band members are, from left to right, as follows: Kerr Pepper, James F. Kerner, David Kerner, Carl R. Kerner, H.C. Korner, and Percy Kerner (in front). (KB)

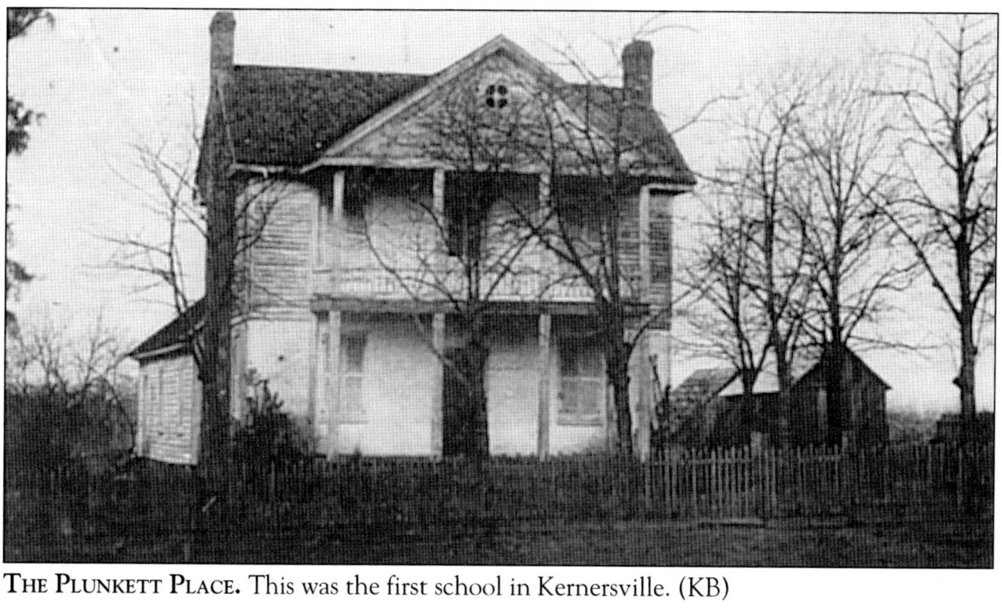

THE PLUNKETT PLACE. This was the first school in Kernersville. (KB)

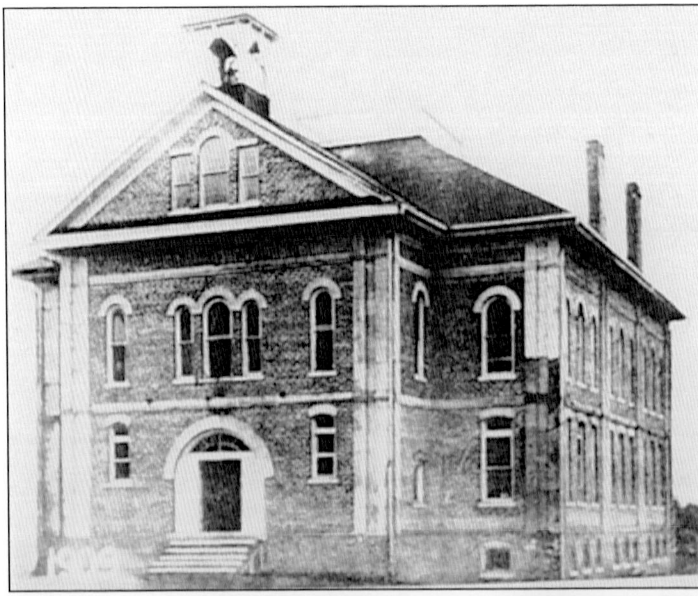

PUBLIC SCHOOL BUILDING IN KERNERSVILLE, 1906. (KB)

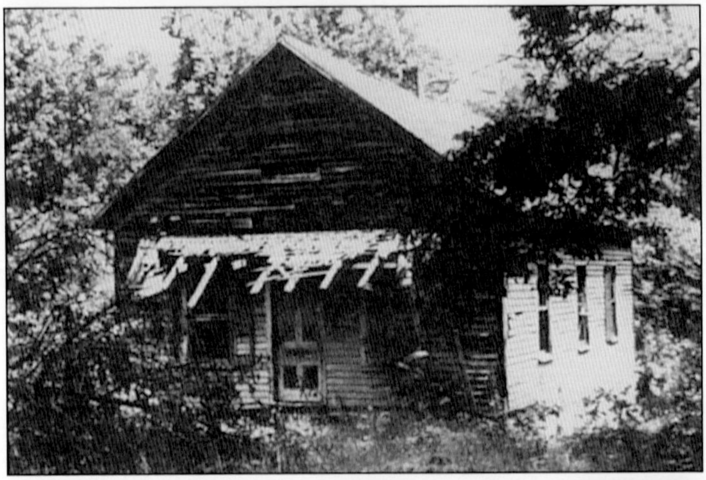

AN 1870S PHOTOGRAPH OF THE BLUFF SCHOOL IN KERNERSVILLE. (FF)

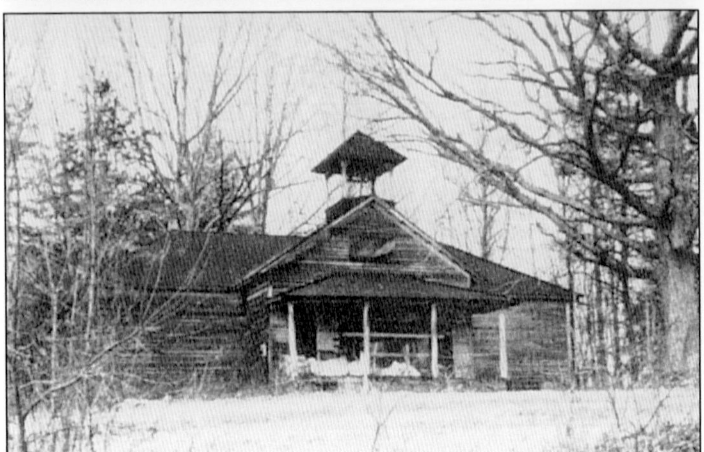

ROCK HILL SCHOOL IN THE BELEWS CREEK VICINITY, AS SEEN IN THE EARLY 1900S. (FF)

Seven

Education

Build It and They Will Come

On August 27, 1859, Winston organized the Forsyth County Educational Association. The state superintendent, Calvin Wiley, gave ideas as to how to insure the best selection of prospective teachers and curriculum, but to no avail. In 1868, the conservative government abolished the position of state superintendent of common schools, thereby allowing public education to be managed by local communities. New laws mandated public instruction, which resulted in a system of free schools for both blacks and whites. That year, Forsyth County had 22 public schools and 22 teachers, but only a small percentage of children attended school. Winston's "negro schools" offered only a primary education, in addition to little or no industrial instruction. This changed in 1892, when Simon Green Atkins interested the leaders of Winston to found the Slater Industrial School, which opened later that year.

Outside of the Winston town limits, Forsyth County had 54 white public schools and 19 black public schools by 1884. Salem's district school for whites witnessed little growth. When the two cities of Winston and Salem officially merged in 1913, so did the school systems. This consolidation resulted in the construction of new schools and increased attendance in schools.

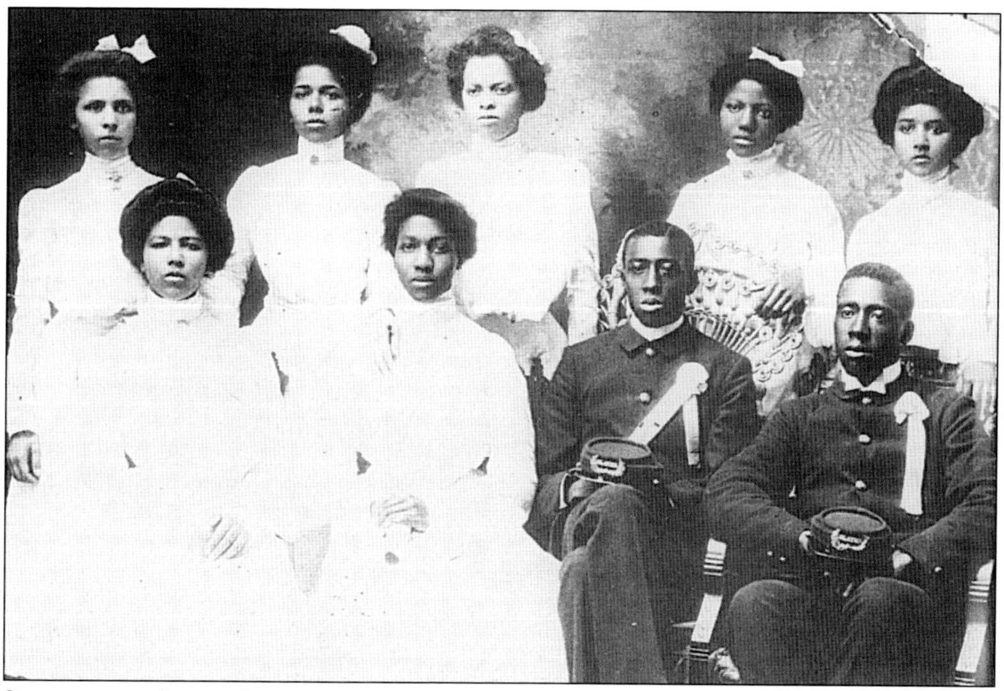

STUDENTS AT SLATER INDUSTRIAL SCHOOL. This school was opened in 1892 in a small frame building with a handful of students. This photograph shows what could be the first graduating class at Slater. (FCL)

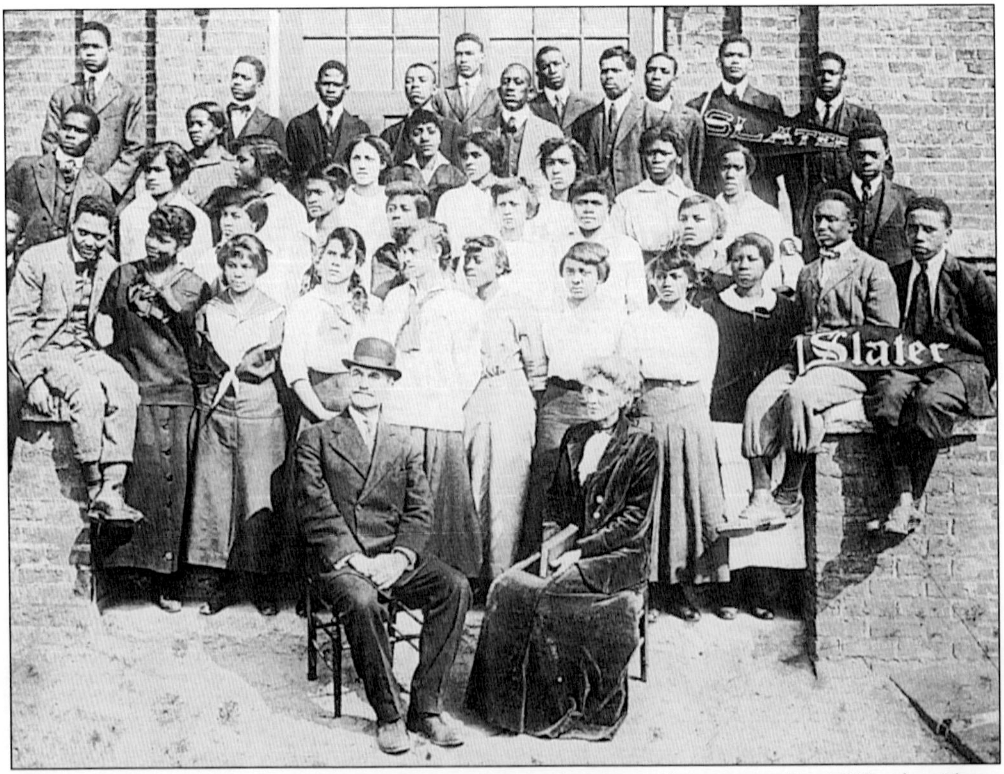

SIMON GREEN ATKINS WITH SLATER INDUSTRIAL ACADEMY STUDENTS. In 1925, the Slater Normal School went under state control as a four-year institution for African-American students and was renamed Winston-Salem Teacher's College. Today, it is Winston-Salem State University. (FCL)

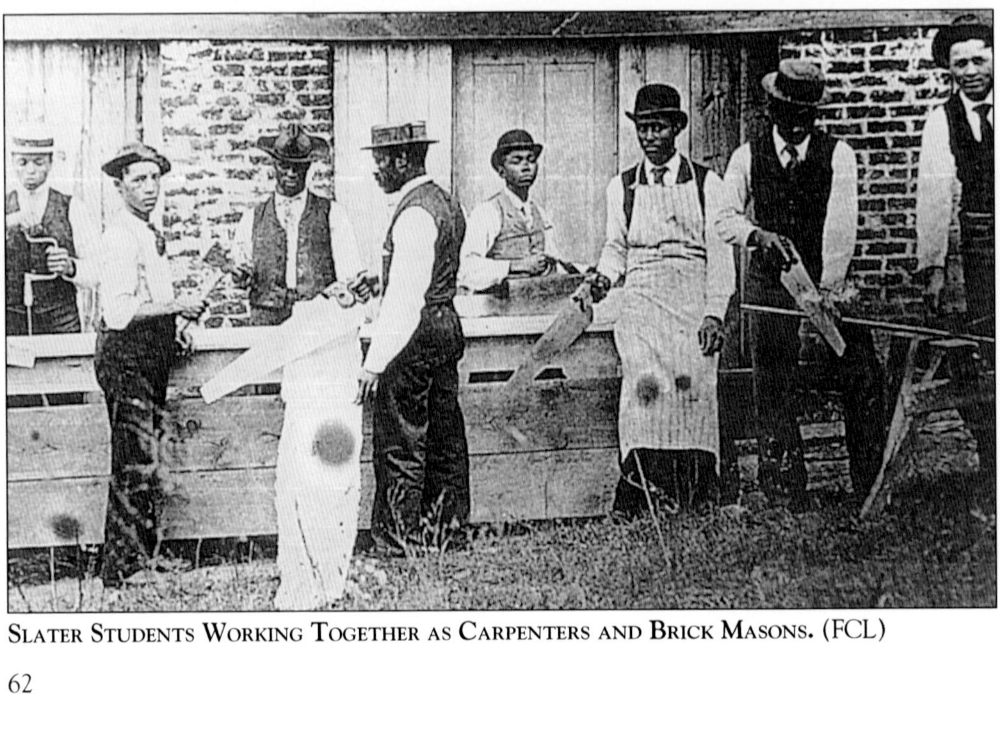

SLATER STUDENTS WORKING TOGETHER AS CARPENTERS AND BRICK MASONS. (FCL)

Davis Military Academy on Parade on Liberty Street between Third and Fourth Streets. (FCL)

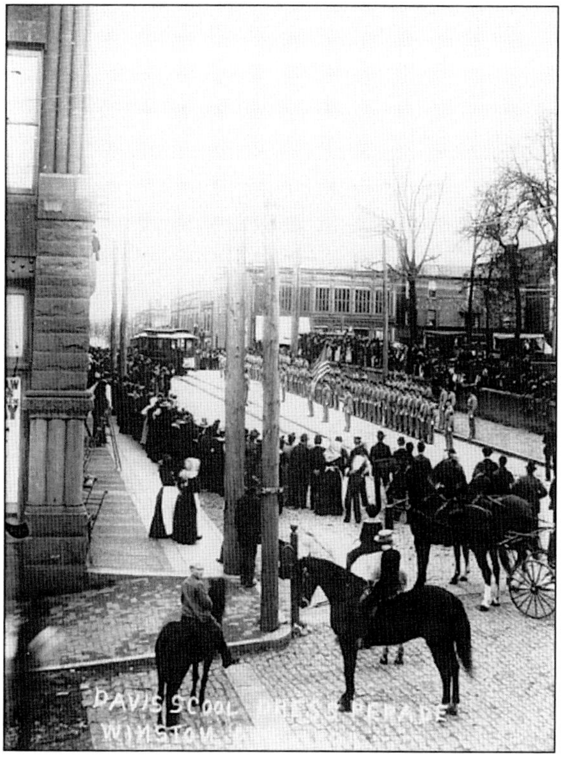

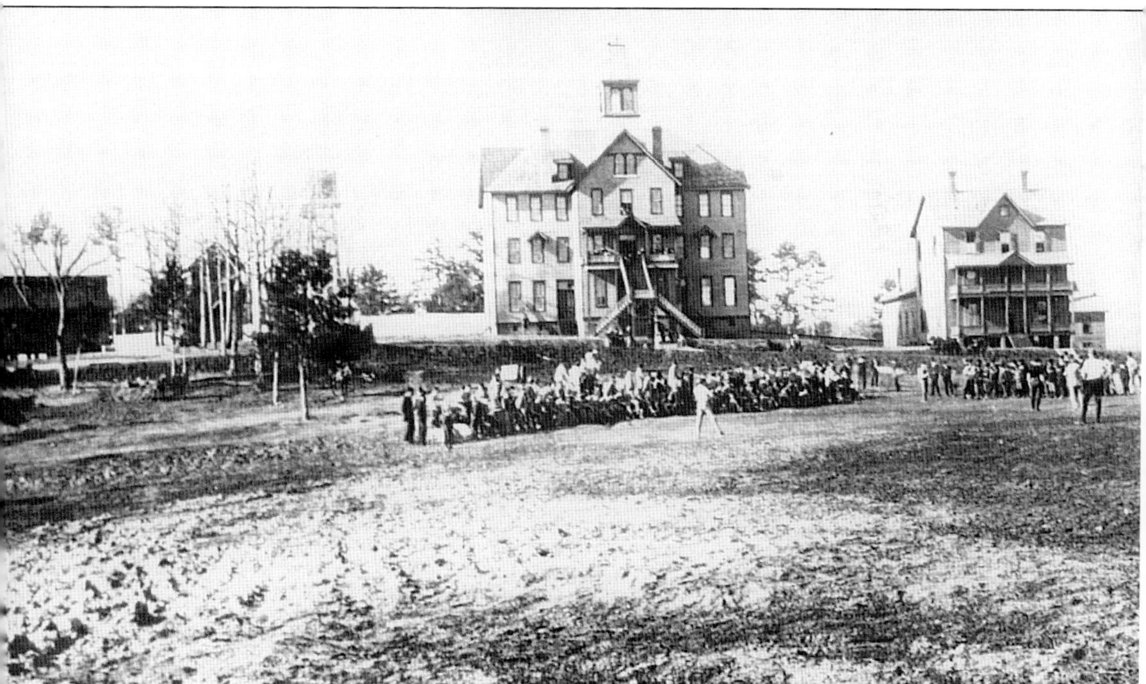

Davis Military Academy. Founded by Col. A.C. Davis in Lenoir County, North Carolina, the academy was located on what is now the Methodist Children Home on Reynolda Road in Winston-Salem. It was relocated to Forsyth County in the 1890s. (FCL)

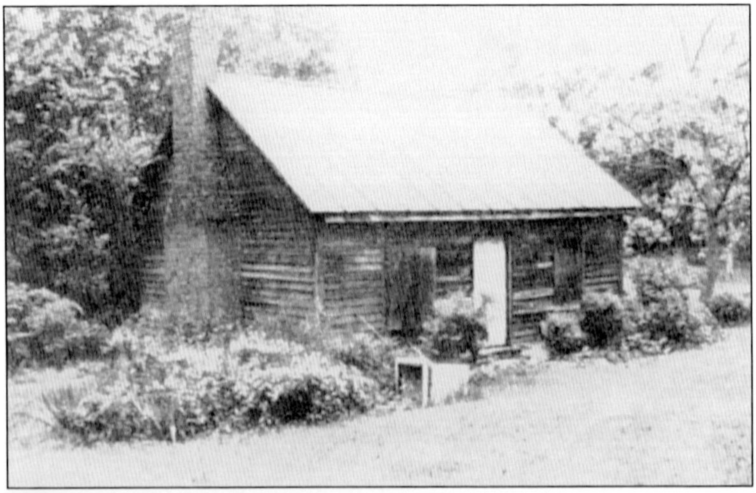

Cool Springs School. This school was built in the late 1800s in the vicinity of Winston-Salem. (FF)

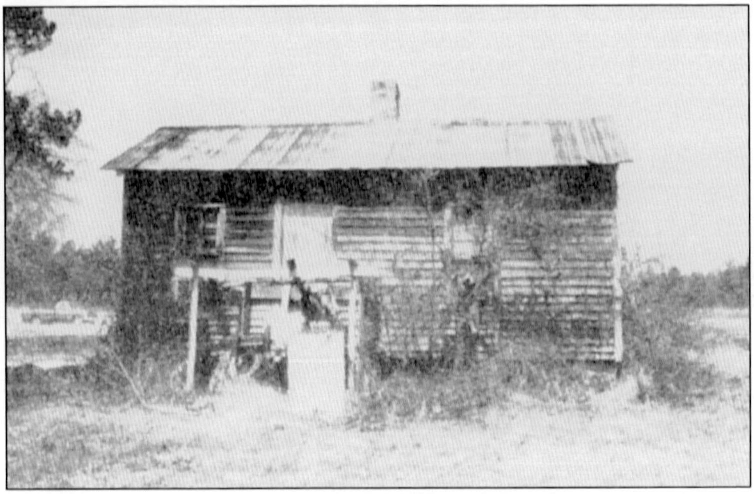

An Unidentified School. This school, which is thought to have been an early-twentieth-century school for African Americans, was located in the Winston-Salem vicinity. (FF)

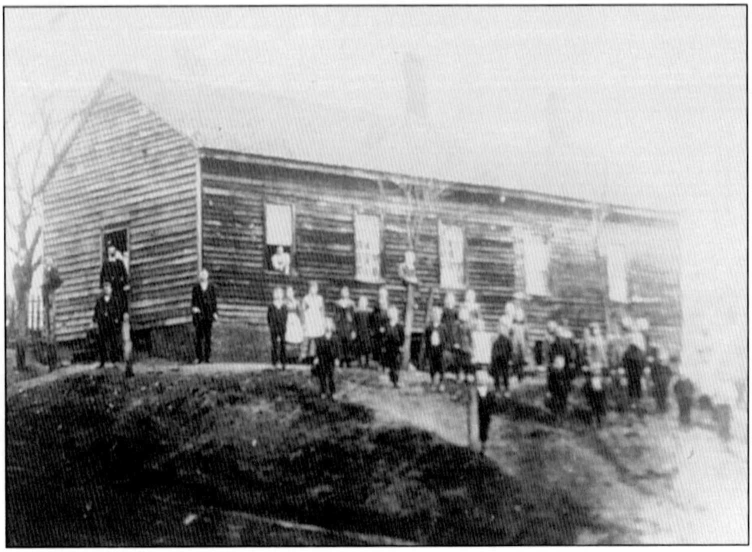

Kreemer's Preparatory School (1863–1868), Located at the Corner of Elm and Bank. (FCL)

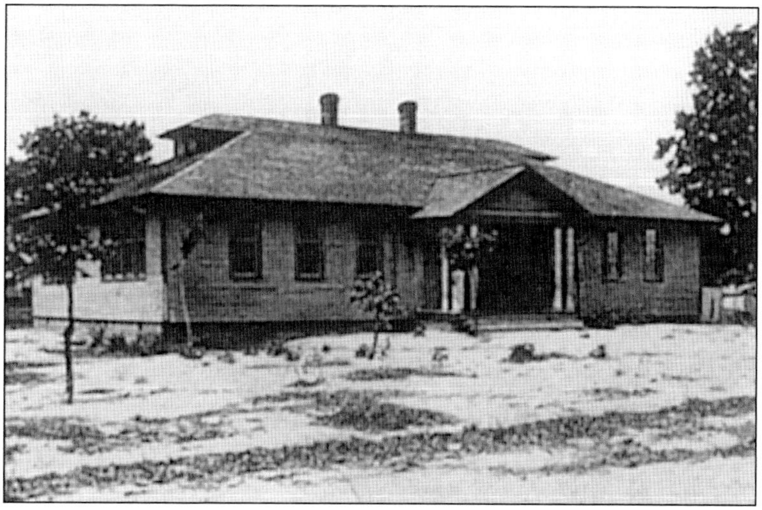

Woodland Avenue Graded School for African-American Students. It was located on the corner of Eleventh Street and opened in 1910. S.A. Smith was the principal. (FCL)

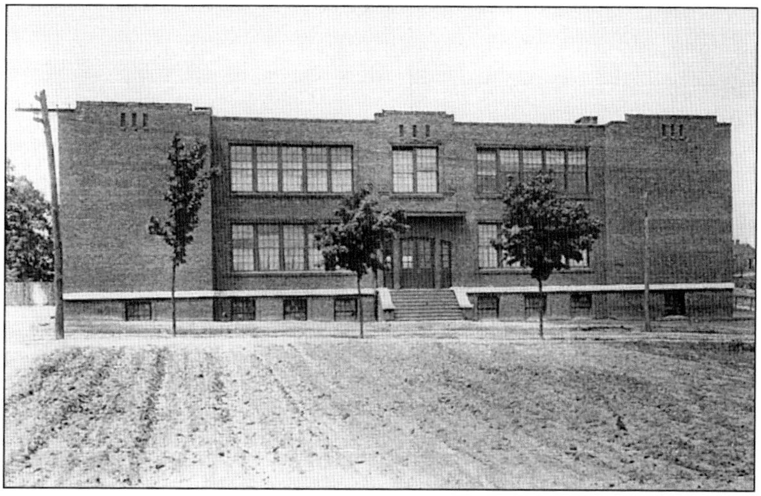

New Woodland Avenue Graded School. It opened in 1914 near the corner of Twelfth Street. R.W. Brown was the principal. (FCL)

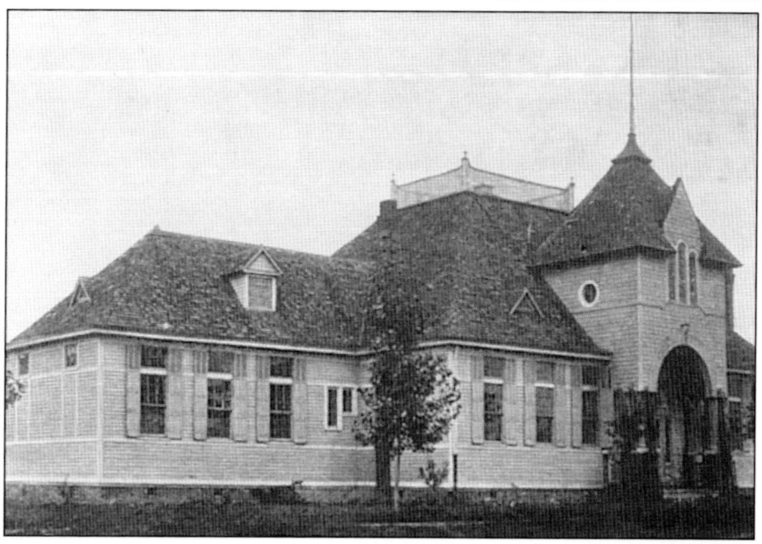

East Graded School, c. 1905. The school was replaced in 1912. (FCL)

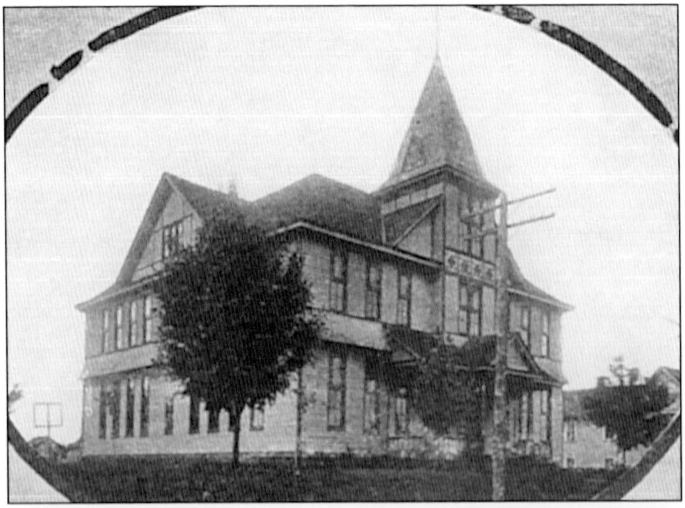

North Graded School, c. 1905. It was built in 1891 and replaced in 1911. (FCL)

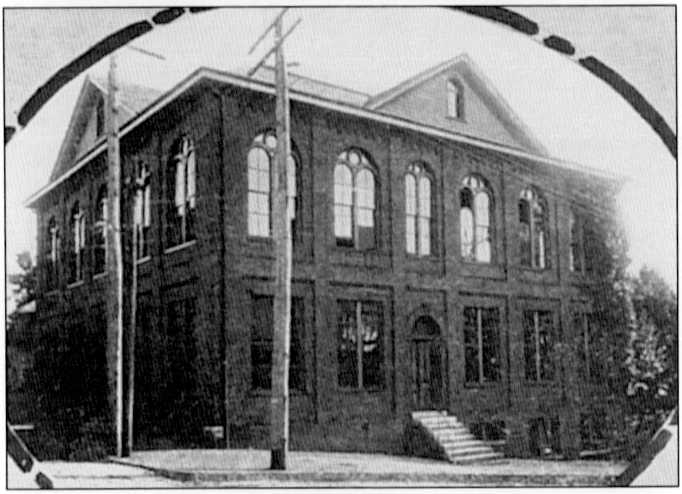

Central Graded School (Formerly the Second Salem Boys School). The school opened in 1913 on Church Street at the corner of Bank Street. Miss Annie Wiley was the principal. (FCL)

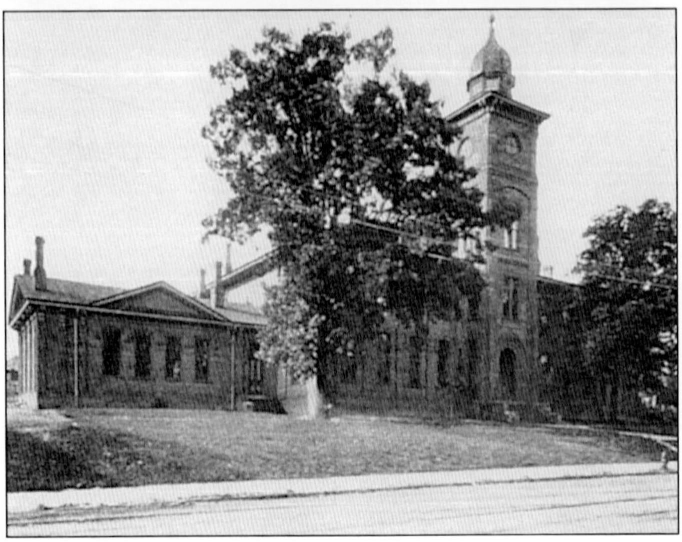

West End Graded School. It opened in 1884 on the corner of Fourth and Broad Streets as Winston Graded School with ten classrooms and had enough room to house the entire school population of the city from the first grade through high school. Mr. Charles D. McIver was the principal. The school was demolished in 1946 to make room for a Sears-Roebuck Department Store. (FCL)

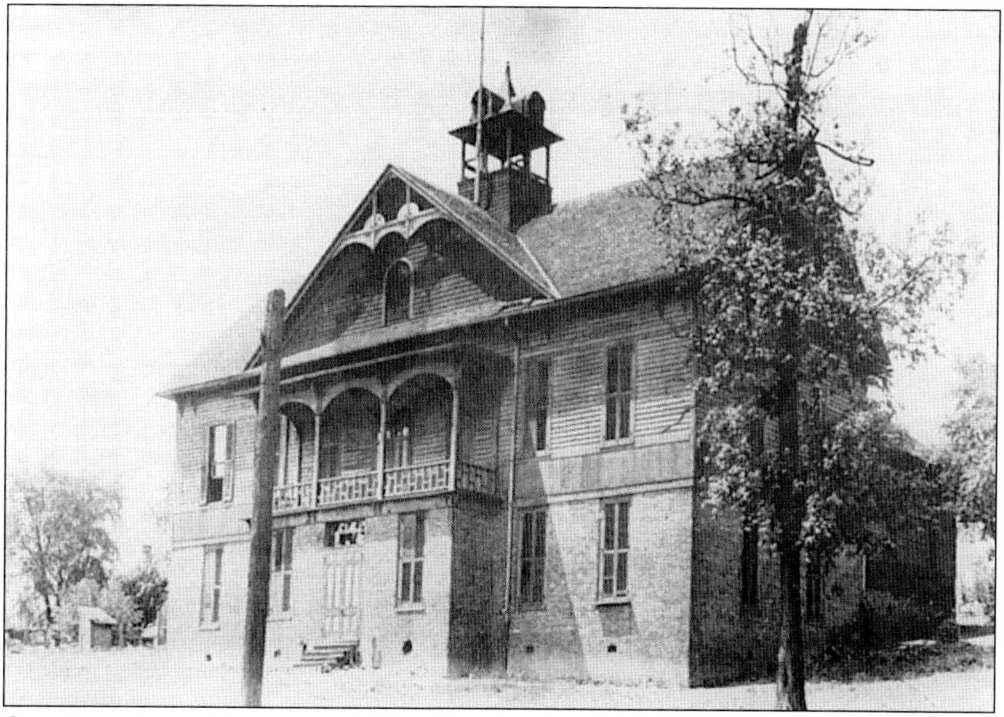

Old West Salem School, c. 1915. Abandoned in 1916 for New Granville School, the old school was located at Mulberry and Laurel Streets. Academy Street ran alongside the building. (FCL)

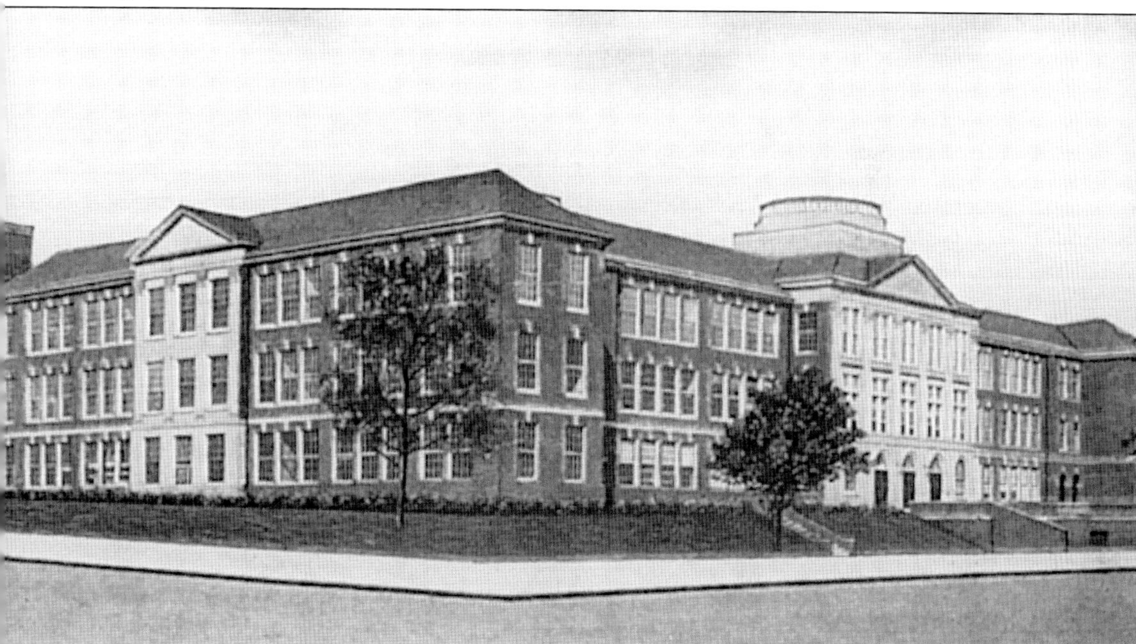

Winston High School. Located on Cherry Street, it was destroyed by fire on January 1, 1923. Construction of Richard J. Reynolds High School on Silver Hill was completed in 1924. The Silver Hill site was donated by Mrs. R.J. Reynolds. (FCL)

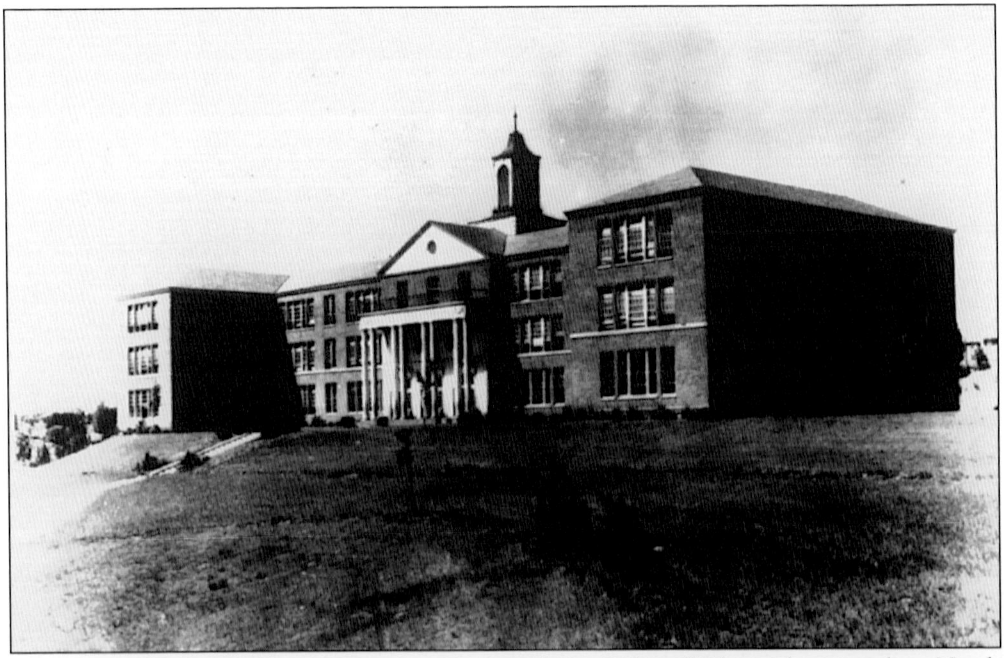

Calvin Wiley School, c. 1920. It was named for Calvin Wiley, who served as North Carolina's superintendent of common schools from 1853 to 1865. He was instrumental in enriching Forsyth County's school system. (FCL)

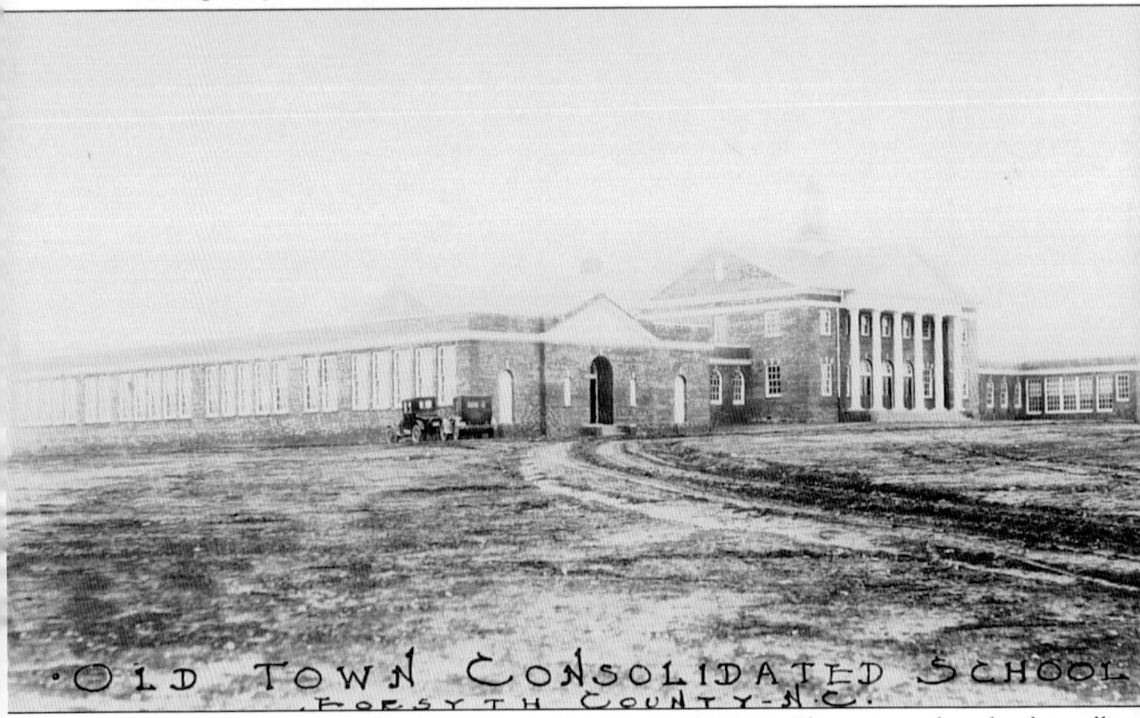

Old Town Consolidated School. Now known as Old Town Elementary, the school is still actively used and is presently being renovated. The school is situated at the corner of Reynolda Road and Shattalon Drive in the Old Town section of Winston-Salem. (FCL)

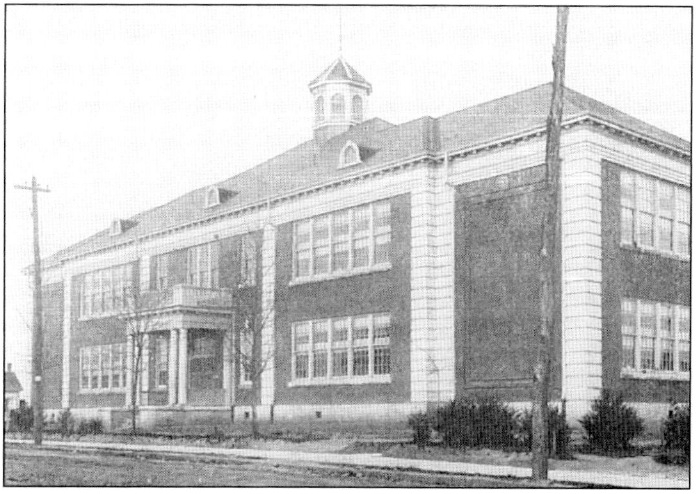

East Winston Grade School. This 1911 photograph shows the East Winston Grade School, which opened in 1901. Miss Ada Roan was principal of this school located at Highland at Seventh Street.

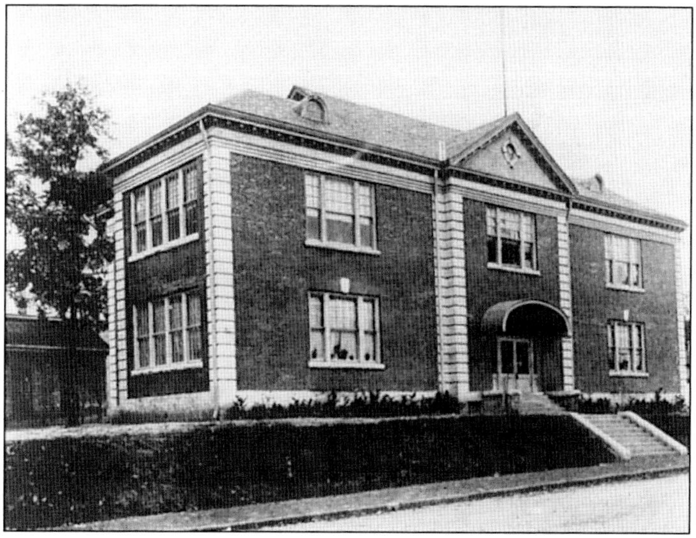

New West End Primary School in 1911. (FCL)

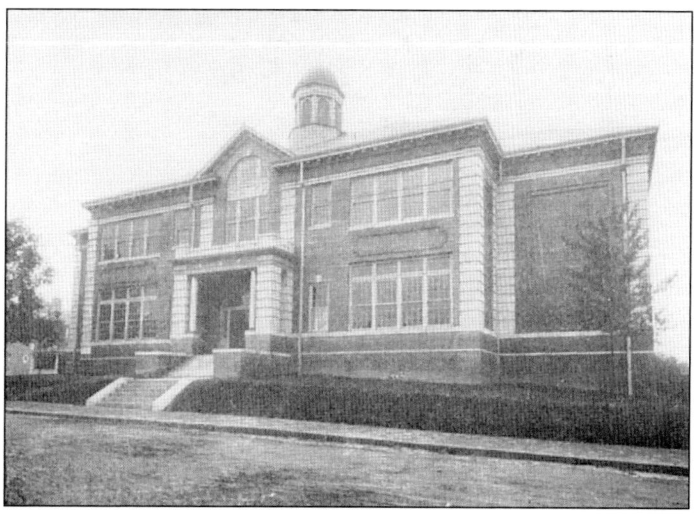

North Winston Grade School in 1912. It was located at 906 Patterson Avenue and also served as an armory, a prison, and Gladiator's Boxing Club. T.H. Cash was the principal.

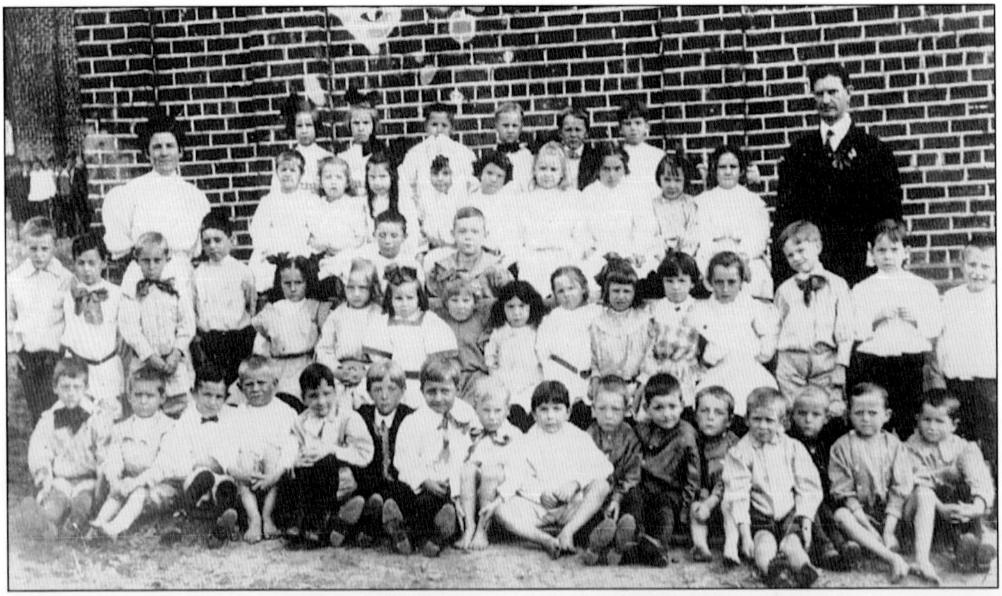

Third Grade Students in West End Graded School, 1900–1901. (FCL)

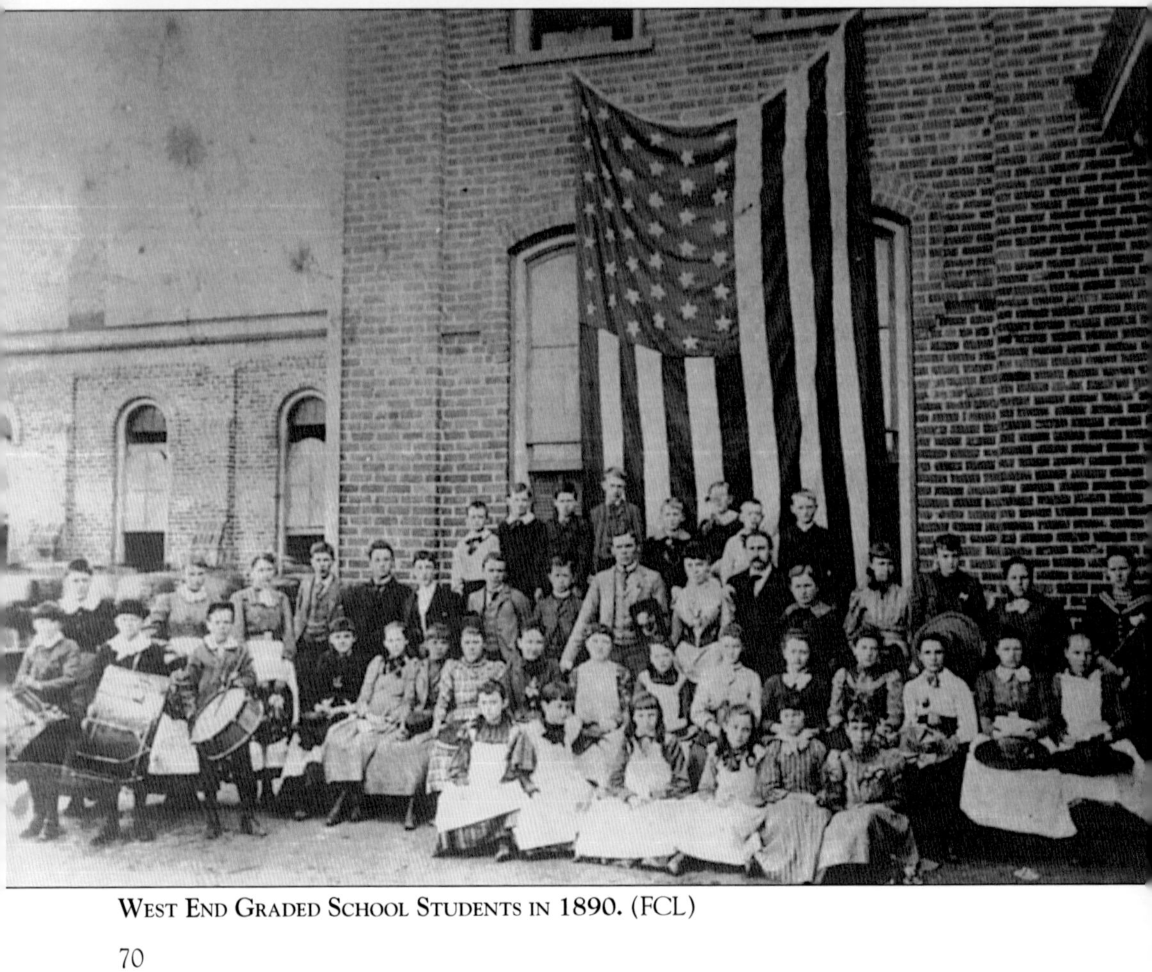

West End Graded School Students in 1890. (FCL)

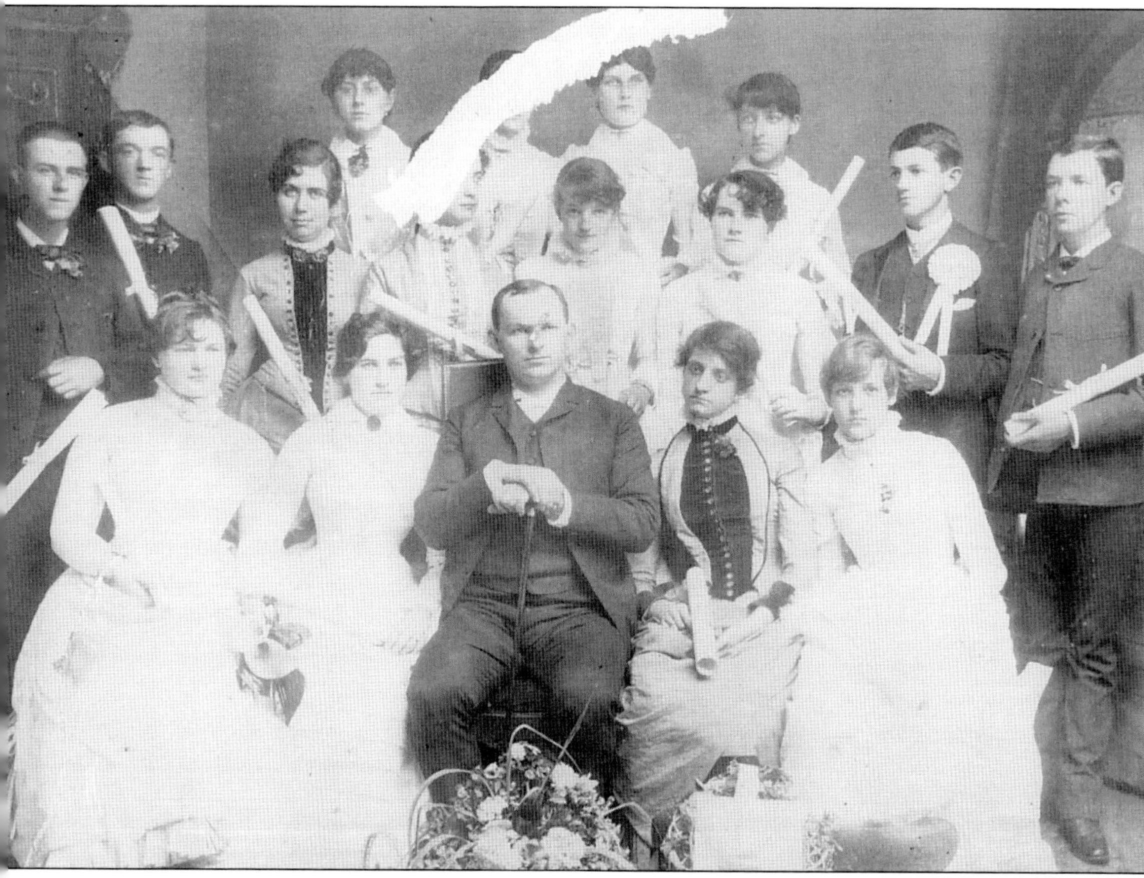

WINSTON HIGH SCHOOL'S FIRST GRADUATING CLASS IN 1886. Principal Charles Duncan McIver left later to teach at the Peace Institute. (FCL)

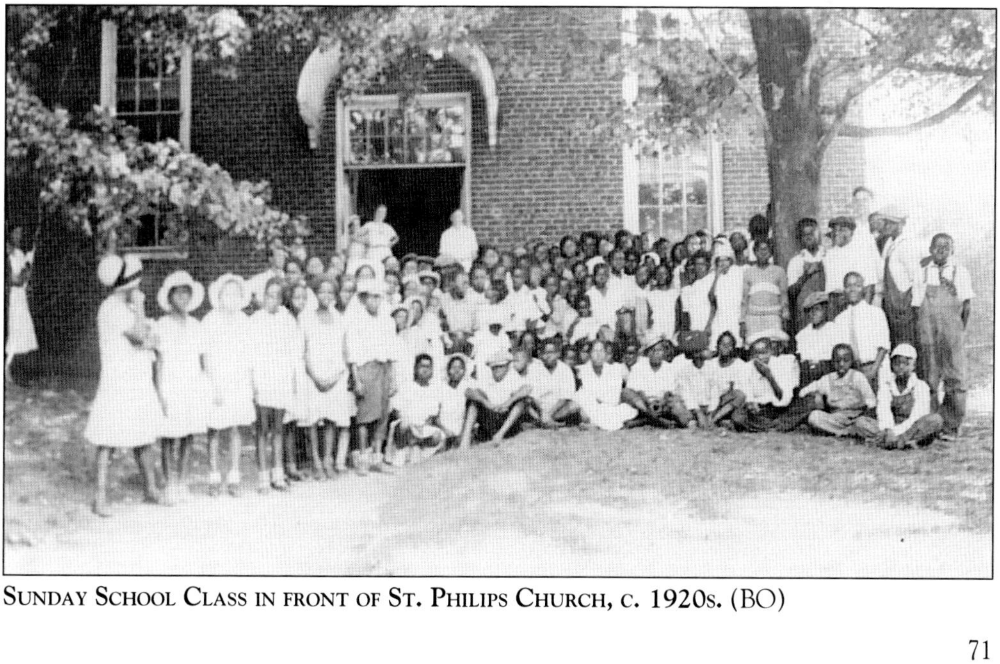

SUNDAY SCHOOL CLASS IN FRONT OF ST. PHILIPS CHURCH, C. 1920S. (BO)

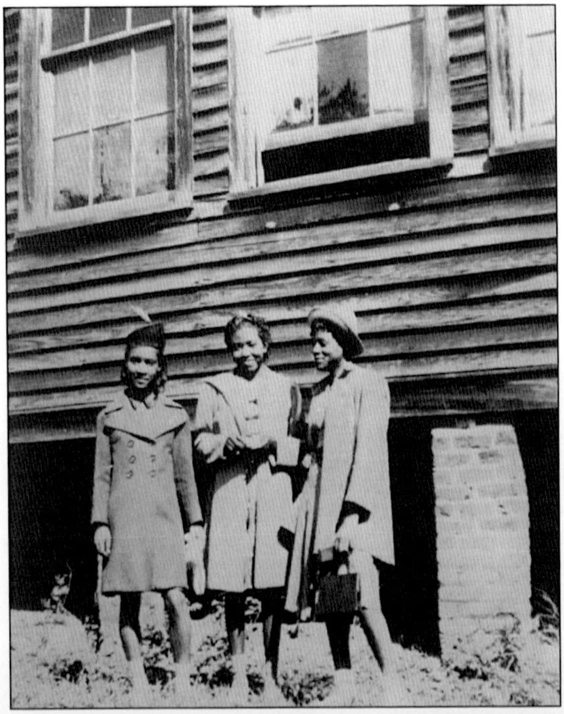

ST. ANDREWS CHURCH IN OLD "SCHOOL IN THE PINES." From left to right are as follows: Nannie Bud, Willette Brendle, and Tilly Latiker. The school faced Pine Street. (WM)

ATKINS HIGH SCHOOL STUDENTS IN 1947. The school was named in honor of Simon Green Atkins. (JRH)

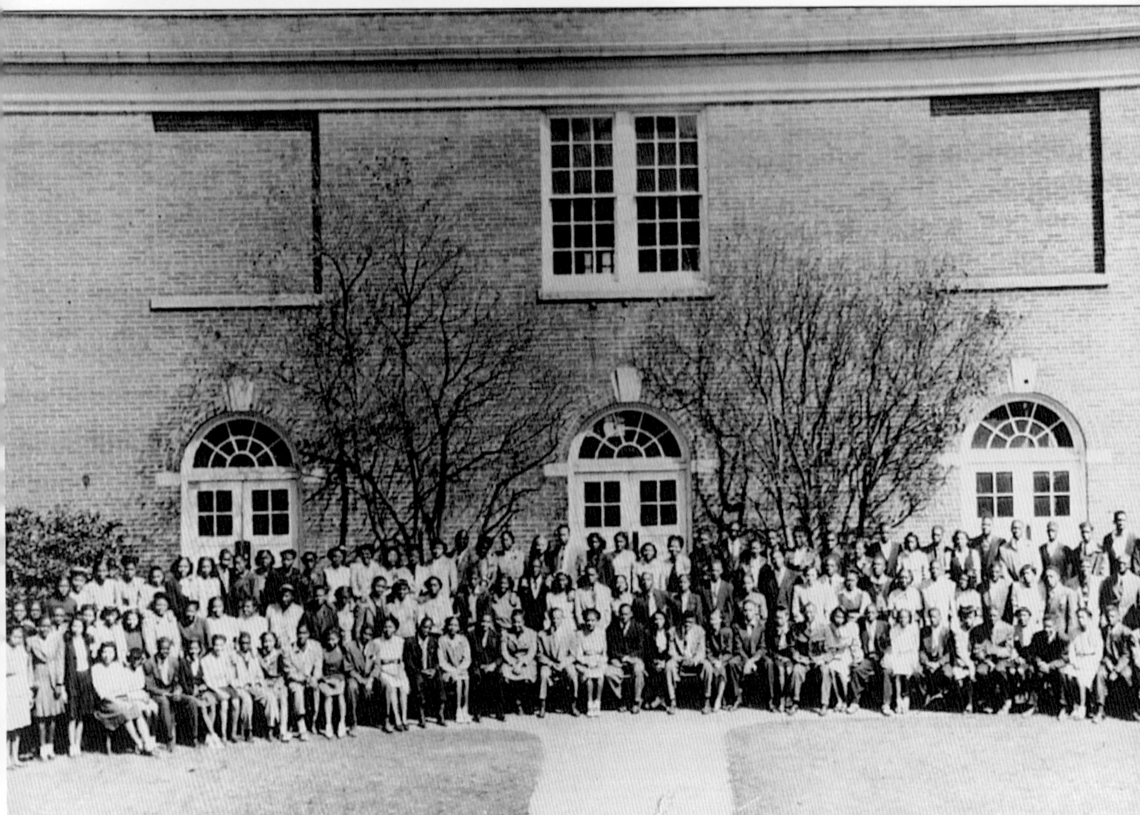

Eight

Time to Relax
Sports and Recreation

No matter how busy one was, there was always time for some friendly competition. Even the most mundane of tasks turned into a social event. A quilting bee could provide some lively gossip as could the old "spit and whittle" club at the old store.

From a friendly neighborhood gathering of "kick-the-can," to a professional baseball game, a crowd was sure to assemble. School and church competitions also offered an opportunity for the community to meet and socialize. At these functions, friends and family shared their picnics. The common goal was always to rally behind the home team and to have a good time.

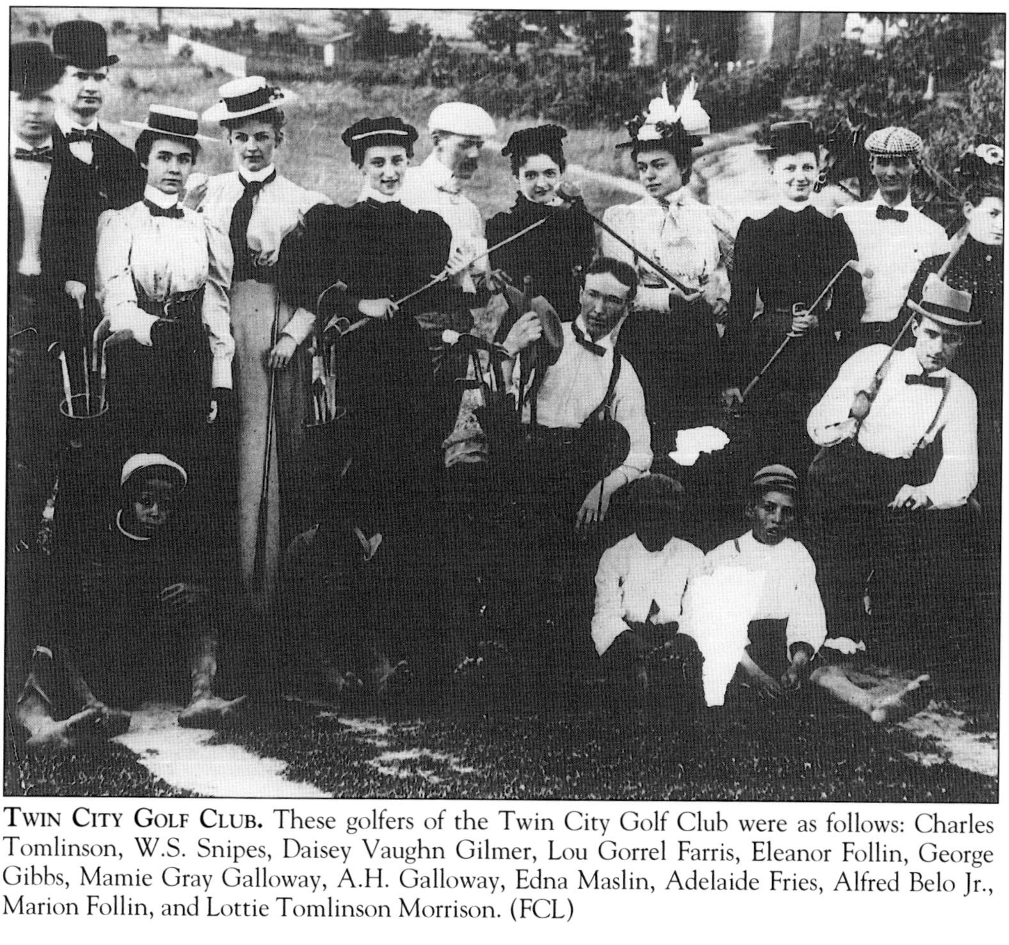

Twin City Golf Club. These golfers of the Twin City Golf Club were as follows: Charles Tomlinson, W.S. Snipes, Daisey Vaughn Gilmer, Lou Gorrel Farris, Eleanor Follin, George Gibbs, Mamie Gray Galloway, A.H. Galloway, Edna Maslin, Adelaide Fries, Alfred Belo Jr., Marion Follin, and Lottie Tomlinson Morrison. (FCL)

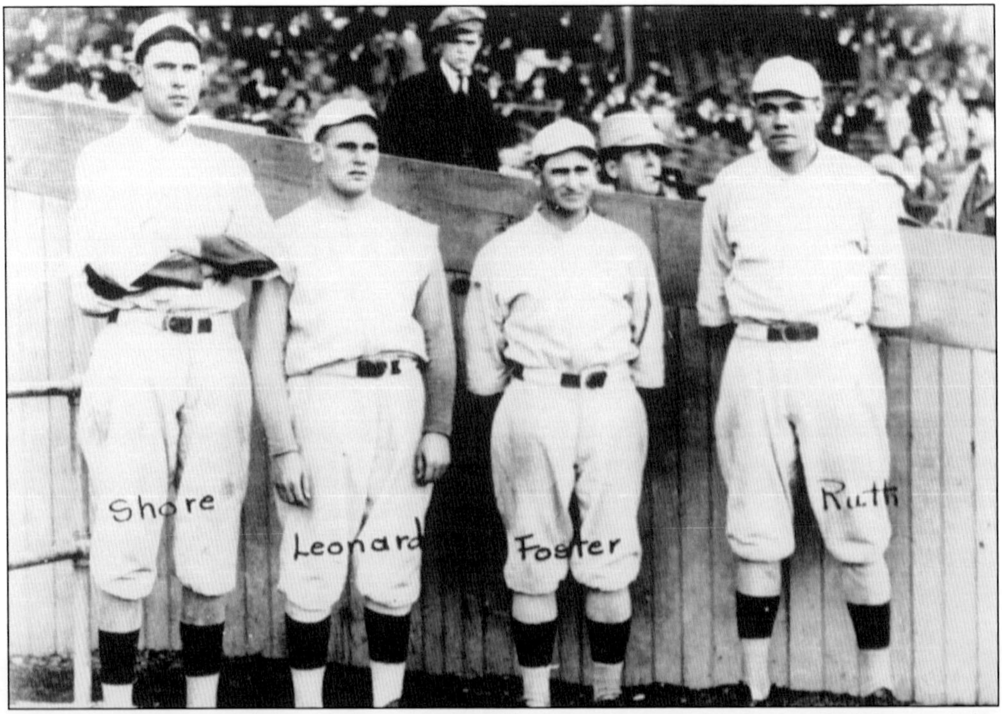

BASEBALL PLAYERS. Pitchers for the 1926 World Series between the Boston Red Sox and the New York Yankees were Ernie Shore, Hubert Benjamin "Duth" Leonard, George "Rube" Foster, and Babe Ruth. (FCL)

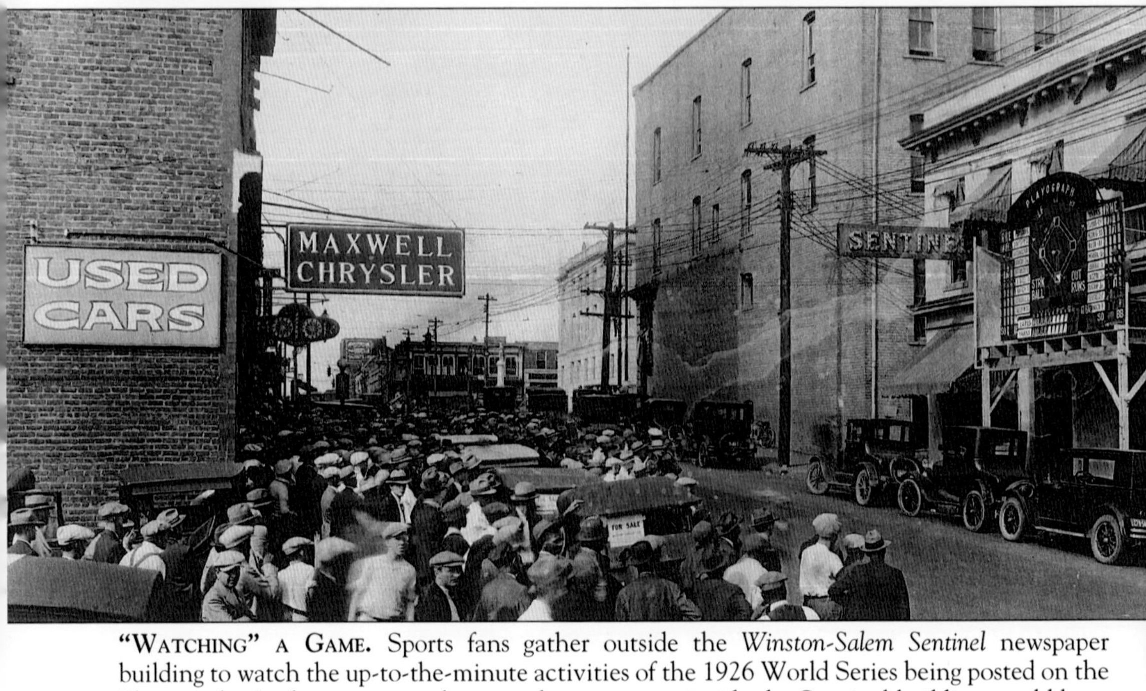

"WATCHING" A GAME. Sports fans gather outside the *Winston-Salem Sentinel* newspaper building to watch the up-to-the-minute activities of the 1926 World Series being posted on the Playograph. As there was no television then, a person inside the Sentinel building would keep the plays of the game current by posting them on the Playograph for everyone to watch. (FCL)

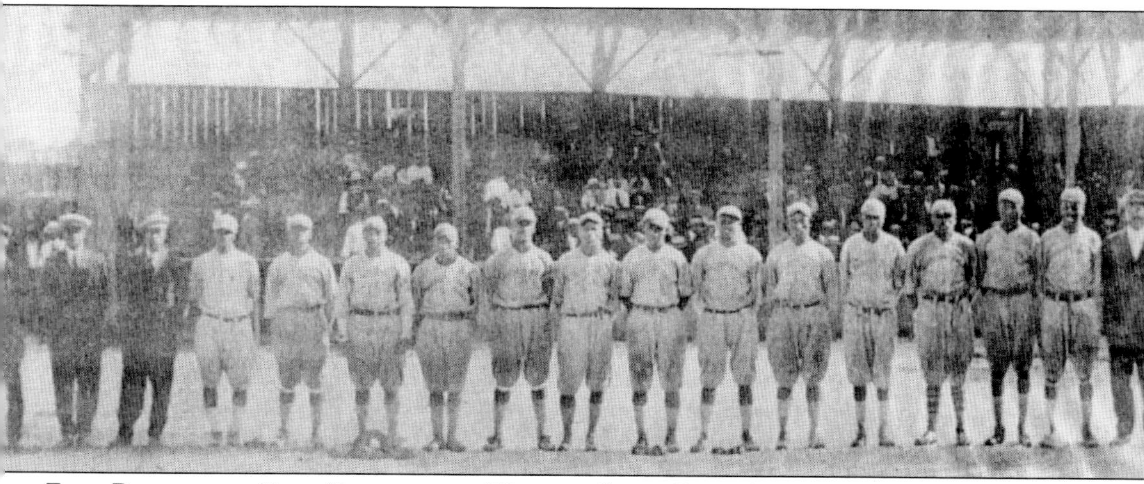

First Photograph Ever Taken of the Winston-Salem Pond Giants, Founded in 1914. This African-American team was the oldest semi-pro baseball team in the nation. Some of the players were Edward Hill, Morris Neely Lawson, Johnny Hopp, Tom Tolliver, and Lefty Gray. Dude Allen was the bat boy. Will Davis was the president of the team, Will Harding, vice president, Morris Lawson, manager, and Wince Rucker, secretary and treasurer. This team was famous for their games played at the Prince Albert Park (where Shiloh Baptist Church is now) against the Atlanta Black Crackers, Washington Potomac's, and Baltimore Black Sox. (FCL)

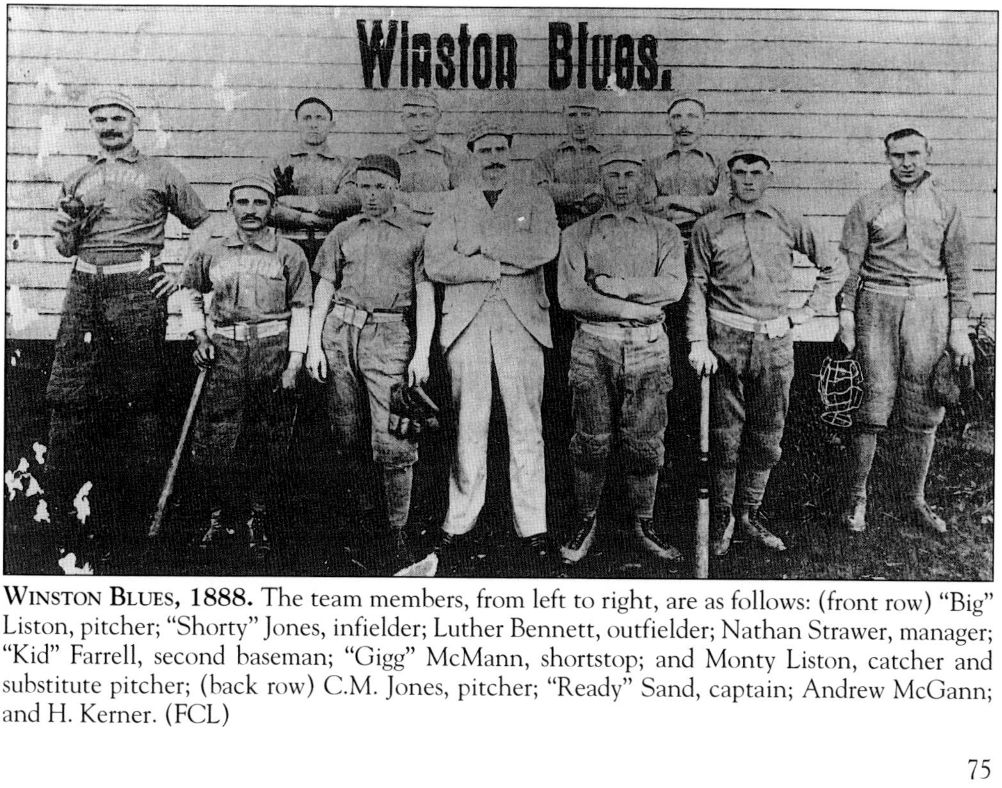

Winston Blues, 1888. The team members, from left to right, are as follows: (front row) "Big" Liston, pitcher; "Shorty" Jones, infielder; Luther Bennett, outfielder; Nathan Strawer, manager; "Kid" Farrell, second baseman; "Gigg" McMann, shortstop; and Monty Liston, catcher and substitute pitcher; (back row) C.M. Jones, pitcher; "Ready" Sand, captain; Andrew McGann; and H. Kerner. (FCL)

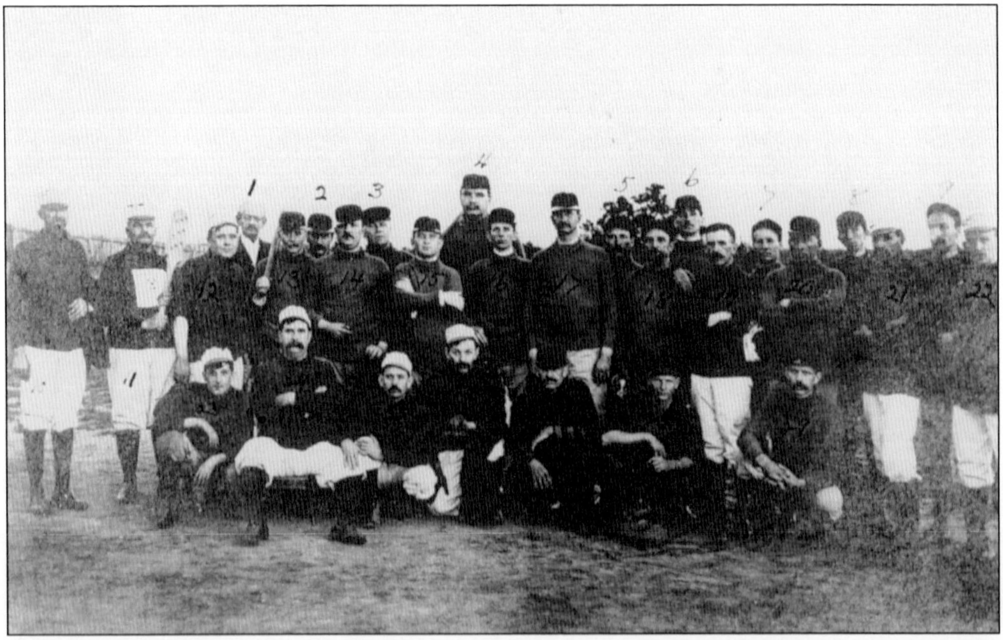

Baseball. On September 11, 1902, local doctors and lawyers engaged in some friendly competition and entertainment for the citizens of Winston-Salem. The doctors won 13-11. (FCL)

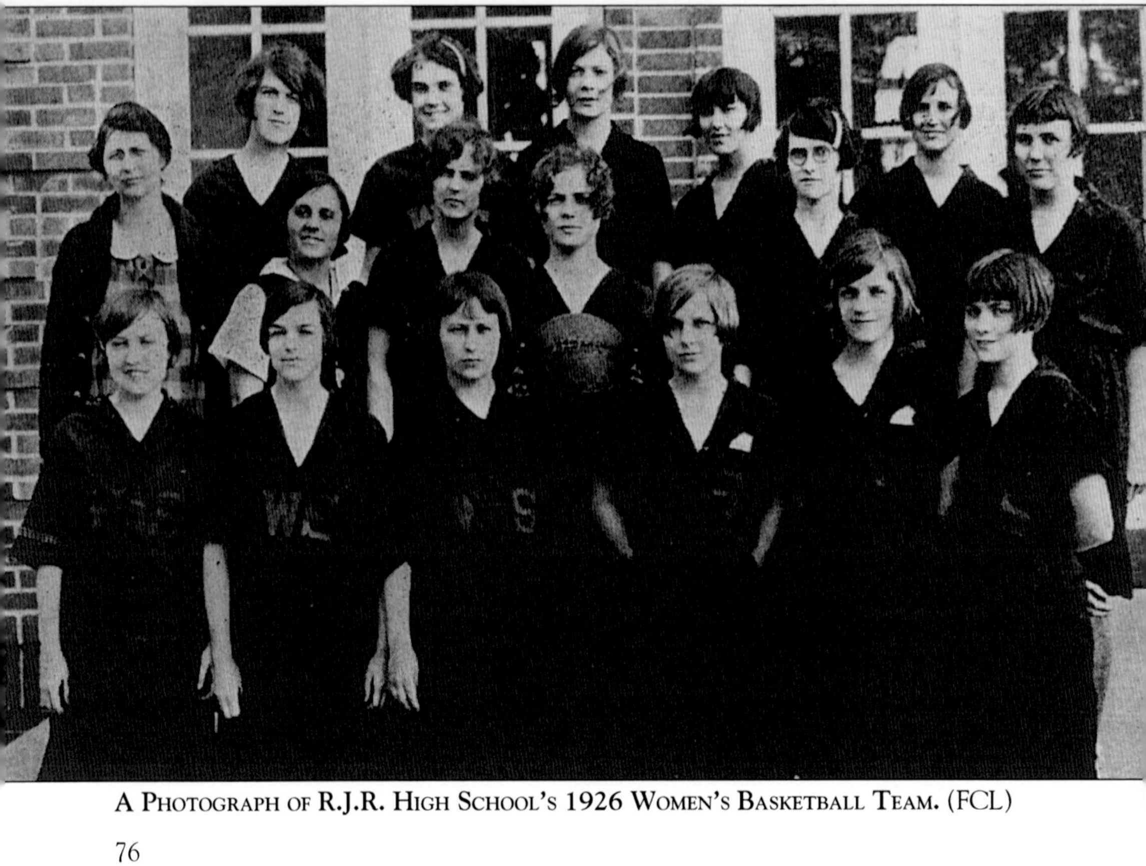

A Photograph of R.J.R. High School's 1926 Women's Basketball Team. (FCL)

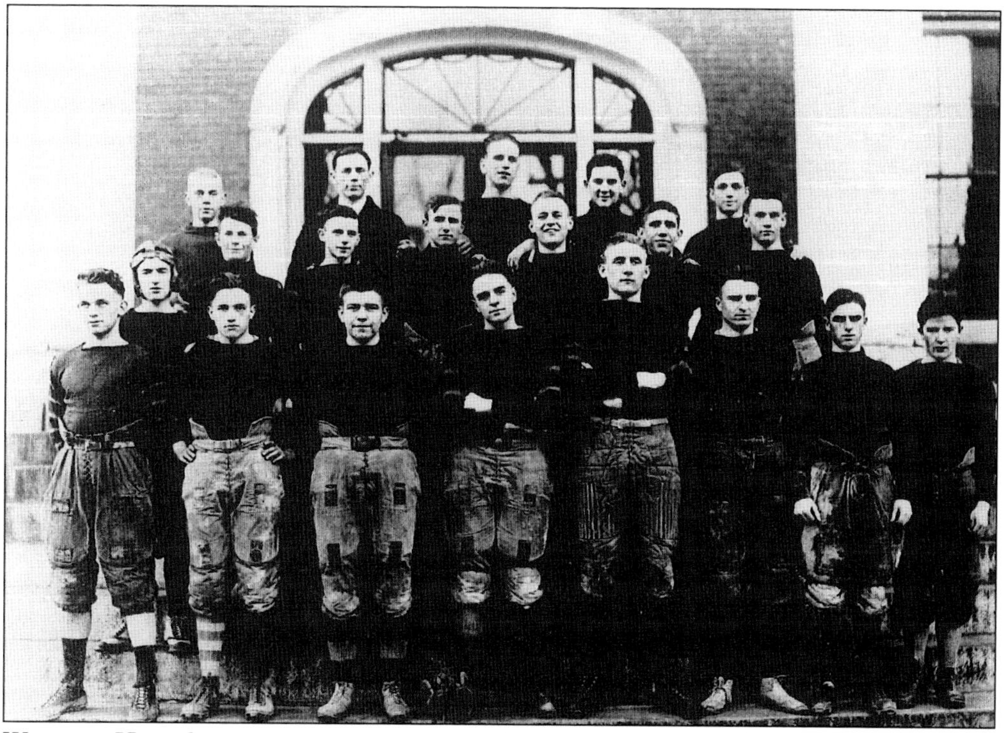

Winston High School Football Team of 1917. The team members are Logan, Wright (coach), Crute (captain), O'Brien, Cooper, Caldwell, Fulton, Connelly, Langley, Shepherd (manager), Kirk, Davis, Marler, Bolick, Turner, Glenn, McKinnie, Dalton, Pulliam, and Thames. G.H. Caldwell was the only member who could afford a helmet. All players had to buy their own uniform. (FCL)

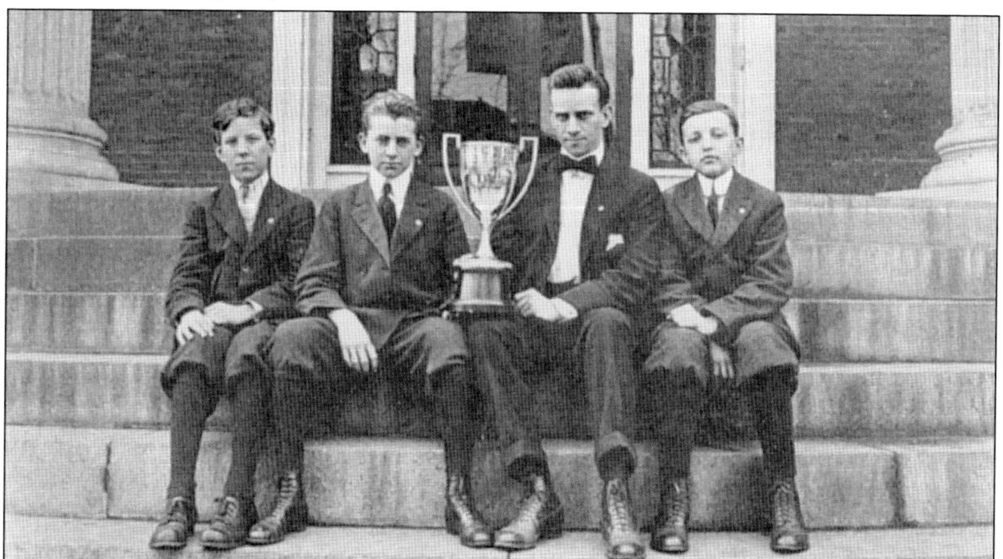

Winston High School Academics. On April 9, 1914, these boys won the Aycock Memorial Cup against 600 other students in the state. The members are Gordon Ambler, Hortus Scott, Charles Roddick, and Clifton Eaton (third from left). (FCL)

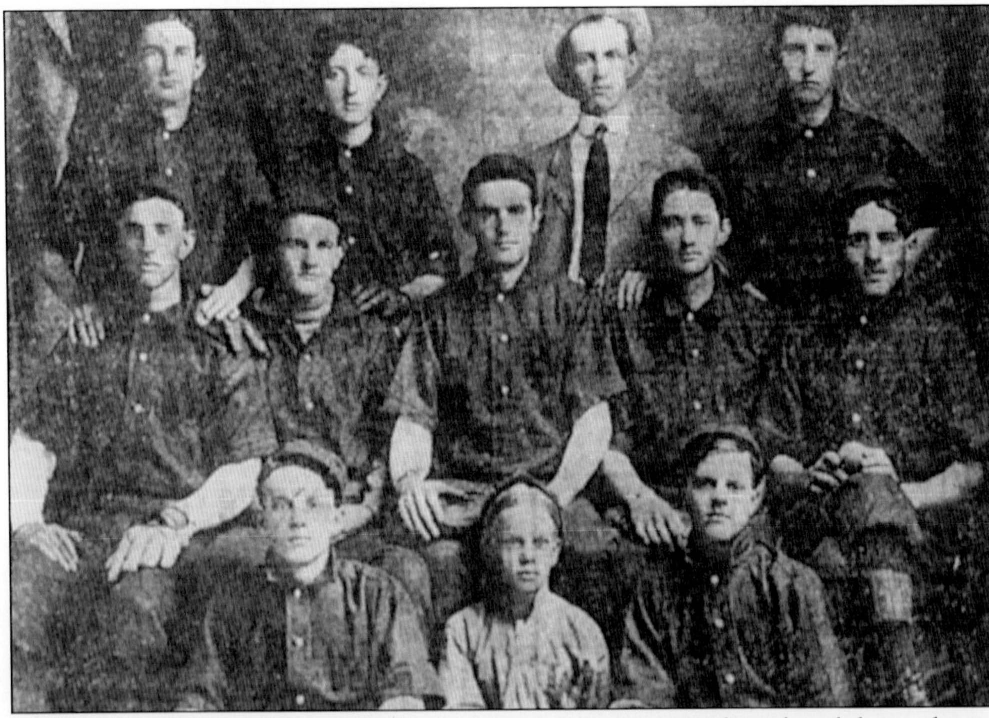

Waughtown Wildcats Baseball Team of 1907. The team members, from left to right, are as follows: (front row) Sid Teague, shortstop; Bernie Teague, bat boy; and Bill Vogler, right field; (middle row) Fate McGee, third baseman; Carl Nissen, pitcher; Hank Nissen, catcher; Tip Crowder, first baseman; and Harvey Cook, utility man; (back row) John Brown, center field; Jim Cofer, second baseman; K.E. (Ned) Shore, utility man; and Charlie Elliott, left field.

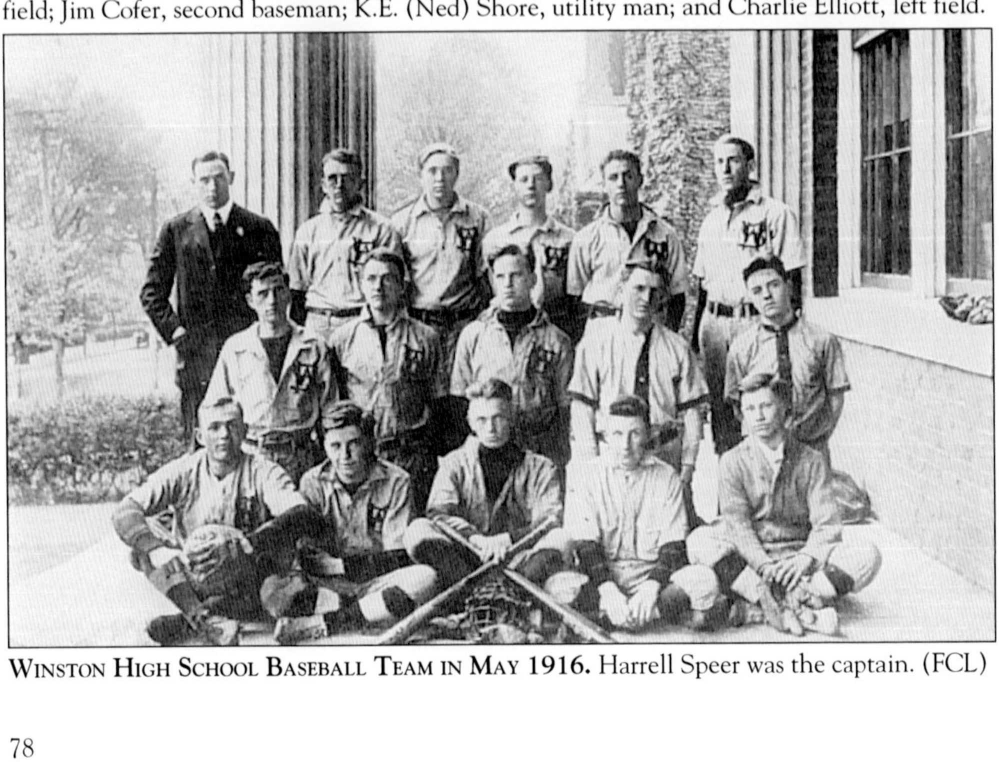

Winston High School Baseball Team in May 1916. Harrell Speer was the captain. (FCL)

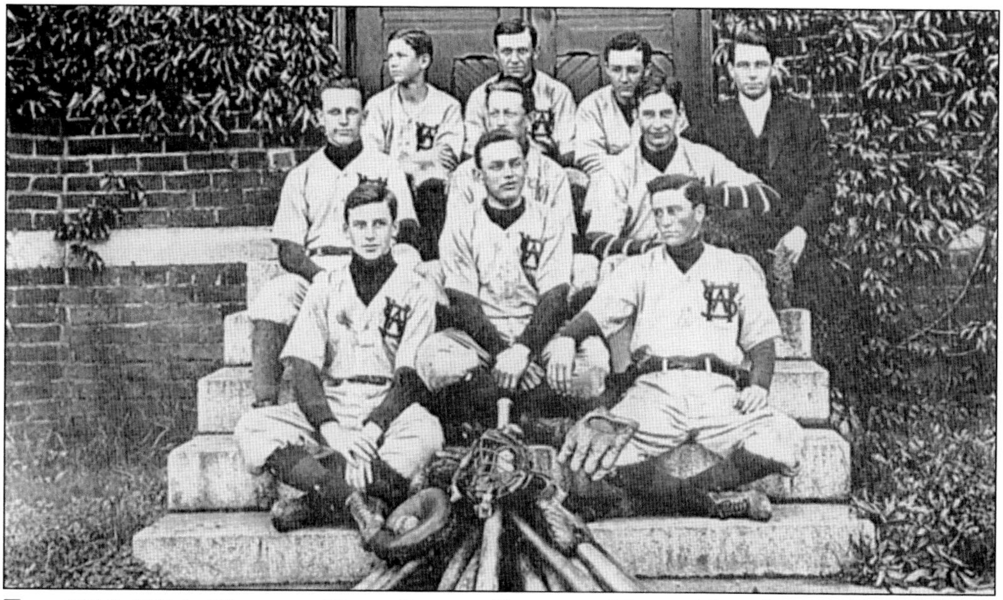

The 1913–1914 Winston High School Baseball Team. The players are as follows: Foglemen, pitcher; Hardin Jewett, pitcher; Hancock, pitcher; Harrel Speer, catcher; Morris, second baseman; Hamilton Horton, shortstop; Raymond Dean, third baseman; Patrick Henry, captain and first baseman; Martin, left field; Weatherman, center field; and Douglas, right field. The substitutes were Wilson and Gregory Graham. (FCL)

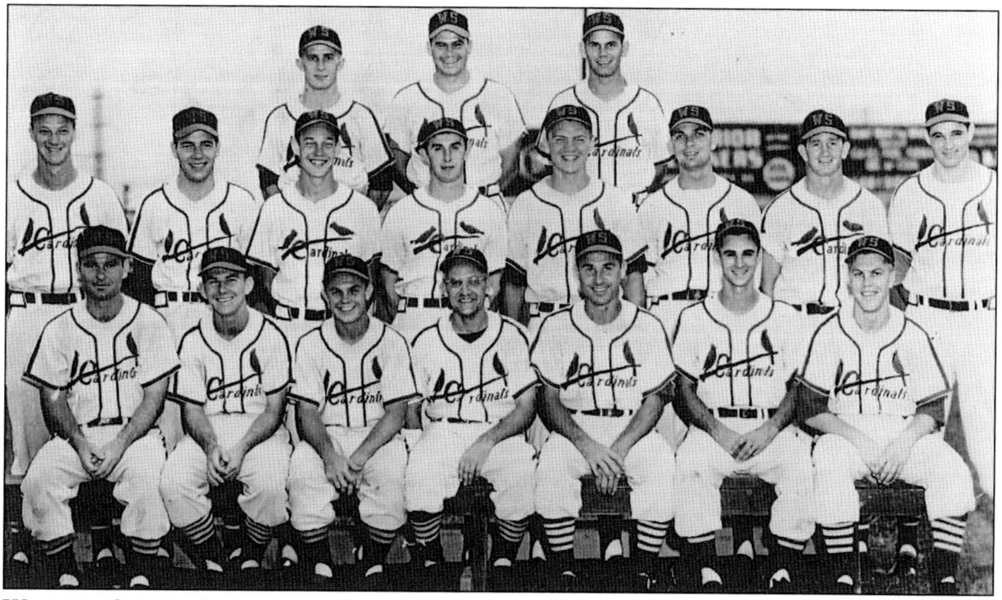

Winston-Salem Cardinals Baseball Team Who Won the 1950 Carolina League Championship. It was the first Winston-Salem professional baseball pennant won in 22 years. The players, from left to right, are as follows: (front row) Ed Polak, Jack Huesman, Earl Weaver, George Kissell (manager), Lee Peterson, Jim Neufeldt, and Bob Bills; (middle row) Dick Umberger, Bobby Tiefenauer, Neal Hertweck, George Condrick, Gene Barth, Hal Atkinson, J.C. Dunn, and Wilmer Mizell; (back row) Ken Morgan, Bill LaFrance, Russell Rack, and Hoyt Benedict (not shown). (FCL)

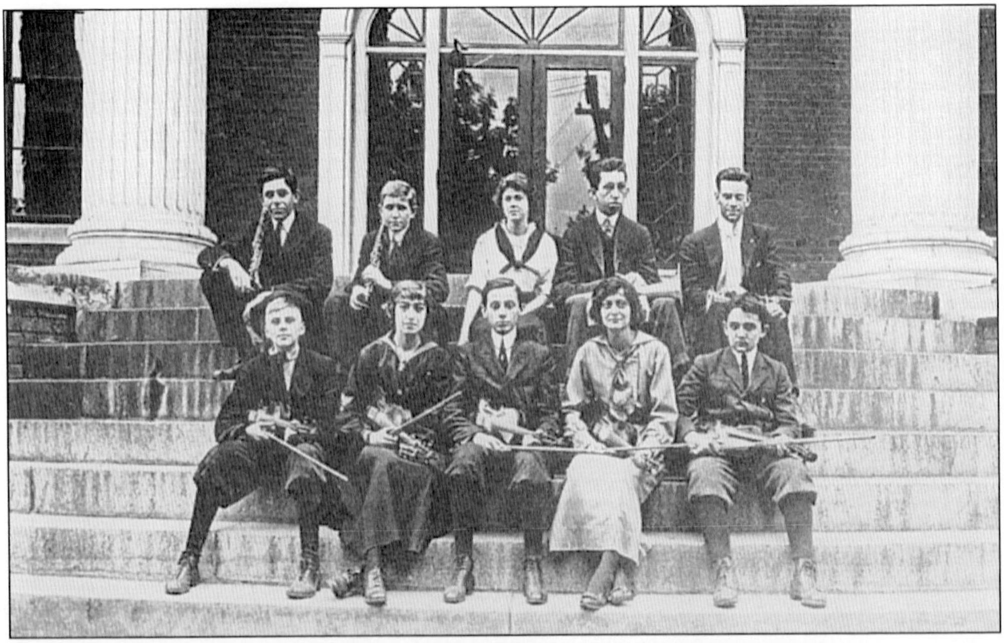

WINSTON HIGH SCHOOL ORCHESTRA IN MAY 1914.

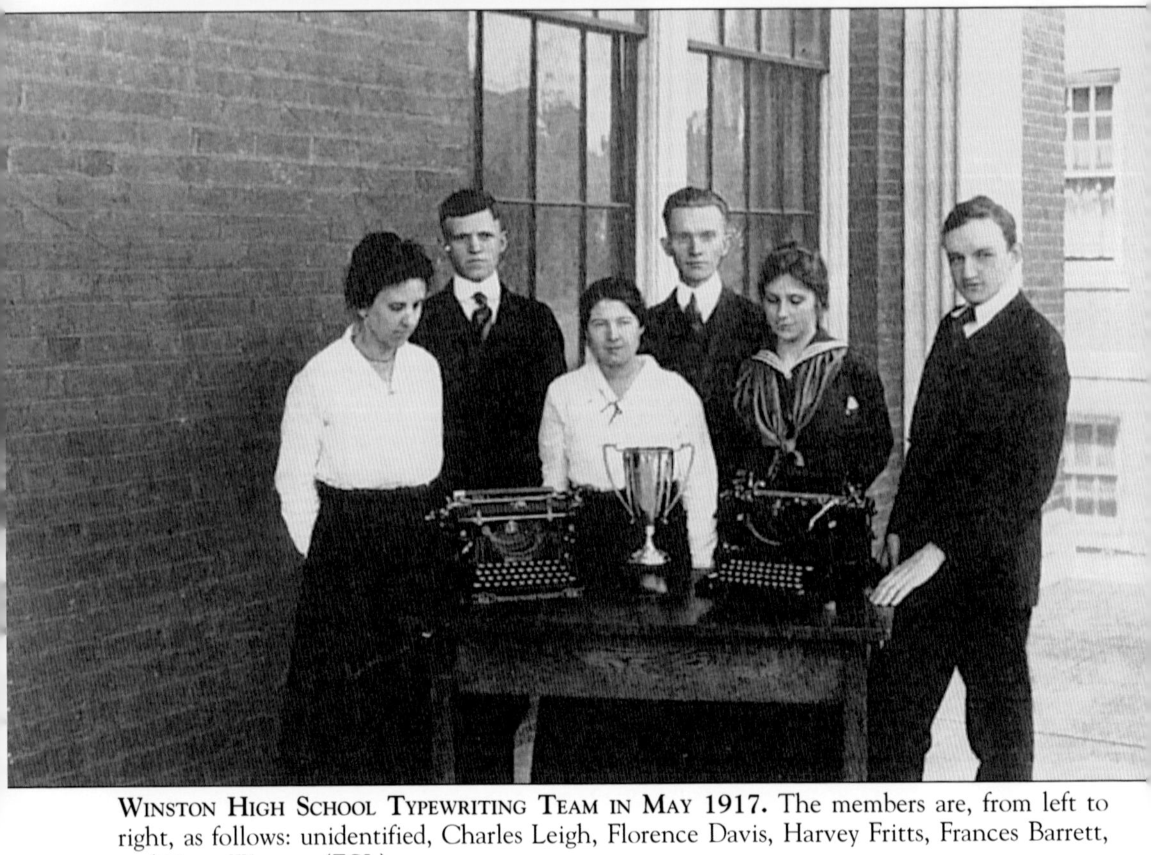

WINSTON HIGH SCHOOL TYPEWRITING TEAM IN MAY 1917. The members are, from left to right, as follows: unidentified, Charles Leigh, Florence Davis, Harvey Fritts, Frances Barrett, and Harry Weaver. (FCL)

Nine

Transportation
Wheels of Progress

Before the luxury of modern-day transportation, people in the country relied on basic conveyances pulled by horse, mules, oxen, and sometimes even goats. Travel was difficult in even the best of circumstances, and a heavy rain could destroy even the best of footpaths.

In the 1850s, two wagon builders, Spach and Nissen, competed for customers. Their strong Conestoga wagons, admired by the tobacco farmers, hauled tons of tobacco and crops from farm to factory. In the late 1890s, transportation became more modernized. The citizens of Forsyth found themselves traveling around the town of Winston by electric streetcar and then by bus. If the train wasn't going your way, Camel City Bus line was.

In the twentieth century, transportation and roads improved by leaps and bounds to meet the needs of families who wanted to escape to the countryside in their own vehicle. From the humble beginnings of Old Plank Road in Bethania, to modern-day Interstate 40, the citizens of Forsyth County have always been able to easily access the great state of North Carolina.

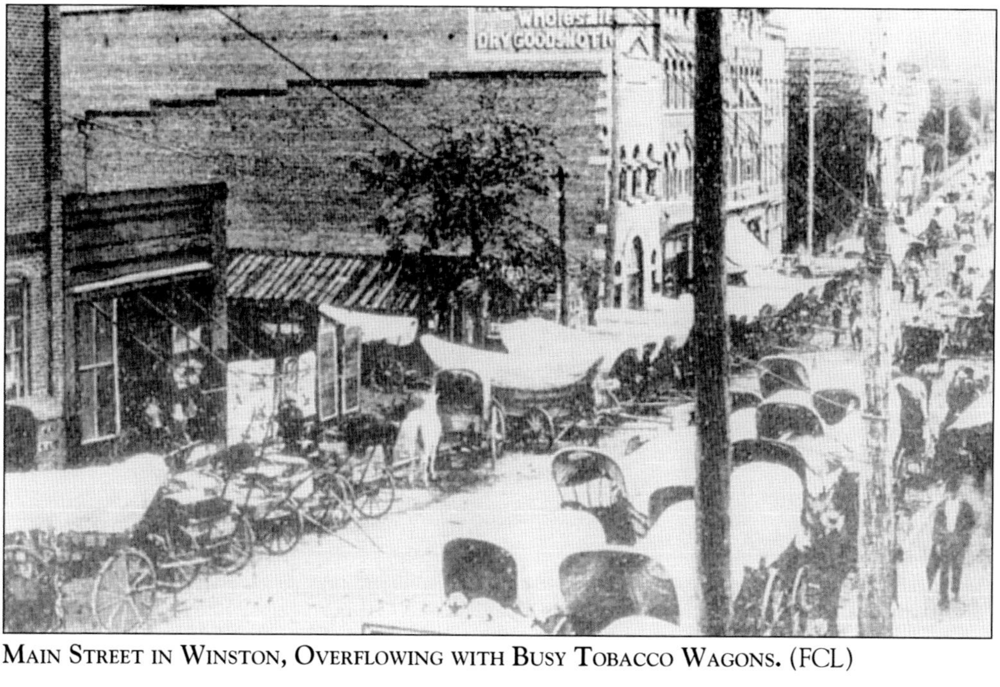

MAIN STREET IN WINSTON, OVERFLOWING WITH BUSY TOBACCO WAGONS. (FCL)

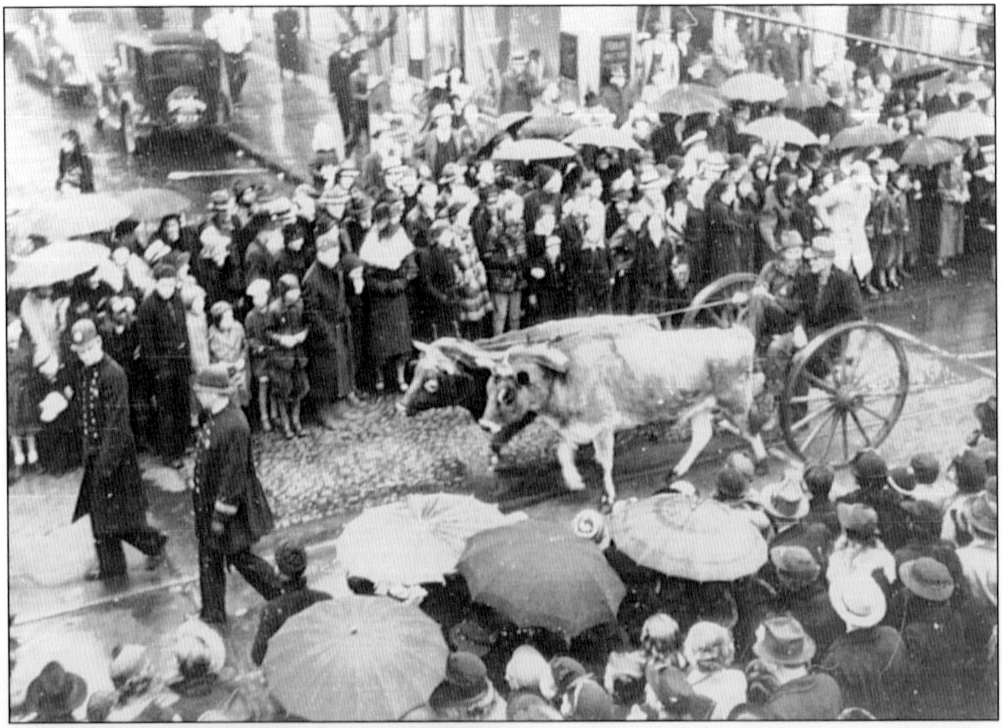

POLICE AND OXEN IN A 1936 PARADE. (FCL)

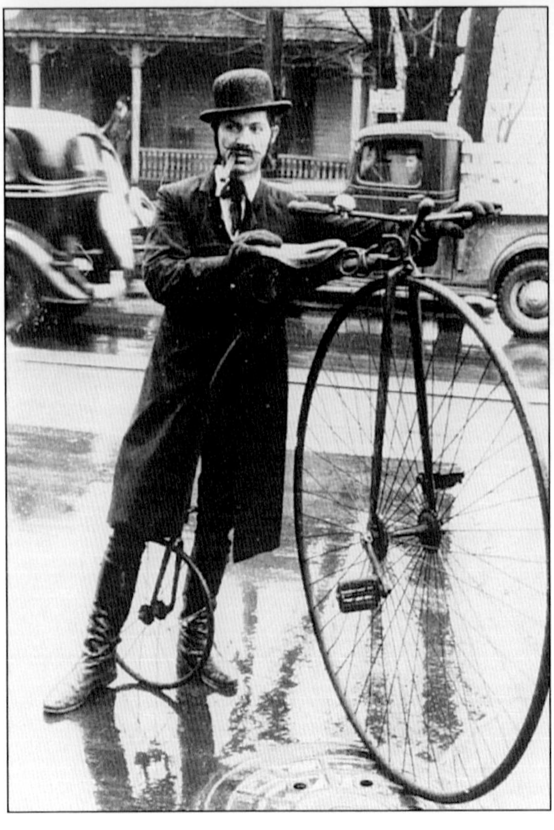

CYCLING. An unidentified cyclist takes on damp weather for this sophisticated pose. (FCL)

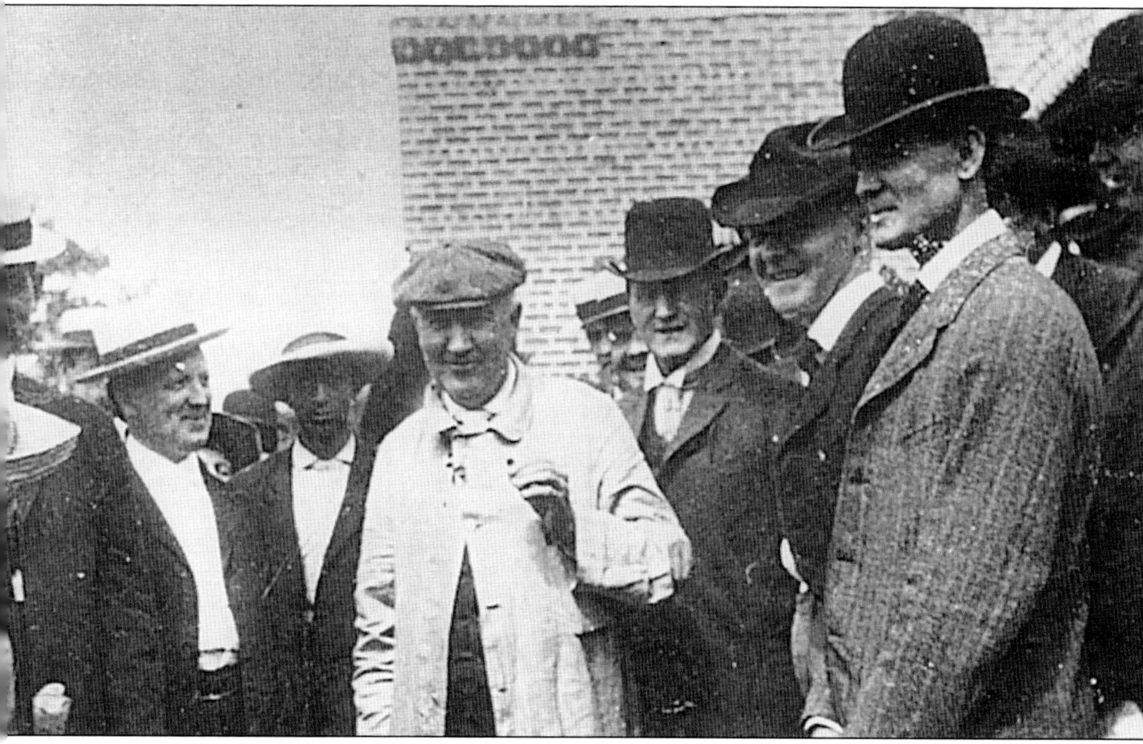

Edison Visiting Winston. When Winston's electric streetcar system began in 1890, Thomas Edison attended the festivities. (FCL)

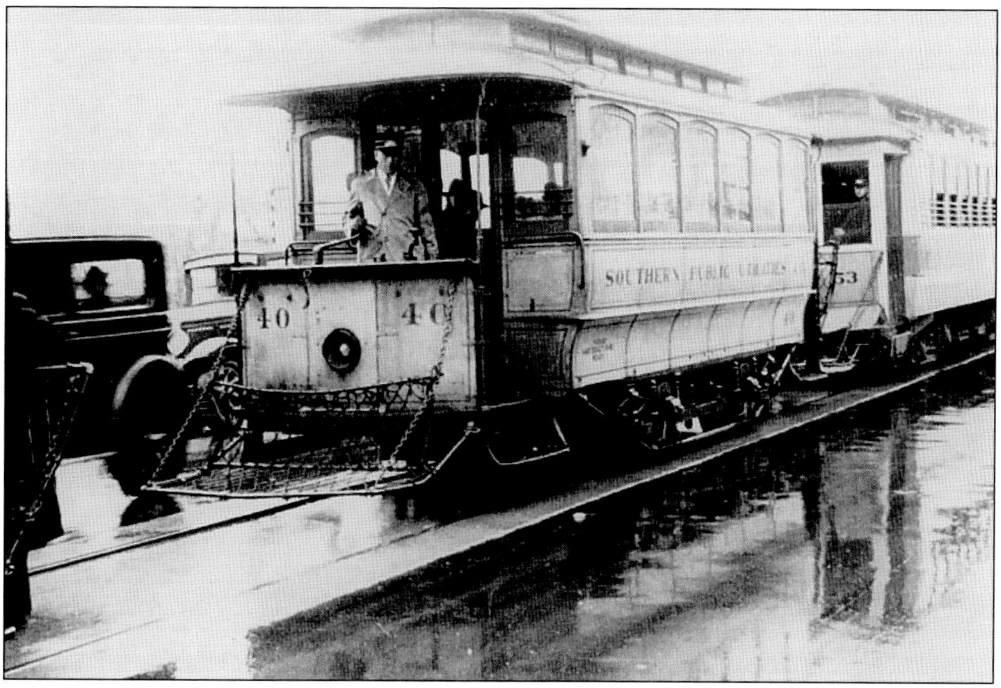

Streetcars Owned by the Southern Public Utilities. This mode of transportation served downtown Winston-Salem. (FCL)

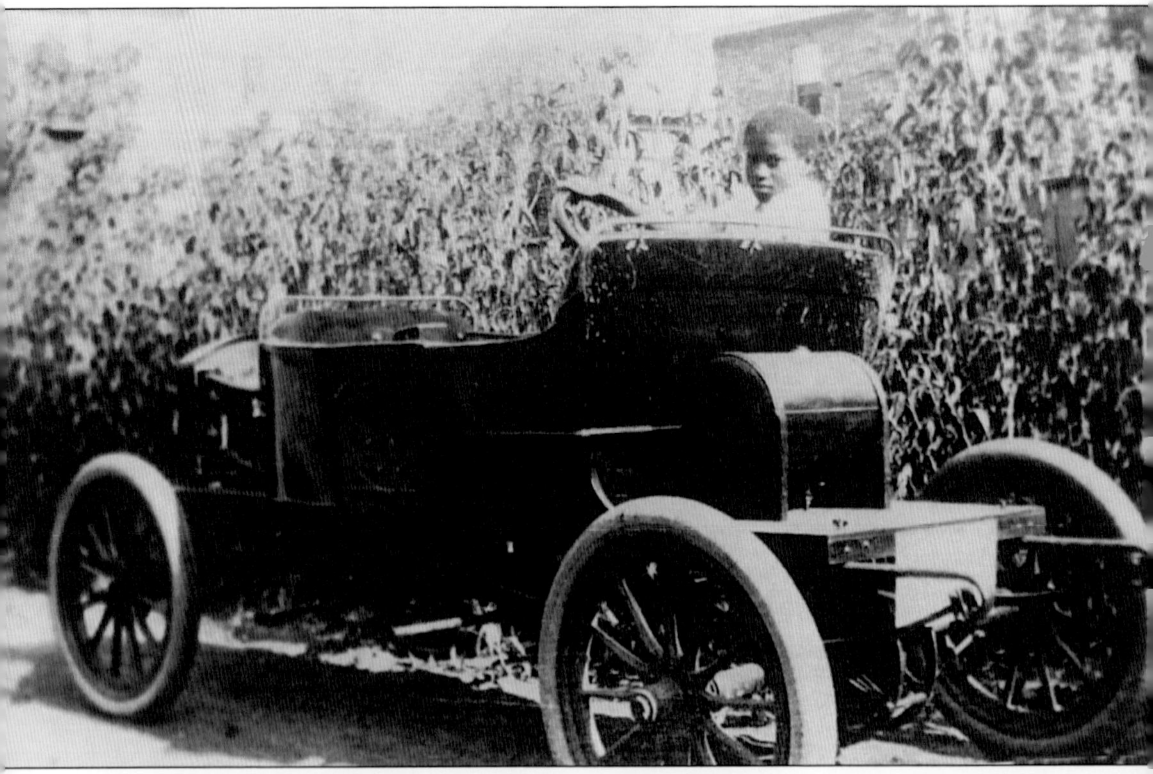

PAUL FRIES AS A LAD YEARNING TO TRAVEL, C. 1912. (CC)

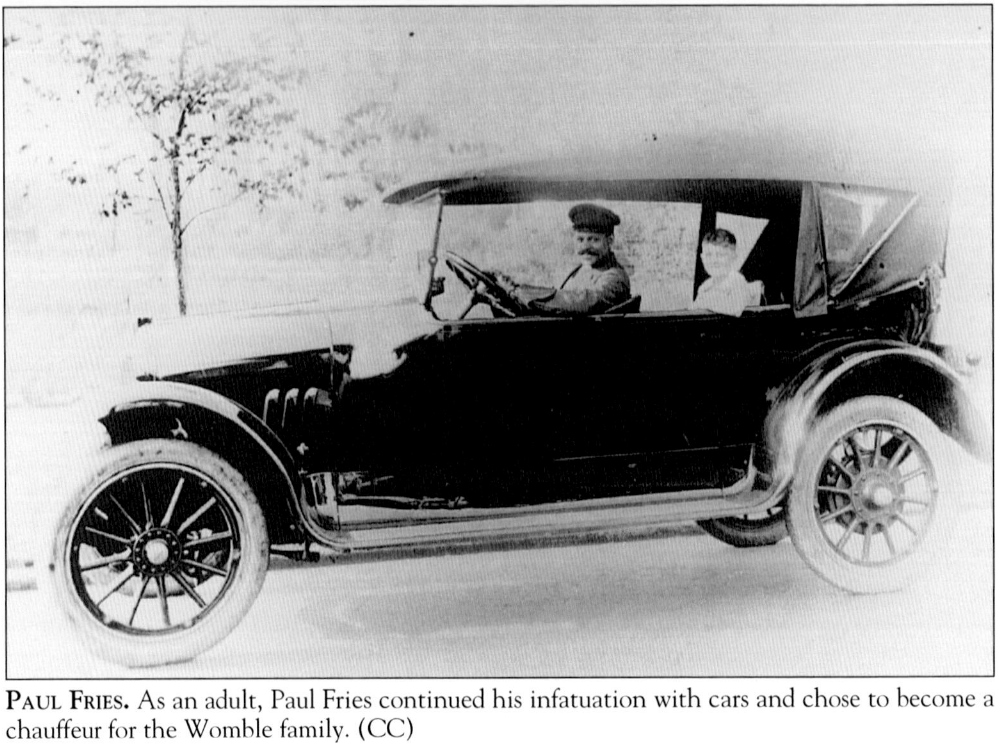

PAUL FRIES. As an adult, Paul Fries continued his infatuation with cars and chose to become a chauffeur for the Womble family. (CC)

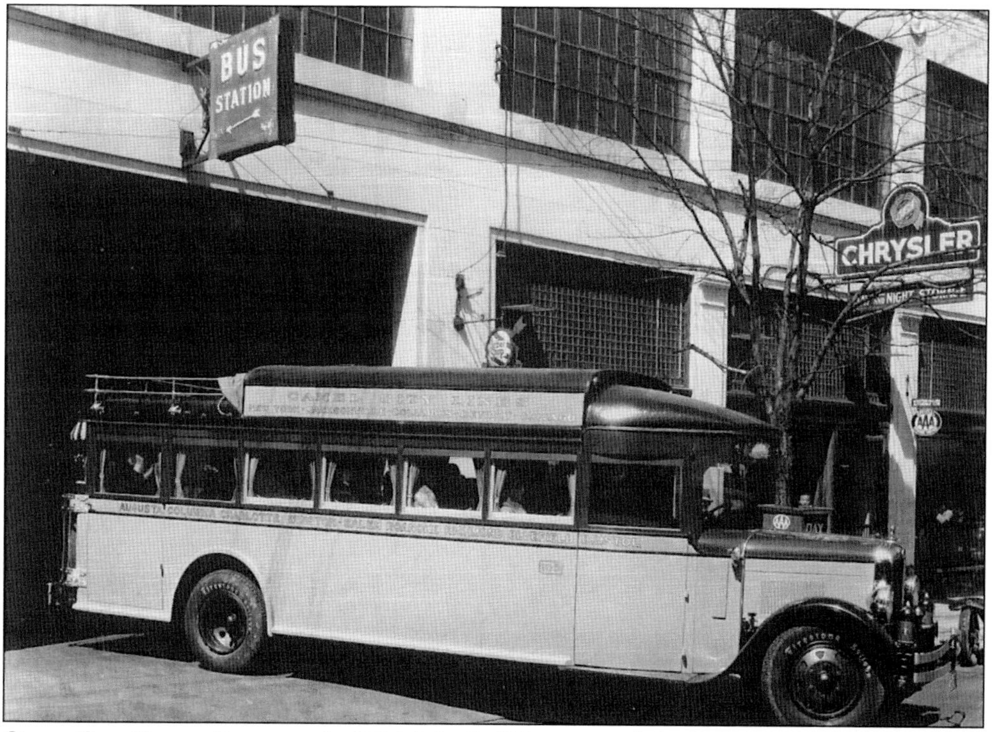

CAMEL CITY COACH COMPANY. In 1926, John L. Gilmer started the Camel City Coach Company with six 21-passengers buses. (FCL)

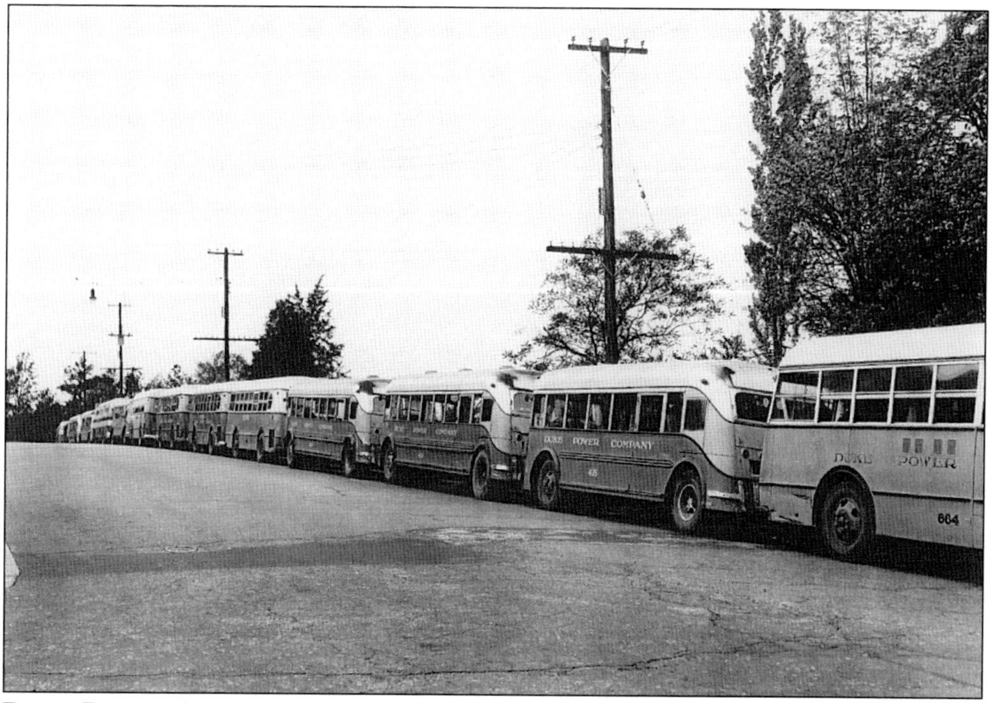

DUKE POWER COMPANY CITY BUSES, C. 1936. These buses replaced the electric streetcars. (FCL)

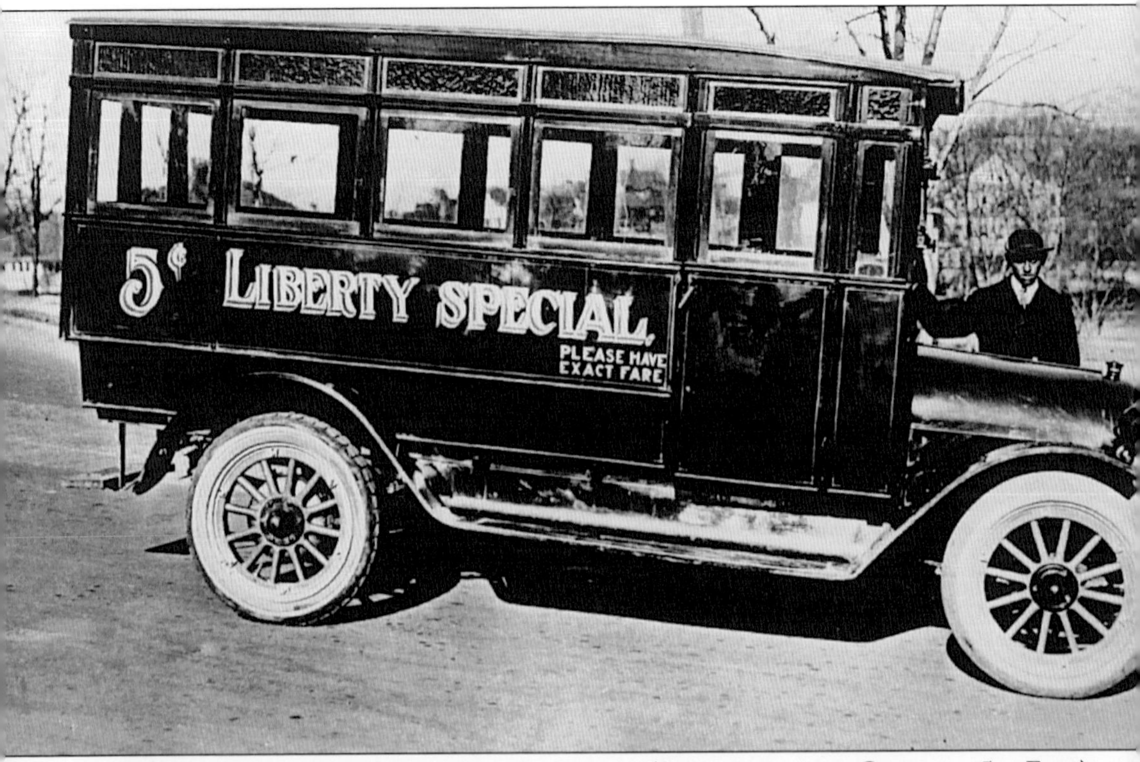

LIBERTY SPECIAL BUS LINES CALLED JITNEYS (SLANG FOR THE ORIGINAL 5¢ FARE). These buses provided transportation in the African-American neighborhoods during the 1920s. (FCL)

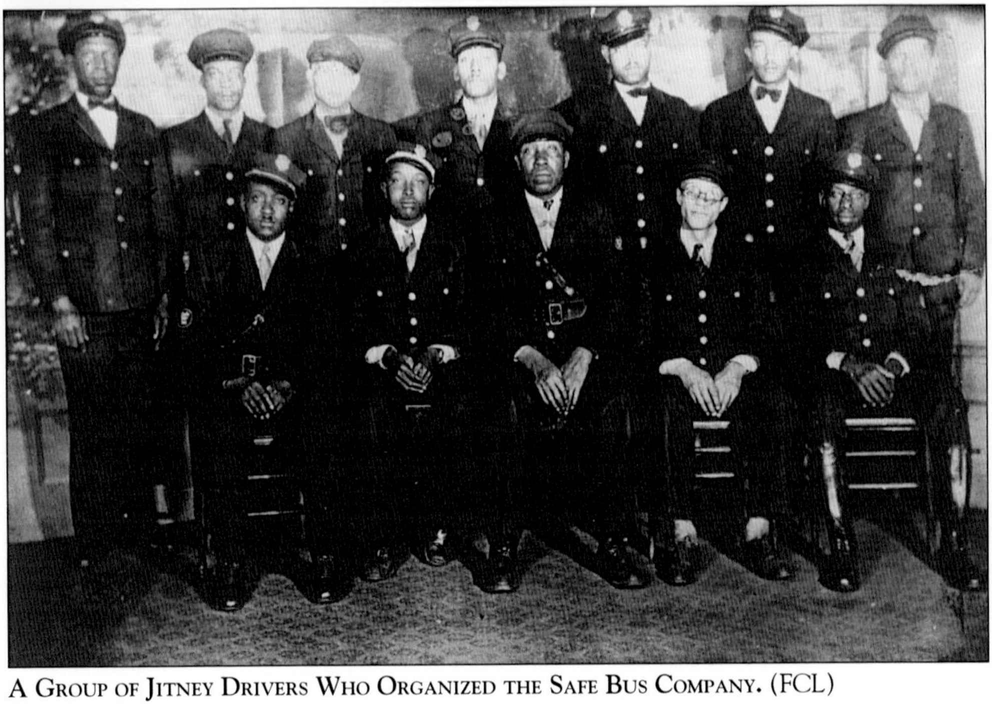

A GROUP OF JITNEY DRIVERS WHO ORGANIZED THE SAFE BUS COMPANY. (FCL)

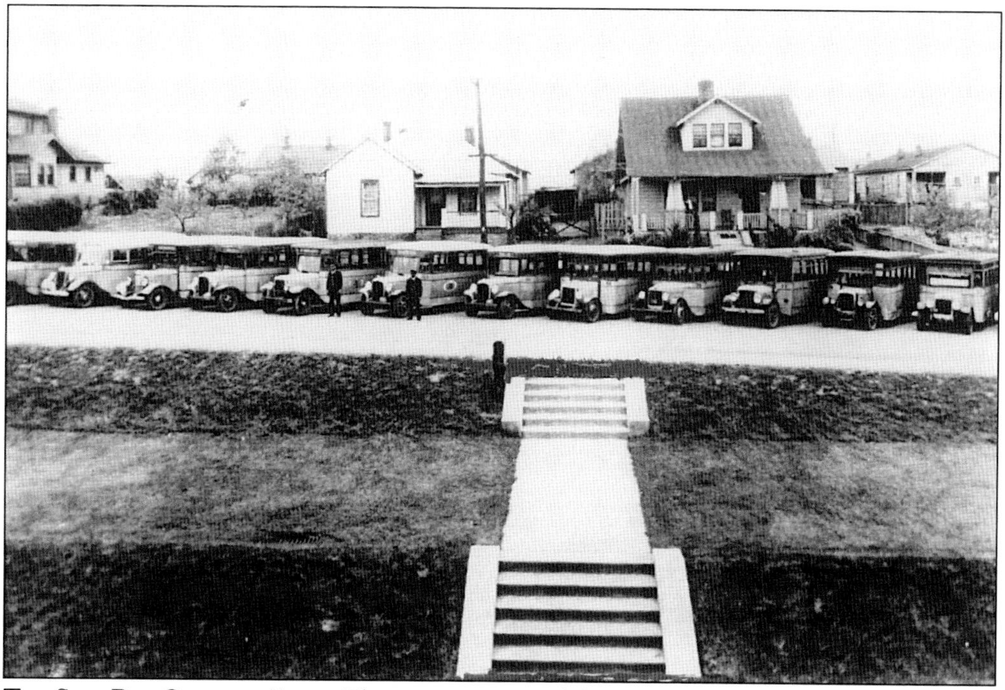

THE SAFE BUS COMPANY FLEET. This company served the community for 50 years before it was purchased by the Winston-Salem Transit Authority. (FCL)

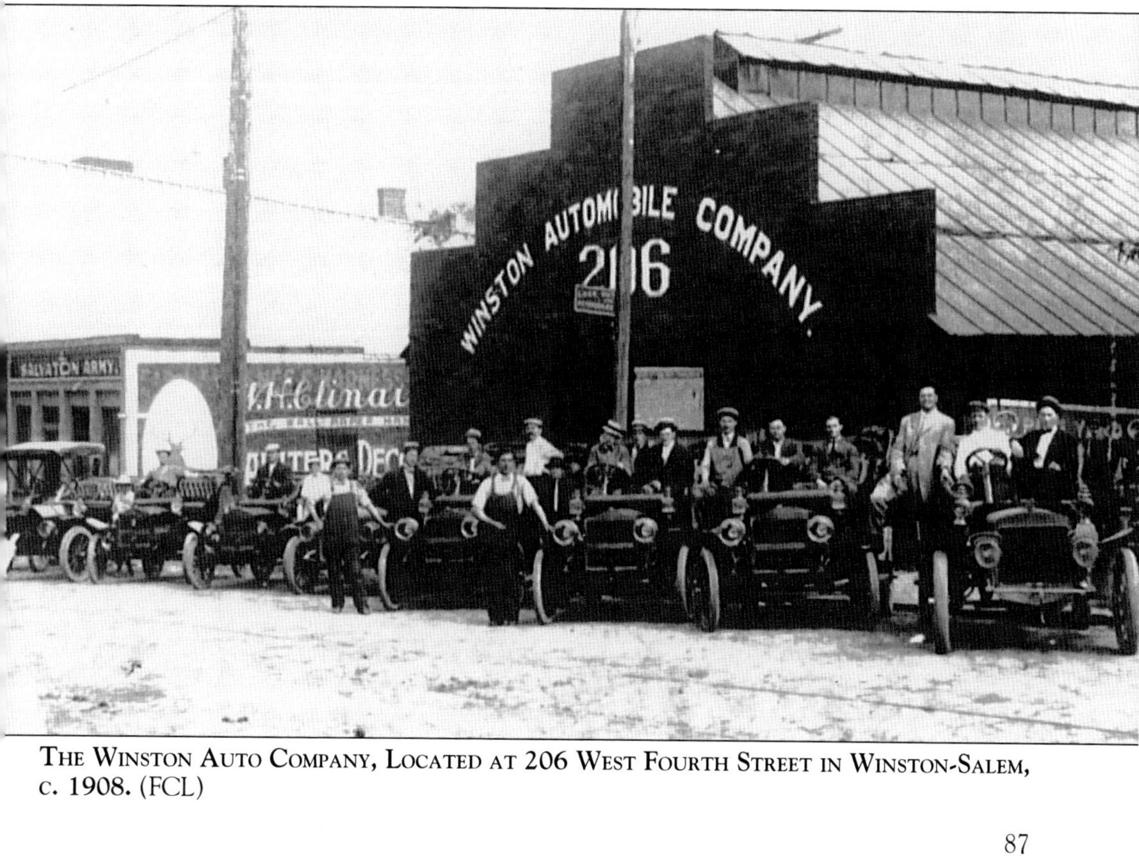

THE WINSTON AUTO COMPANY, LOCATED AT 206 WEST FOURTH STREET IN WINSTON-SALEM, c. 1908. (FCL)

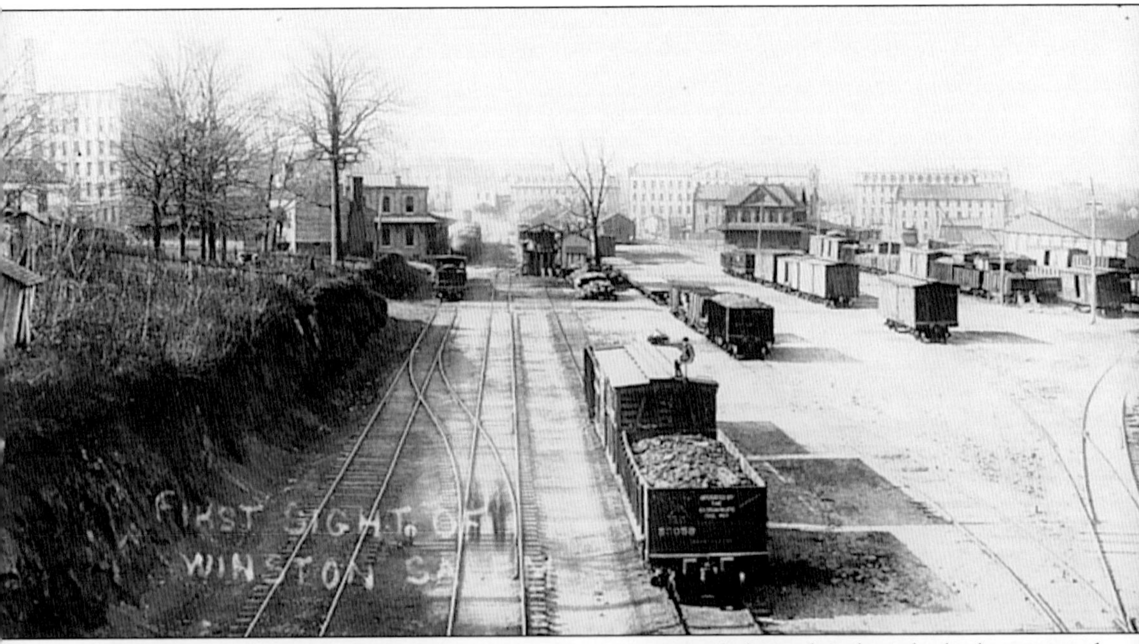

TRADE AND COMMERCE, C. 1890. First Street intersected the railroad yard which is viewed from Belews Street to the north, with the R.J.R. building No. 256 being on the left. Tobacco companies, W.B. Pollard and Co., Harvey and Rintels, W.F. Smith and Sons, and the Brown Brothers Tobacco Company, are scattered in the background. Smaller businesses included wholesale grocery Edgar D. Vaughn and Company and S.E. Allen's Hardware. (FCL)

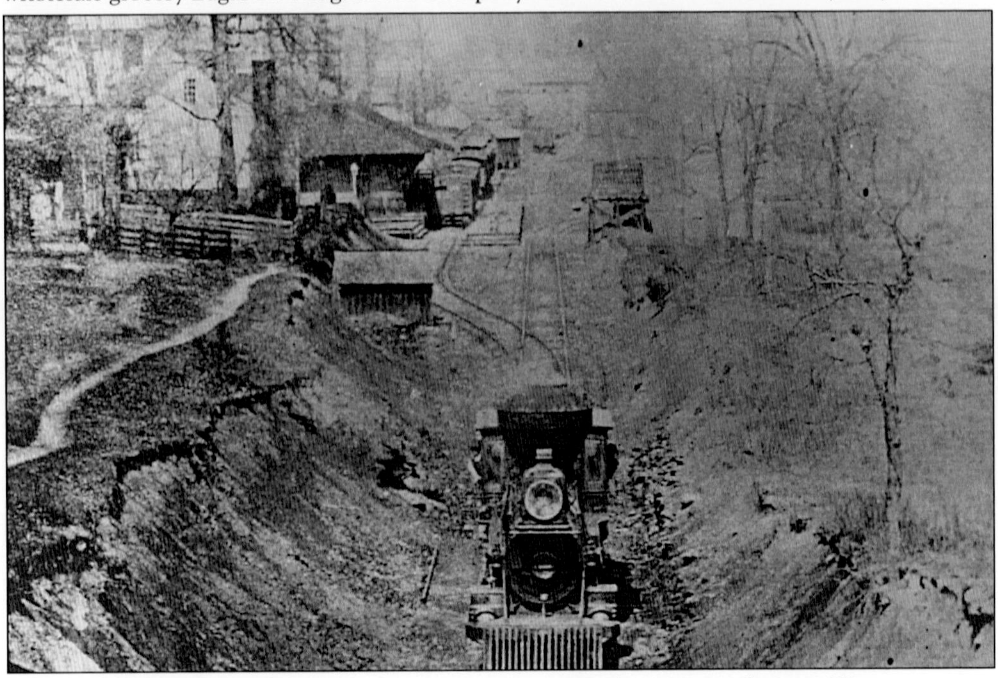

ENGINE LEAVING TRAIN YARD. As depicted in this 1880 photo, trains leaving Winston were a common site. This was one of the earlier engines of the Richmond and Danville Railroad. The engineer was E.E. Harris. (FCL)

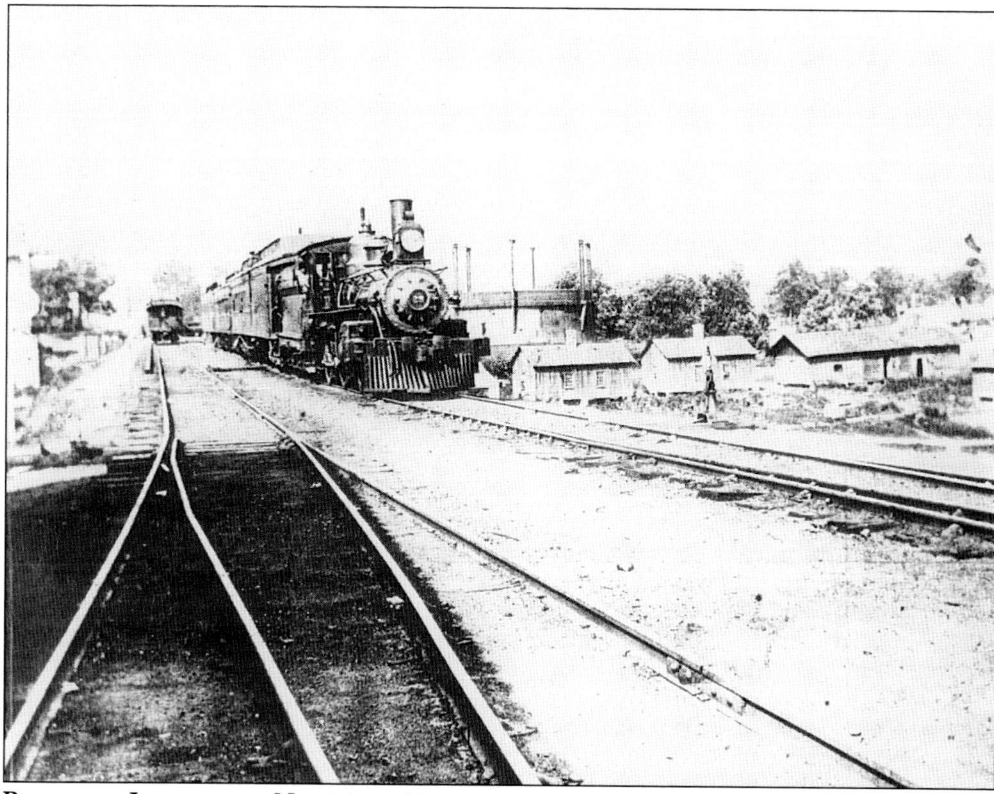

Passenger Locomotive No. 29 of Norfolk and Western R.R. Entering Winston in 1890. (FCL)

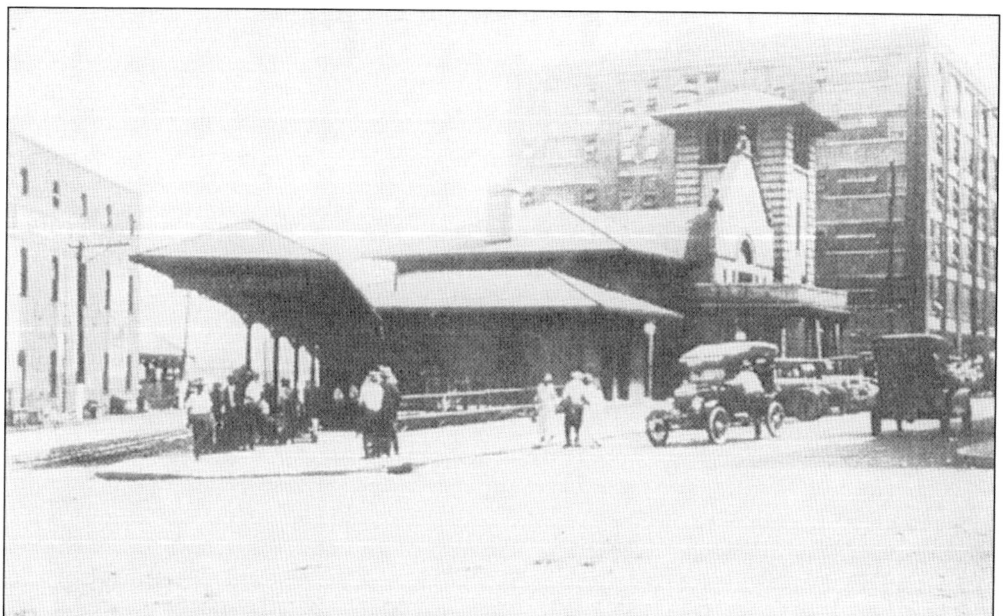

Union Passenger Station, c. 1920. Passengers enjoy more comfort during their wait with this modern Union Passenger Station located at Chestnut and Third. (FCL)

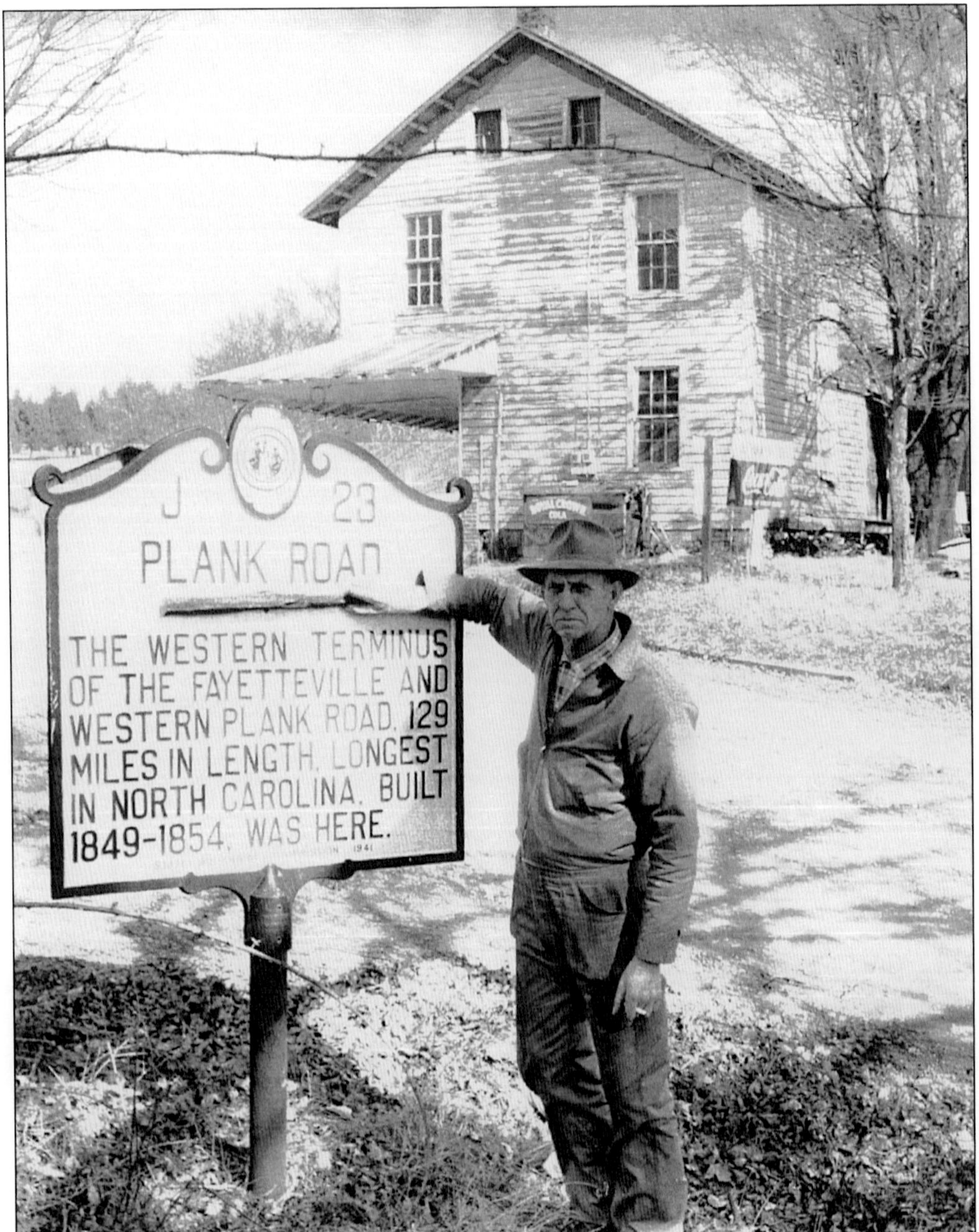

A 1959 PHOTOGRAPH OF J.A. SHORE. He is next to the historical marker describing the Fayetteville and Western Road. This road, chartered in 1849, ran through Winston on its way to the western terminus of Bethania. The tollhouse for the Old Plank Road was located at the intersection of Kent Road and Reynolda. (FCL)

Ten

County Government
Unsung Heroes

The two cities of Winston and Salem merged in 1913. This consolidation required a rearrangement of both county and city government. As a result, this new city witnessed construction of new government buildings, as well as reorganization of the cities' law forces.

Winston and Salem also showcased many heroes. Citizens who served either on a local front or on a national front selflessly risked their lives to protect others from harm. From the late 1800s to the present, this selection of photographs documents the growth experienced in the public sector of Winston and Salem.

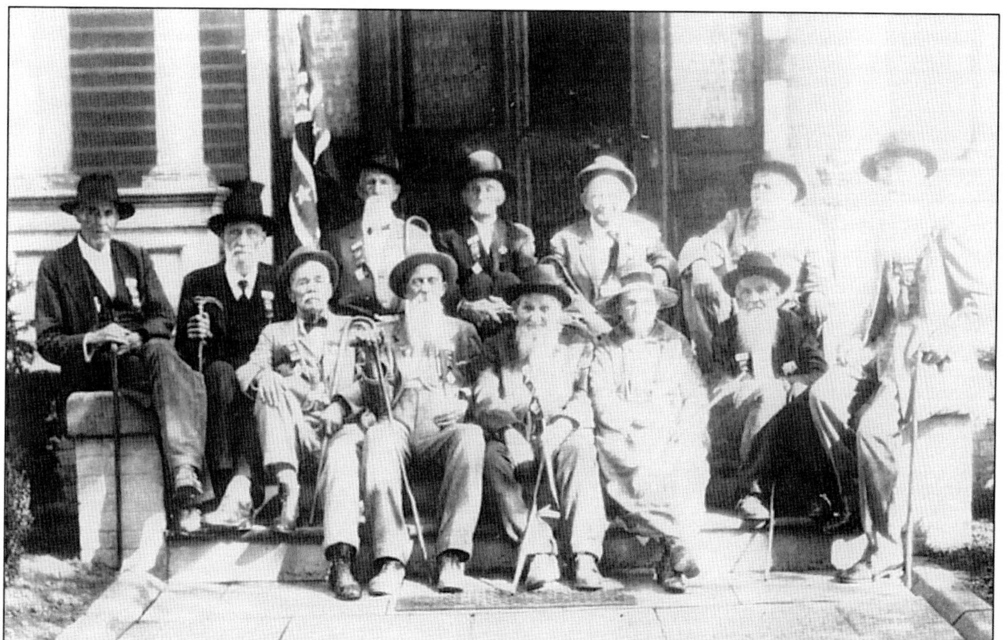

CONFEDERATE VETERAN REUNION IN 1930. These veterans are, from left to right, as follows: I.A. Cowan, W.C. Meadows, A.J. White, J.A. List, J.F. Hatley, J.M. Story, D.E. Honeycutt, C.S. Holton, Mrs. D.E. Honeycutt, S.S. May, G.H. Hall, and M.J. Short. (FCL)

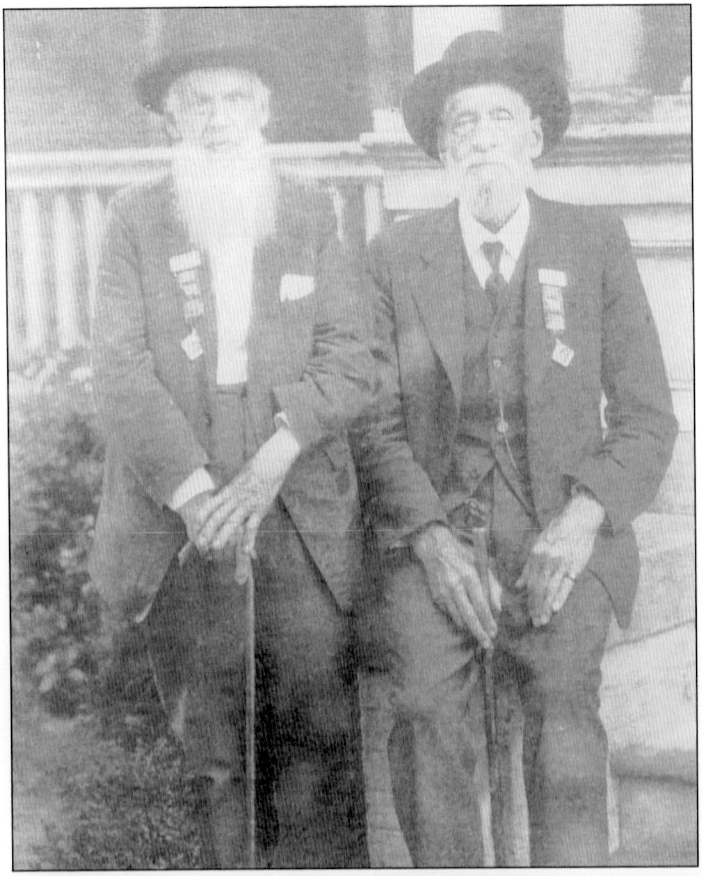

Old Soldiers, c. 1930. Reverend Stanley E. May (left) and Reverend W.C. Meadows pose for their Confederate Veterans Reunion photograph. (FCL)

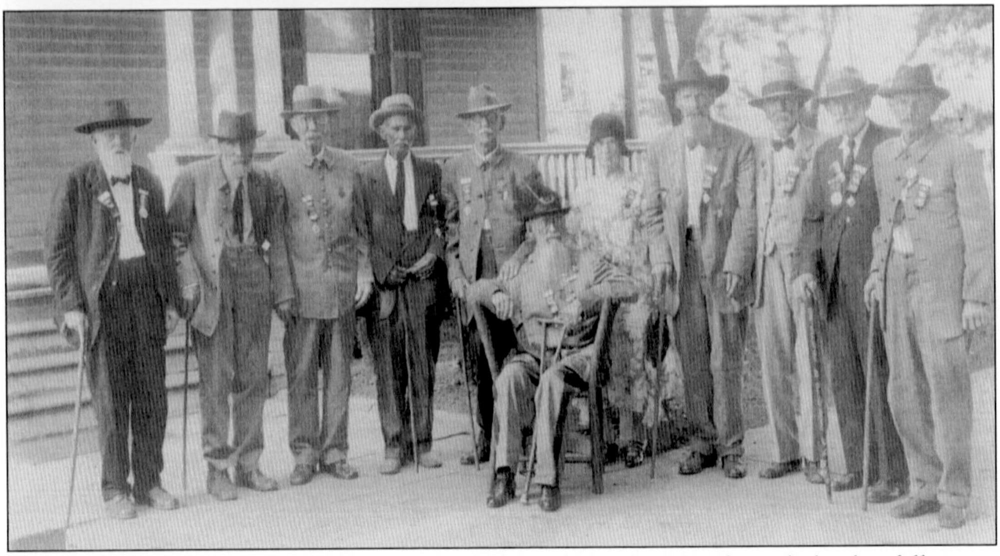

Confederate Veterans, 1930. The veterans in this photograph include the following: Maj. Gen. W.A. Smith (seated), W.S. Grisson, Capt. N.W. Bernhardt, J.A. McAskill, M.D. McNeill, Mrs. W.A. Smith, T.N. Alexander, W.G. Johnson, J.H. Shore, and W.M. Barwick. (FCL)

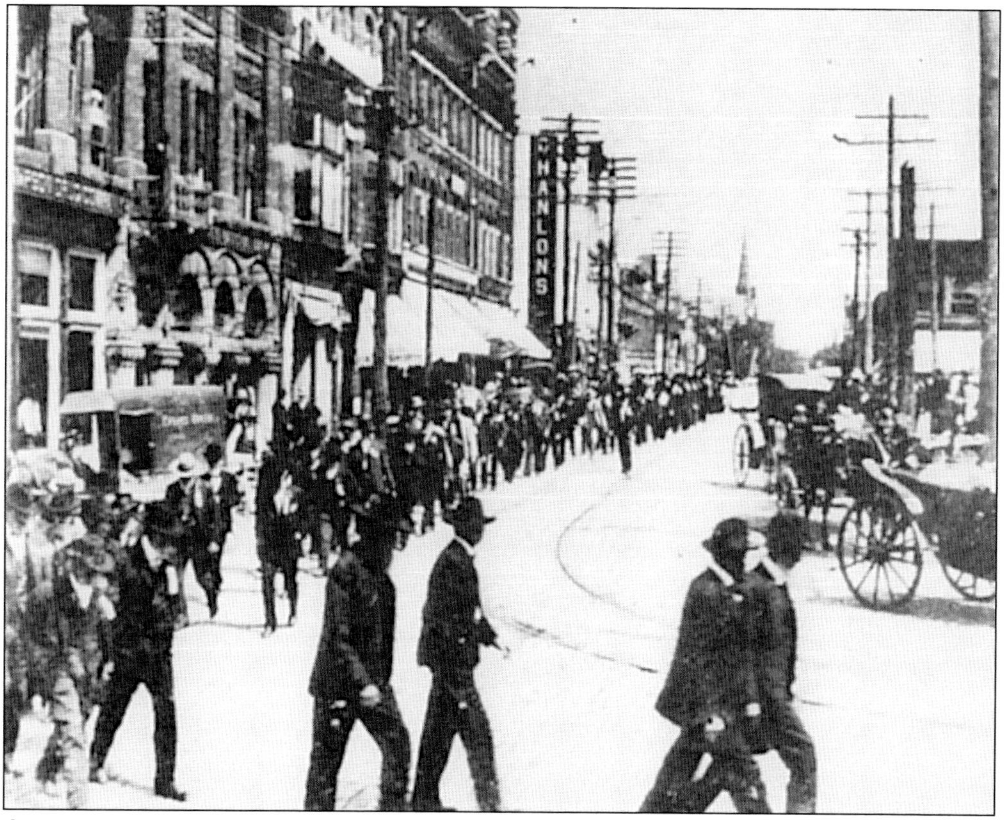

CIVIL WAR VETERANS MARCHING DOWN LIBERTY FROM FOURTH STREET IN 1910. (FCL)

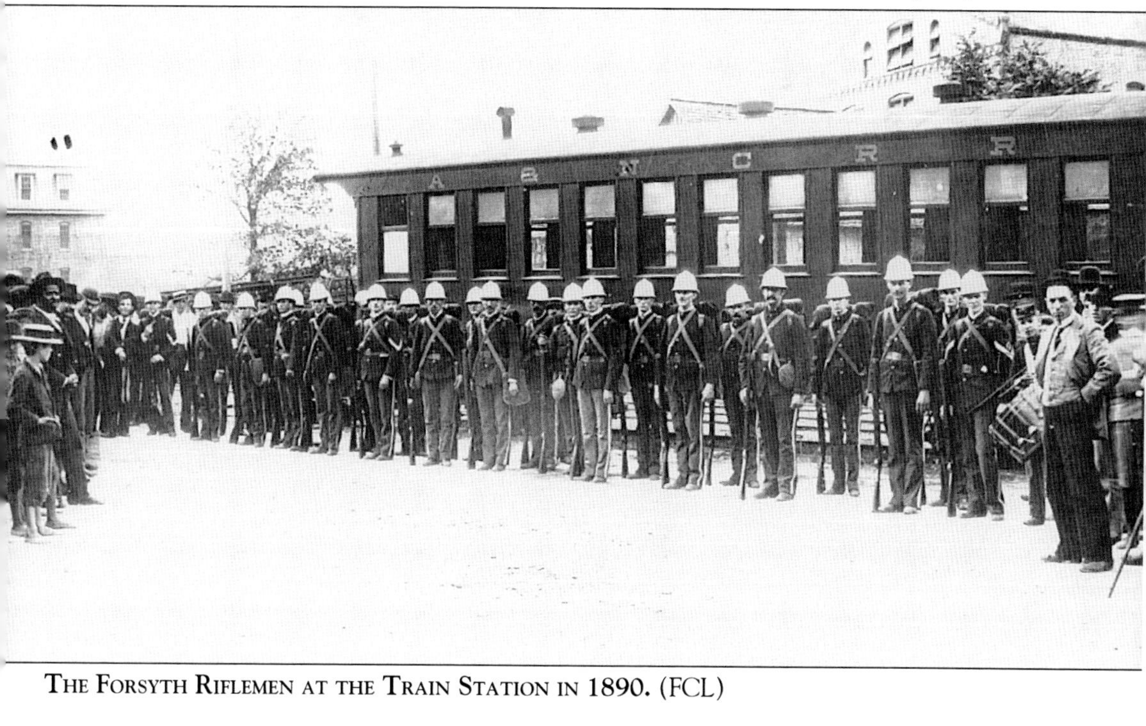

THE FORSYTH RIFLEMEN AT THE TRAIN STATION IN 1890. (FCL)

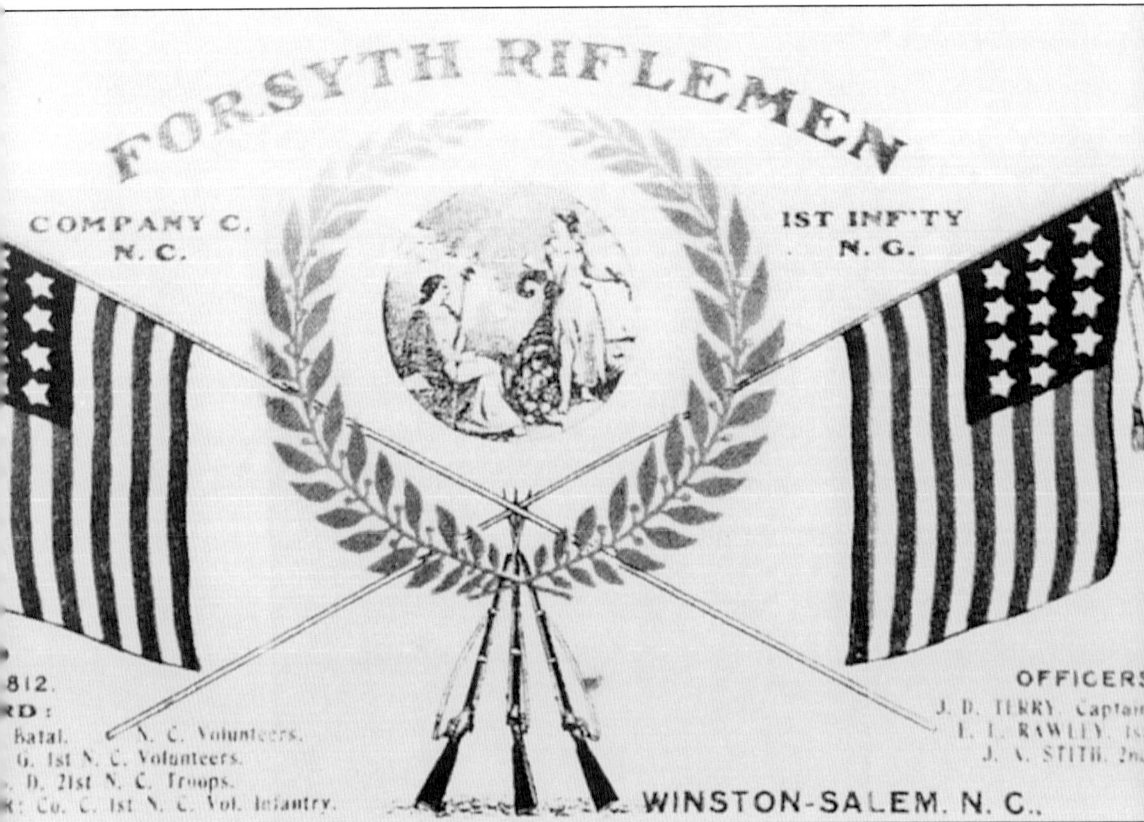

THE FORSYTH RIFLEMEN. They were the first permanent military organization in the county. Its existence dates back as far as the War of 1812. The Riflemen were involved in both the Spanish-American War and with the Third Infantry in World War I. The Riflemen's flag, as shown here, was proudly displayed. (FCL)

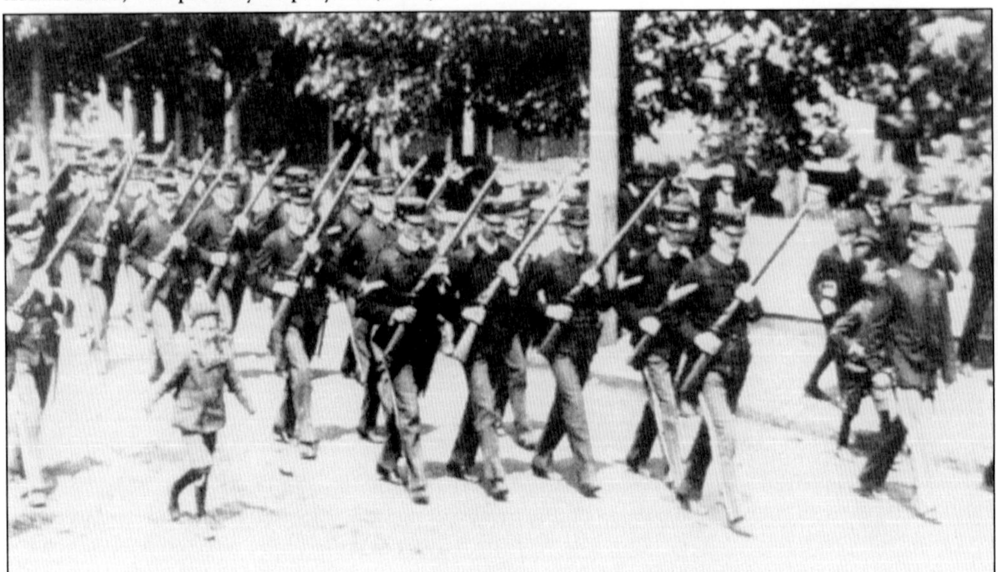

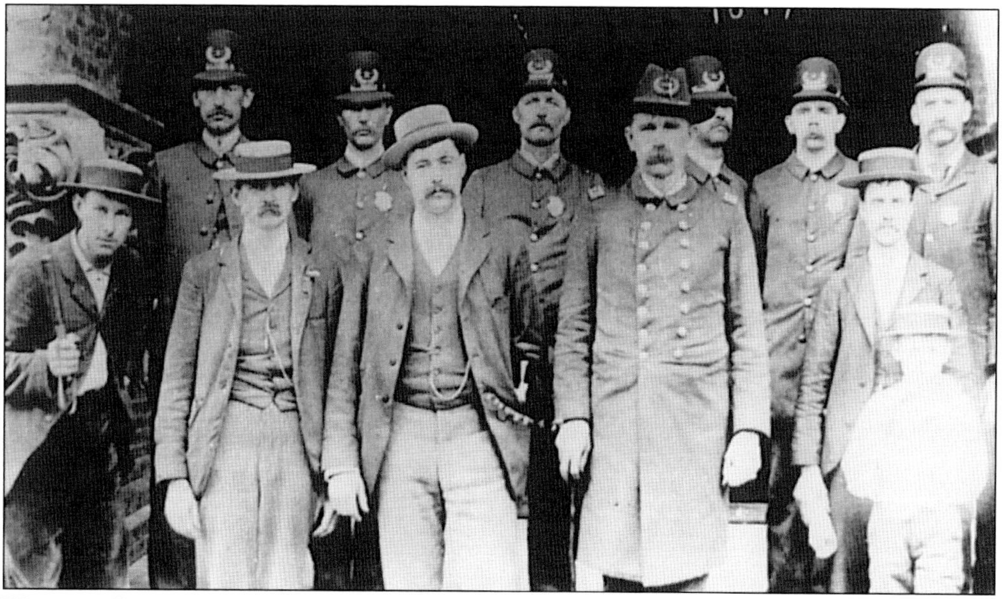

WINSTON POLICE, 1894. The members include the following: Chief J.M. Wilson, Tom Hege (back row, left), former Chief J.W. Bradford (back row, far right), and members of the police commission. (FCL)

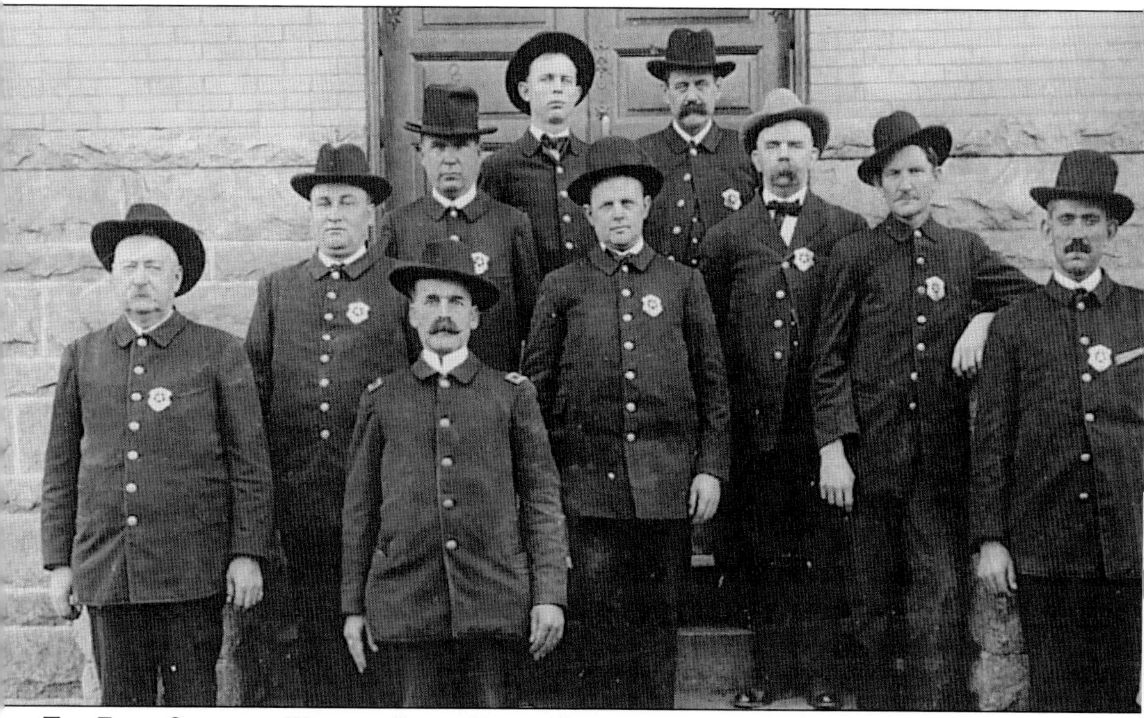

THE FIRST COMBINED WINSTON-SALEM POLICE DEPARTMENT, 1913. The members are, from left to right, as follows: (first row) Luther Kimball, formerly chief of the Salem force; Chief James A. Thomas; and Columbus A. Wall; (second row) E. Frank Apple; Robert W. Bryant; and Robert Young; (third row) Robert L. Blackburn and John T. Thomas; (fourth row) Norman B. Williams and sanitary inspector Charles A. Pratt. (FCL)

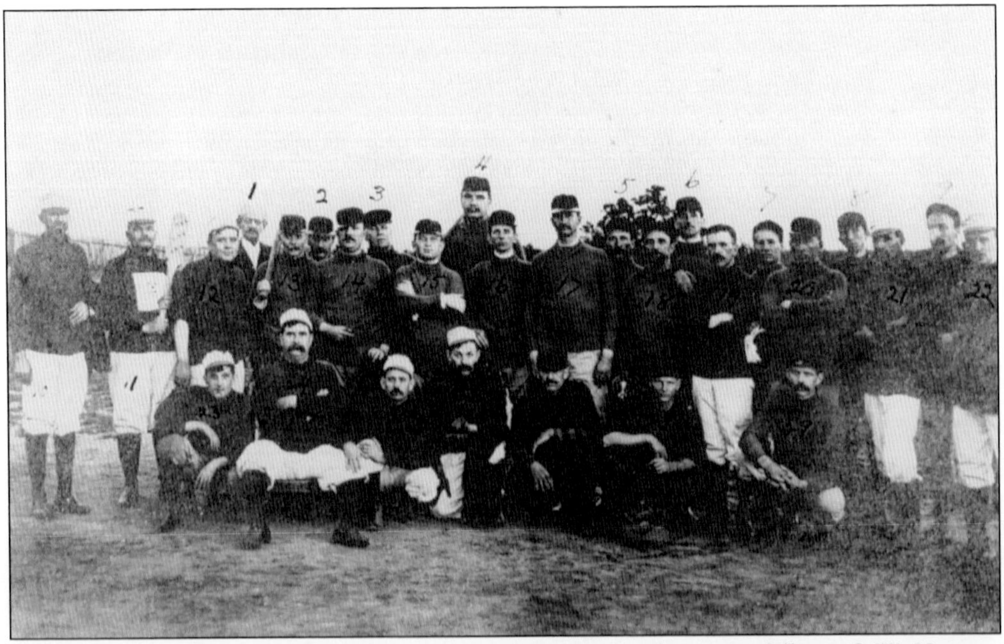

Winston Police Force, 1893. The members, from left to right, are as follows: O.W. Hanner, Frank Martin, J.J. Cofer, W.M. Sugg, Henry Valentine, and John T. Thompson; (seated at left) Chief J.W. Bradford and Jesse C. Bessent. (FCL)

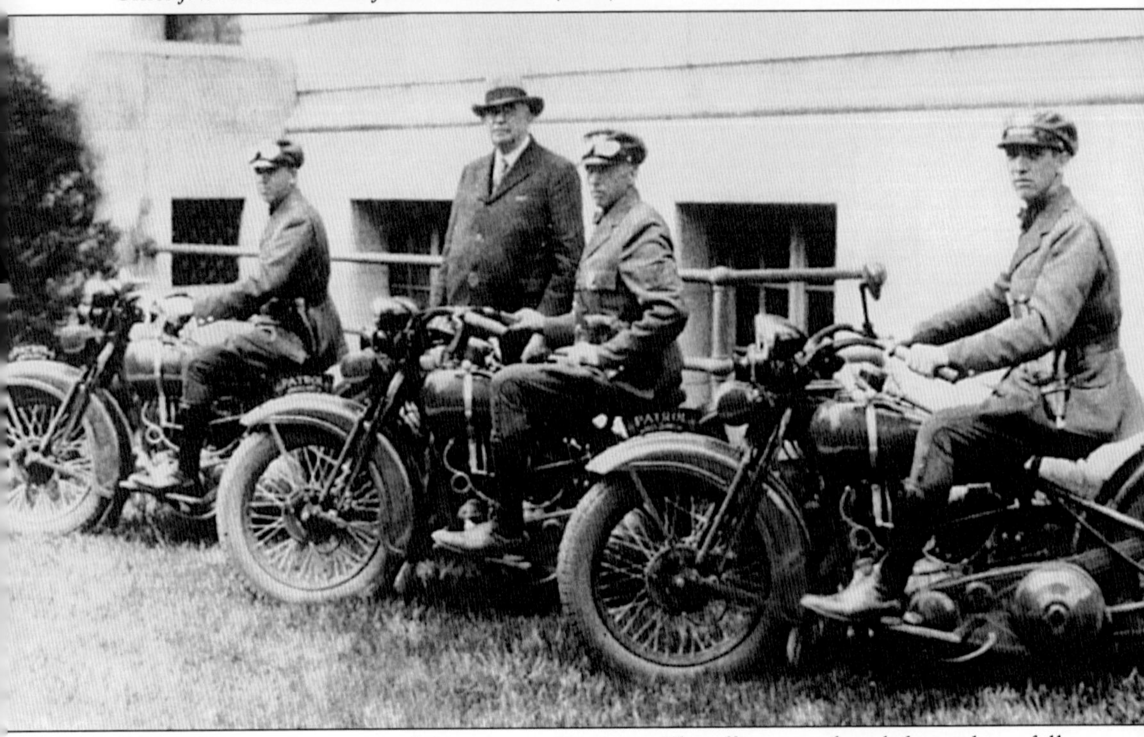

A 1926 Photograph of the Motorcycle Officers. The officers are, from left to right, as follows: Ken Pfaff, Mack Spainhour, A.C. Bovender, and J.B. McCreary, sheriff (standing). (FCL)

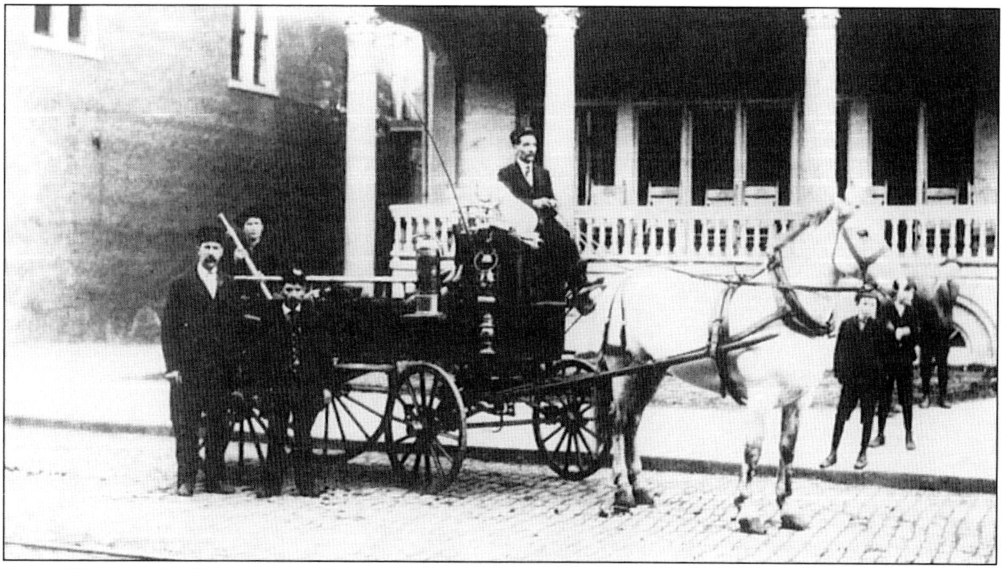

THE WINSTON'S TRUCK-AND-LADDER BRIGADE IN FRONT OF THE JONES HOTEL. Tom Keith holds the nozzle at the rear of wagon; standing at the far left is Bob Shelton and next to him is Winston's first paid fireman, John H. Holmes. In the driver's seat is Watt Knight. The boy under the horse's head is Red Powell. (FCL)

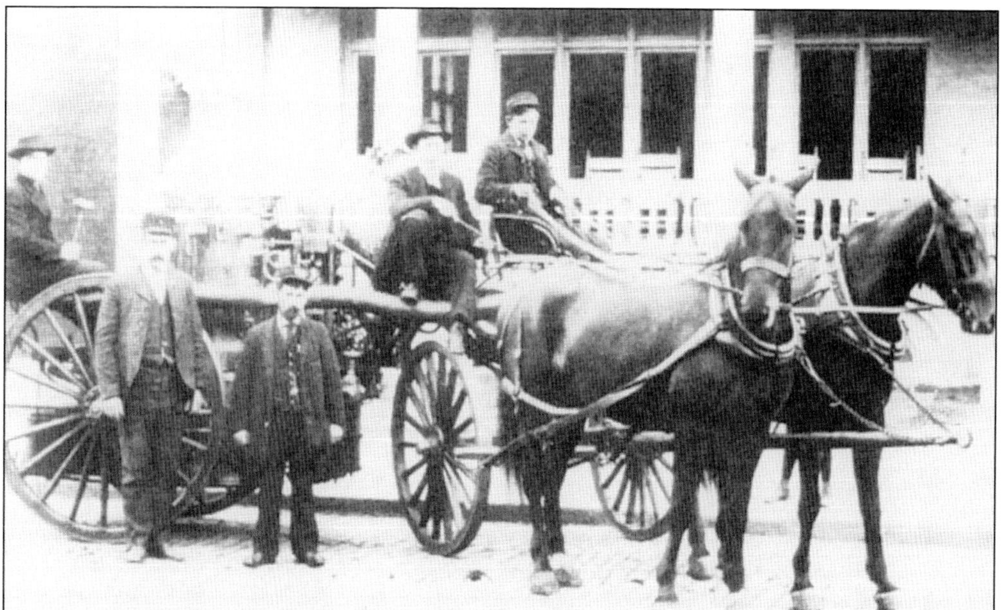

THE PUMPER SQUAD. This squad consists of Tom Keith, Bob Shelton, and John Holmes. On the horse is Jule Stith and in the driver's seat is Tom Graham. (FCL)

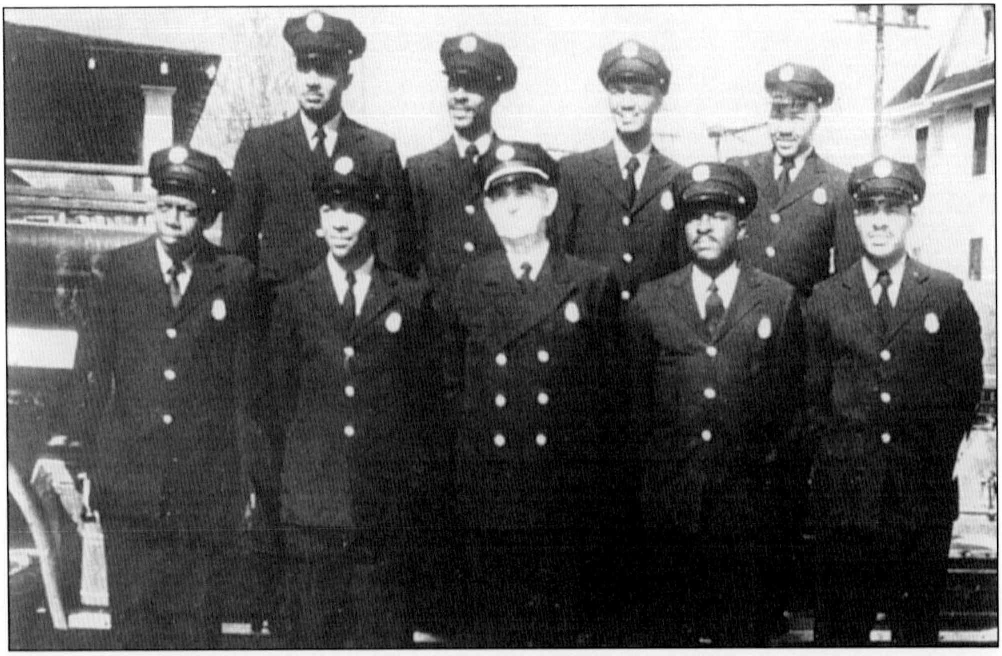

Winston-Salem's First African-American Fire Company, as Seen in 1950. The members are as follows: (front row) John F. Meredith Jr., George W. Penn, Capt. L.C. Williams, Willie J. Carter, and Lester E. Erwin Jr.; (back row) Ralphael O. Black, Robert L. Greer, John Henry Ford, and John Roi Thomas. (FCL)

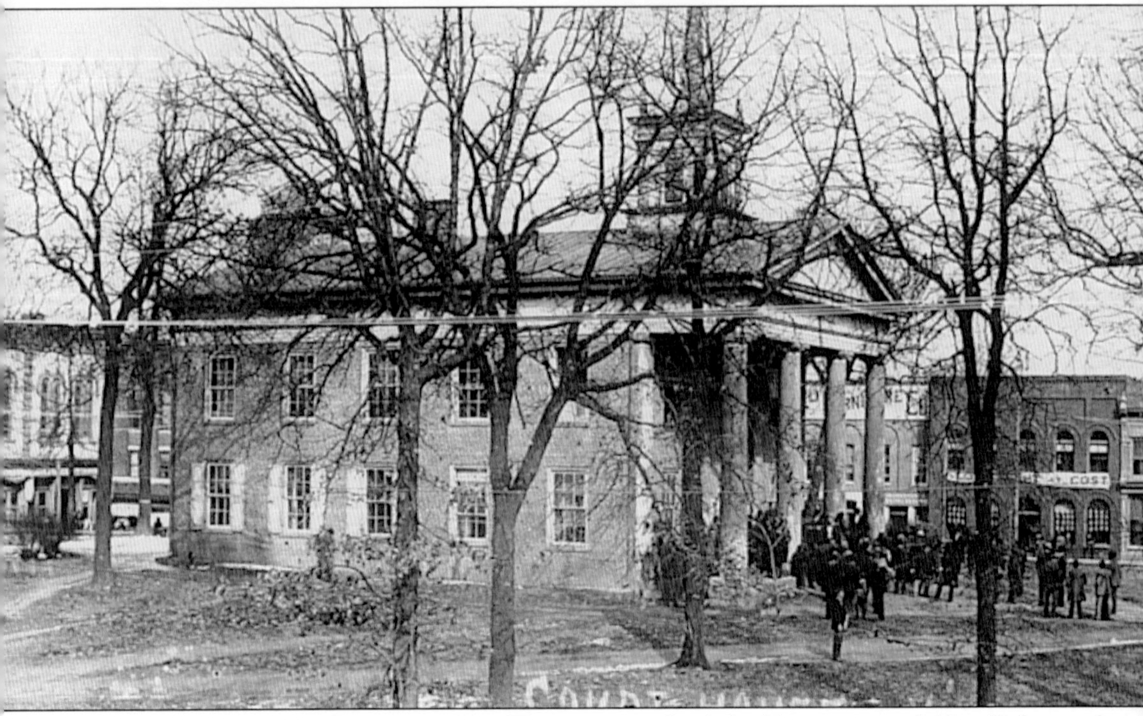

First Courthouse, Built in 1851. This two-story brick building measured 44 x 60 feet and was designed and built by Frances Fries. (FCL)

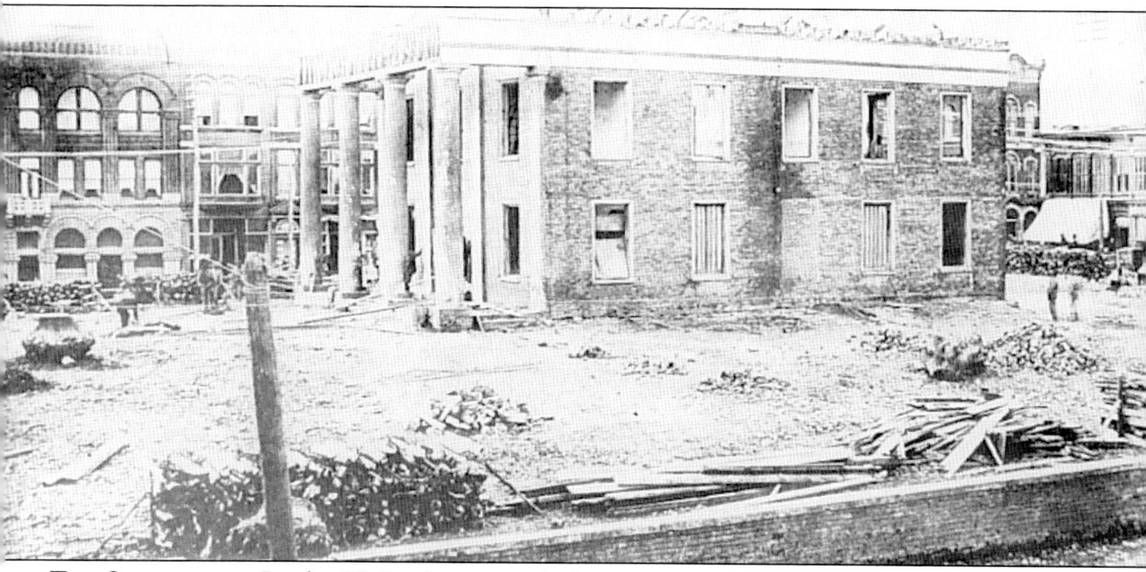

The Courthouse. By the 1880s, the county had outgrown its courthouse, and in 1896, this building was torn down for a new building. (FCL)

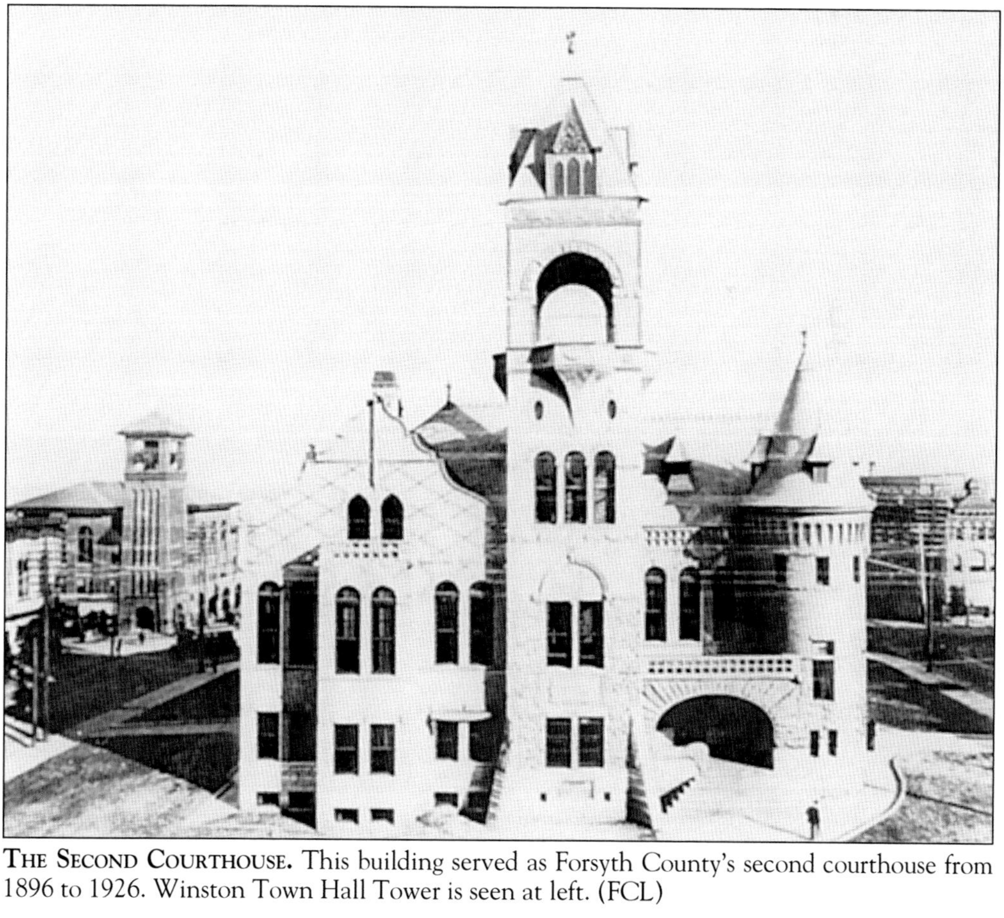

The Second Courthouse. This building served as Forsyth County's second courthouse from 1896 to 1926. Winston Town Hall Tower is seen at left. (FCL)

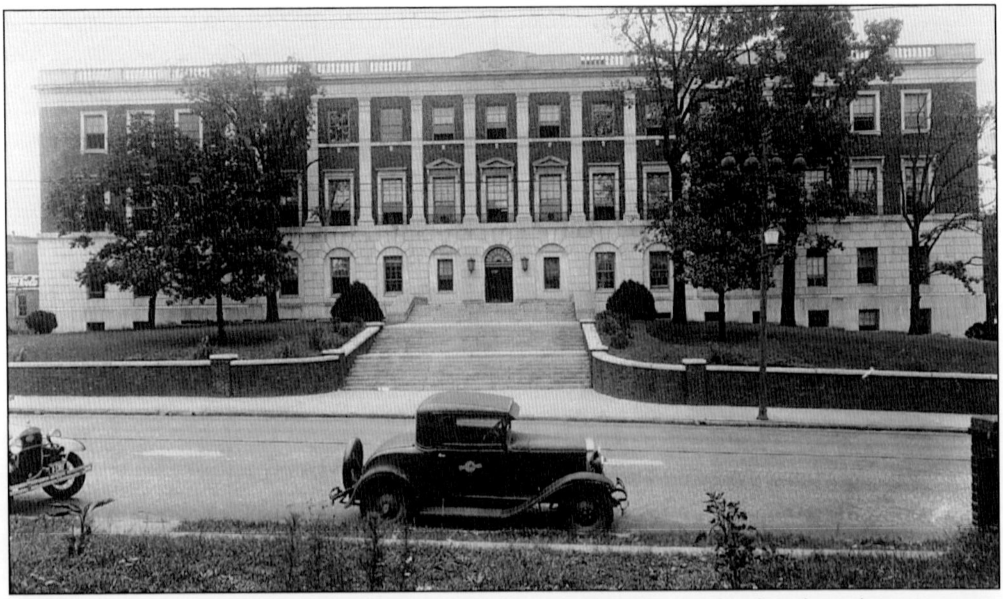

FORSYTH COUNTY'S THIRD COURTHOUSE, BUILT IN 1926. Since the fourth and most recent courthouse has been built, this building now serves as the City Hall Building. (FCL)

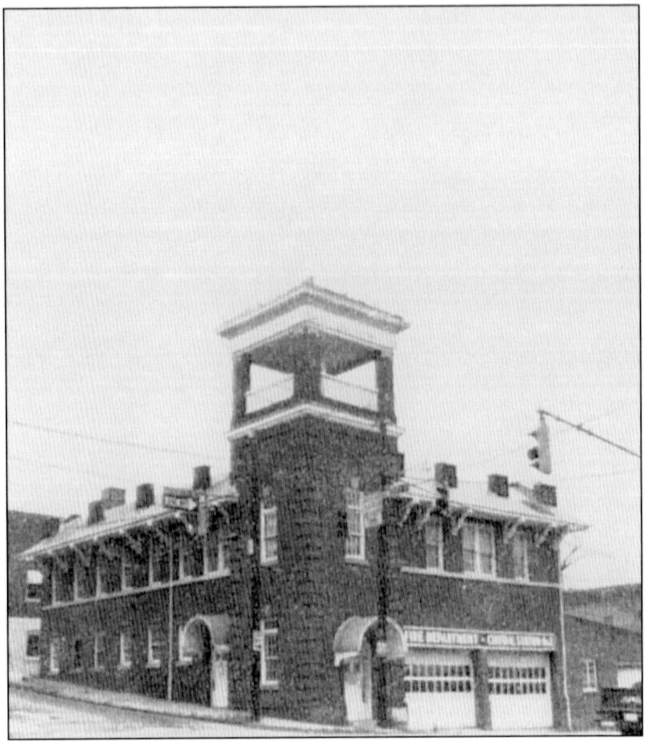

THE SALEM TOWN HALL AND FIREHOUSE, BUILT IN 1909. Horse-drawn fire wagons were stationed here. Town business was conducted above stairs. (FCL)

Eleven

Fields of Dreams

Businessmen and Industry

After the Civil War, the citizens of Forsyth County pulled together and began to rebuild. New business ventures required new buildings. Larger, more accessible mills in town replaced the rural area gristmills, and modern brick mercantile stores replaced the old paint-faded storefronts.

Several industries experienced success in Forsyth County. The tobacco industry was truly "king." It was a thriving industry that provided many jobs to the residents of Forsyth County. Also, the woolen and cotton mill industry grew, thereby replacing the need for the spinning wheel and loom. Consequently, bolts of cloth and sacks of meal became more plentiful as a result of this growth. Coupled with the growth of new industry and the invention of electricity, Forsyth County was entering into a new age of business.

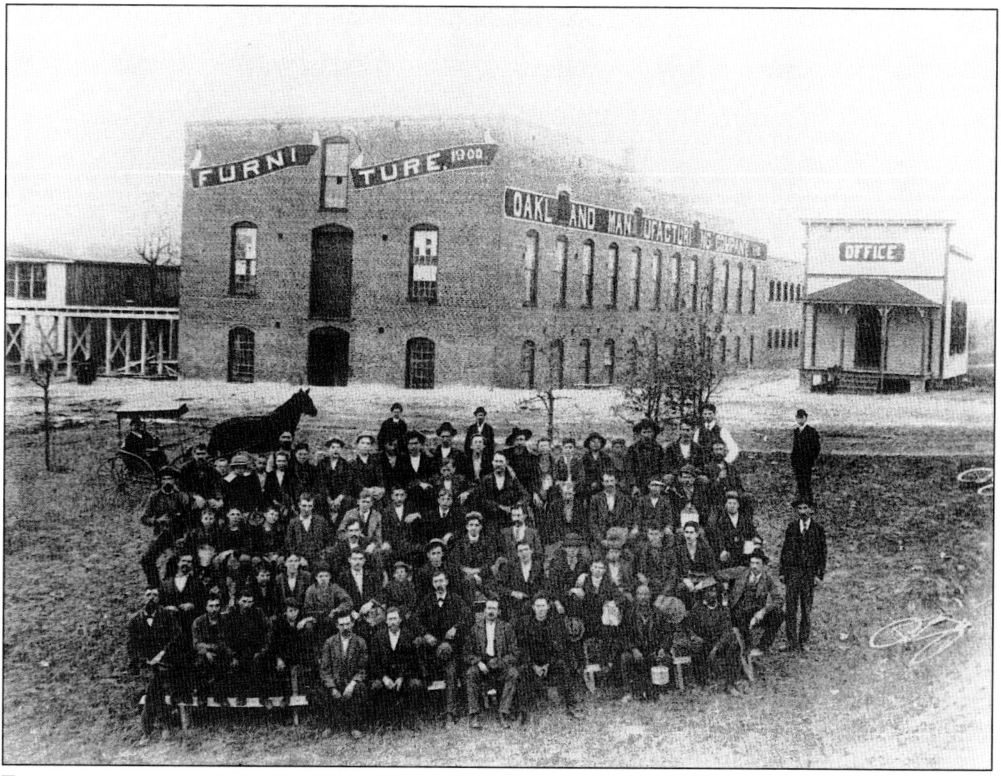

EMPLOYEES OF THE OAKLAND FURNITURE MANUFACTURING CO. For this picture, employees stand in front of the store and office located at 1201 Depot Street in the Fairview area. W.P. Hill served as president, M.D. Stockton, vice-president, C.G. Hill, treasurer, and B.F. Huntley, secretary. (FCL)

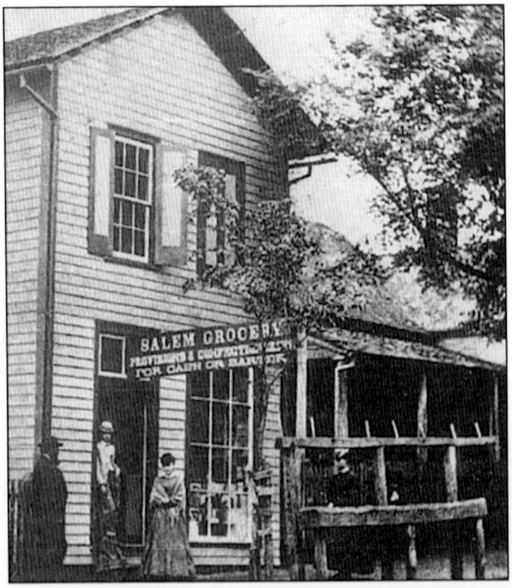

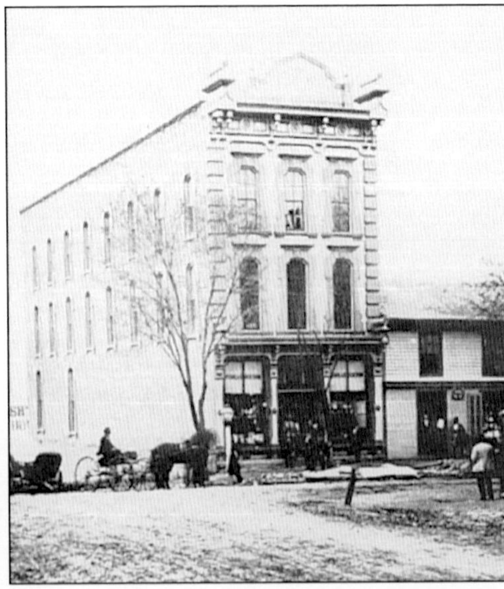

Left: **Salem Grocery, Located on the Corner of Main and Academy, in Winston-Salem.** (FCL)
Right: **Pfohl & Stockton Store.** Built in 1876, the Pfohl & Stockton Store, located on the southeast corner of Main and Third Streets, boasted the first modern three-story building in Winston. (FCL)

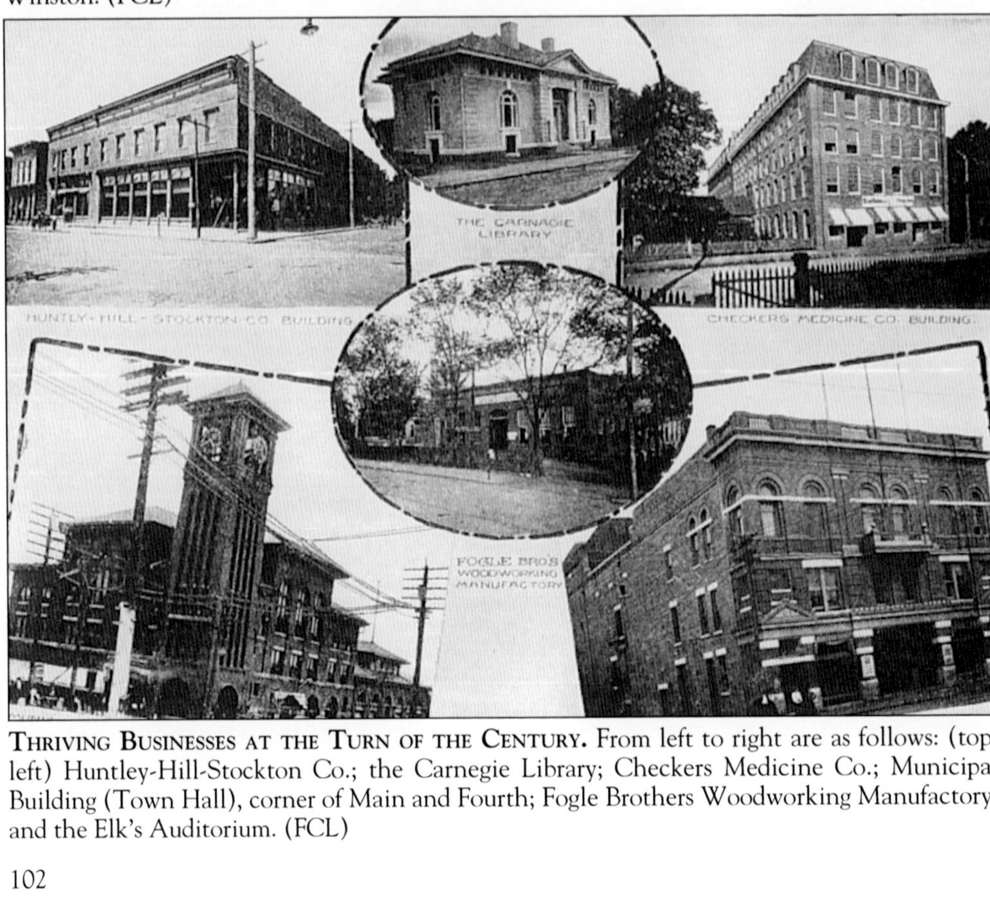

Thriving Businesses at the Turn of the Century. From left to right are as follows: (top, left) Huntley-Hill-Stockton Co.; the Carnegie Library; Checkers Medicine Co.; Municipal Building (Town Hall), corner of Main and Fourth; Fogle Brothers Woodworking Manufactory; and the Elk's Auditorium. (FCL)

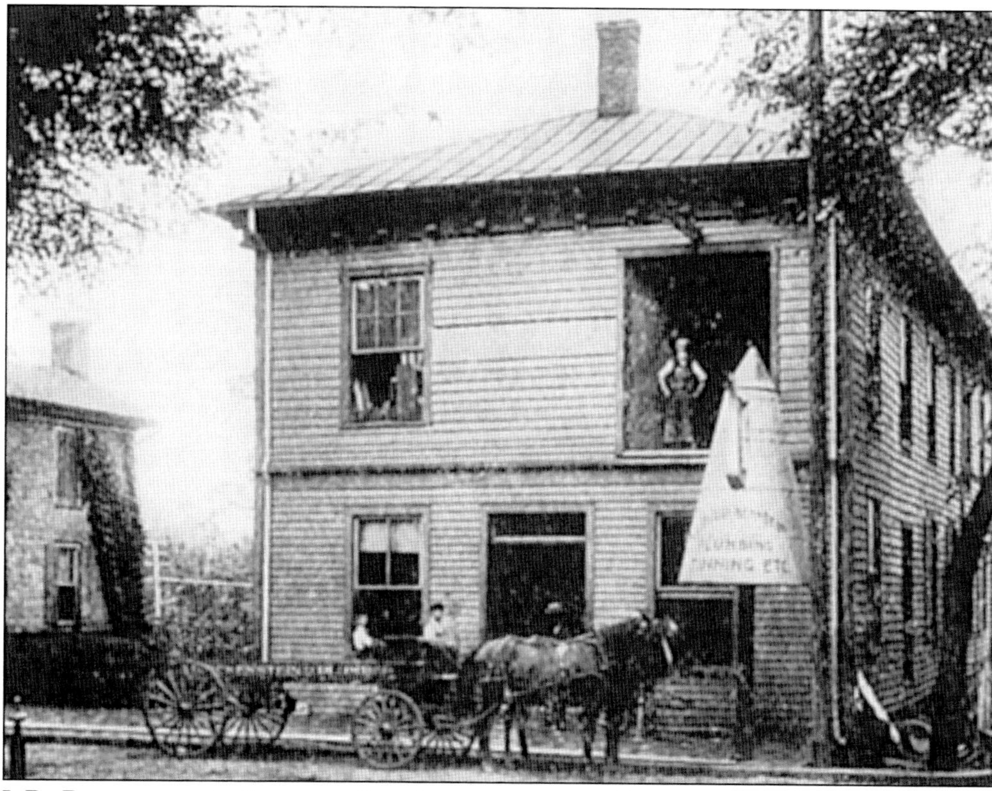

L.B. Brickenstein's Plumbing Est. Lawrence B. and Gevennie R Brickenstein were the owners. (FCL)

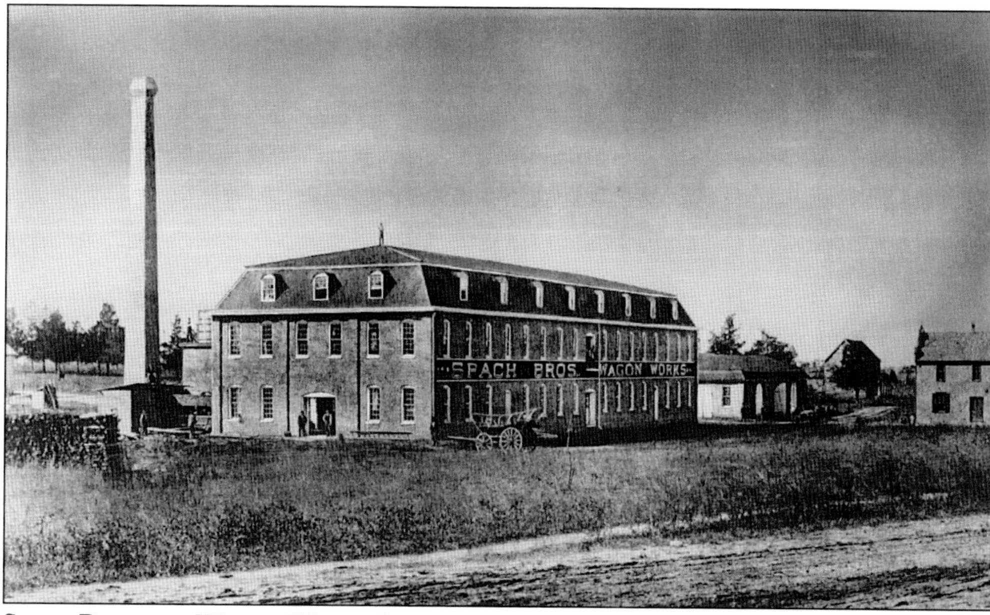

Spach Brothers Wagon Works Company, Opened in Waughtown in 1854. During the 1870s , around 20 wagons a year were produced. In 1928, the company stopped making wagons and began making furniture. (FCL)

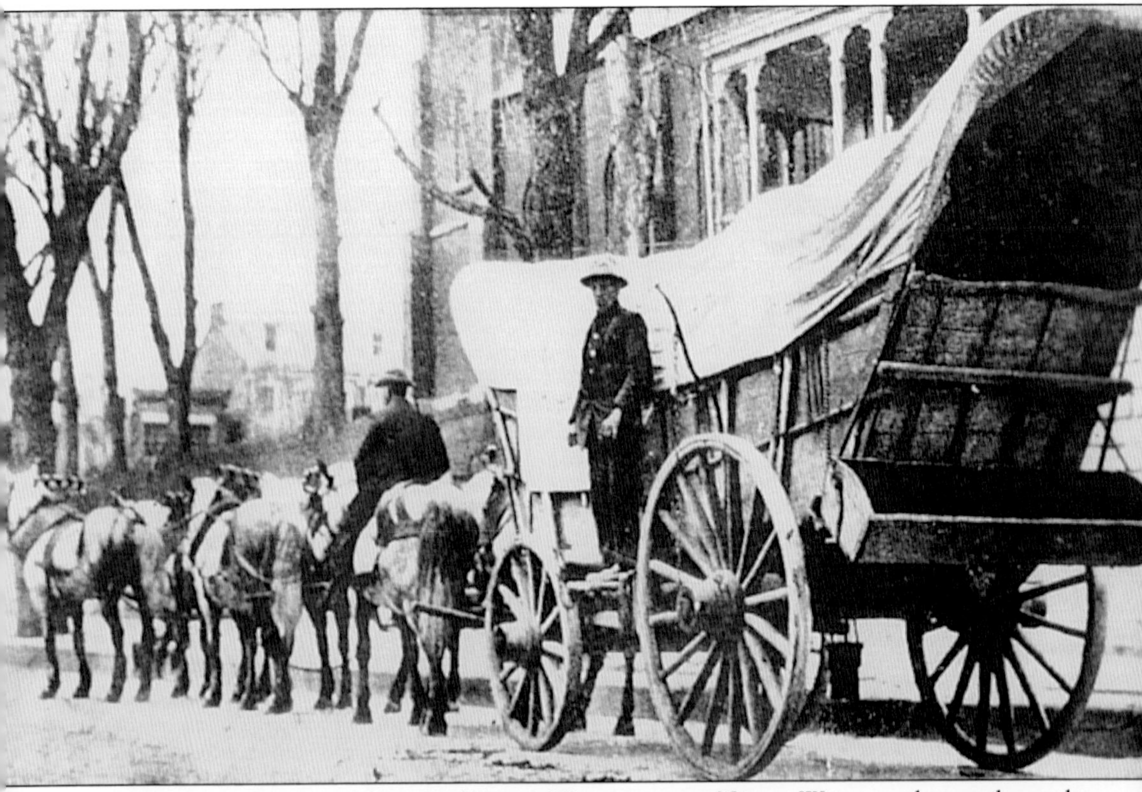

Example of Wagons Made by Nissen Wagonworks. Nissen Wagonworks was located at 2501 Waughtown Street in Waughtown. (FCL)

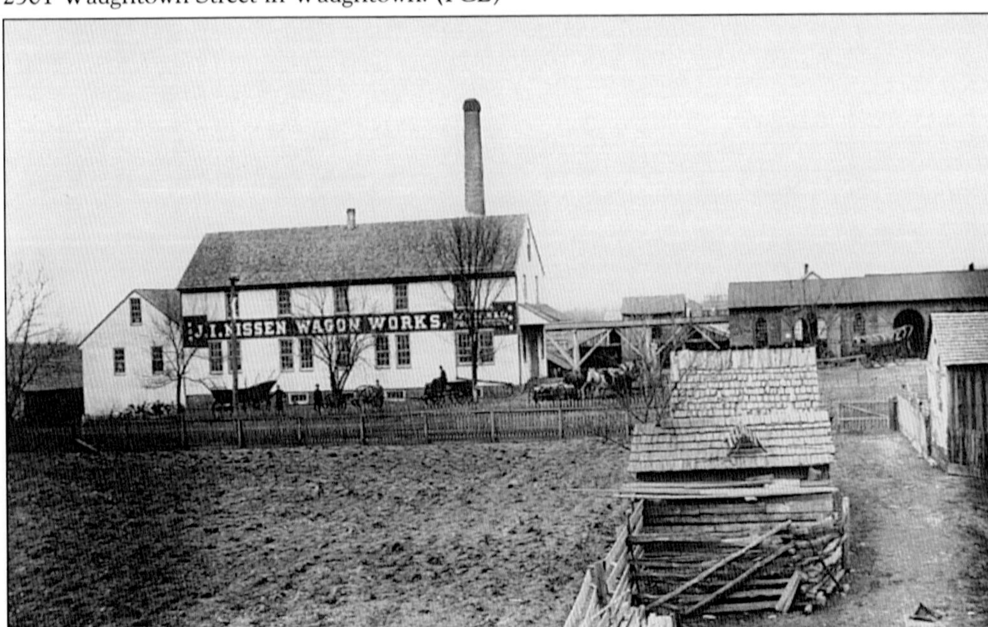

J.I. Nissen Wagonworks. It was organized in 1834, and by 1870, the company covered a 600-acre tract in Waughtown. (FCL)

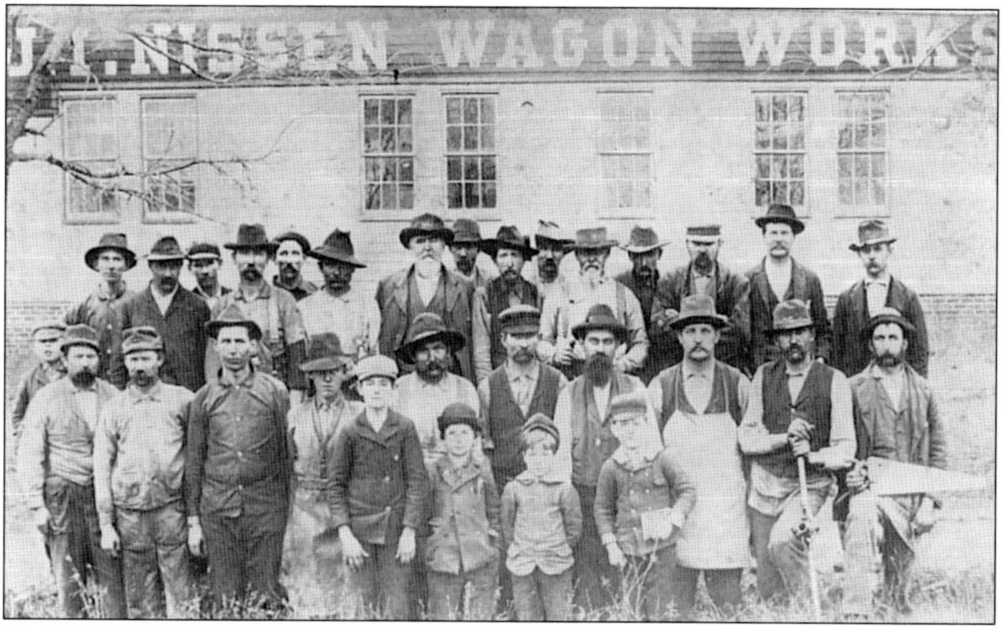

Employees of J.I. Nissen Wagonworks. As depicted in this photograph, all ages worked at the J.I. Nissen Wagonworks. (FCL)

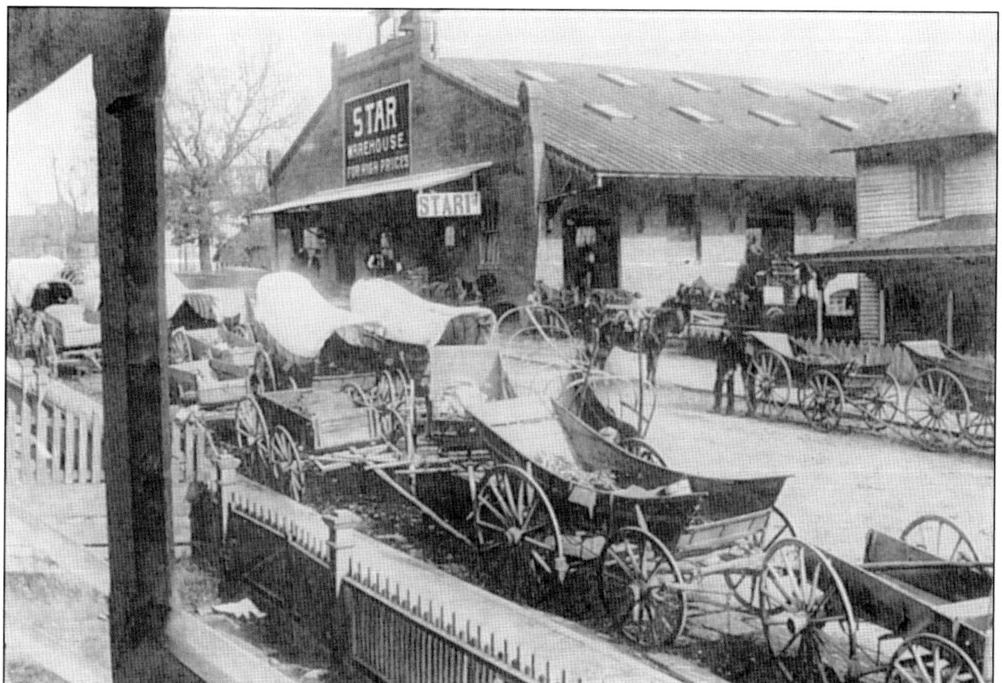

Star Tobacco Warehouse, Located at 541–545 Main Street in Winston-Salem. (FCL)

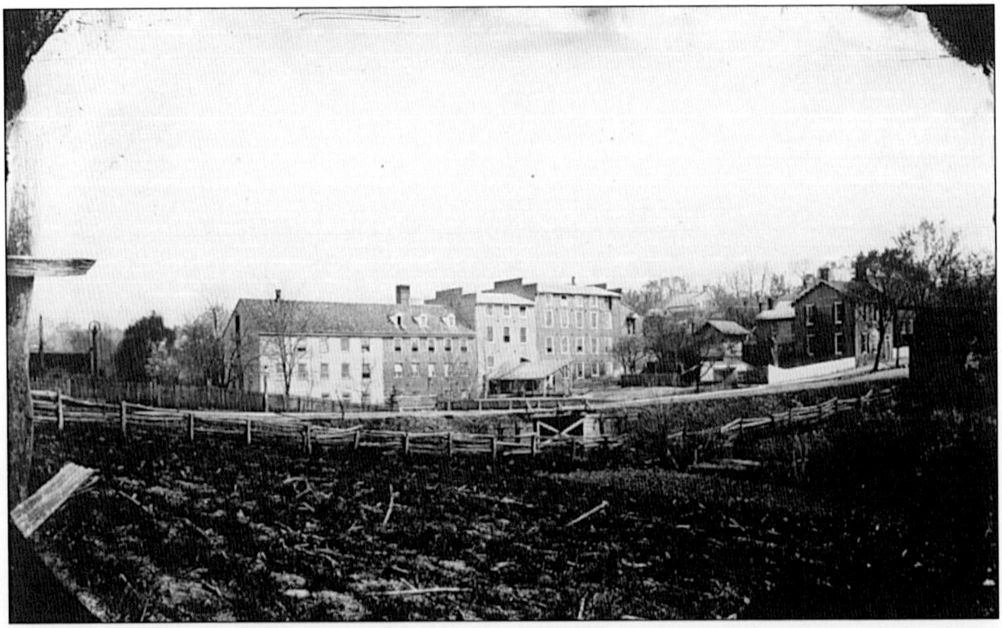

F & H Fries Co., c. 1840. It consisted of a woolen mill, a cotton mill, and a smokehouse. In 1903, he incorporated the Arista Mills, the first textile mill to use electric lighting. His business was located at 107 Shallowford, in Brookstown. (FCL)

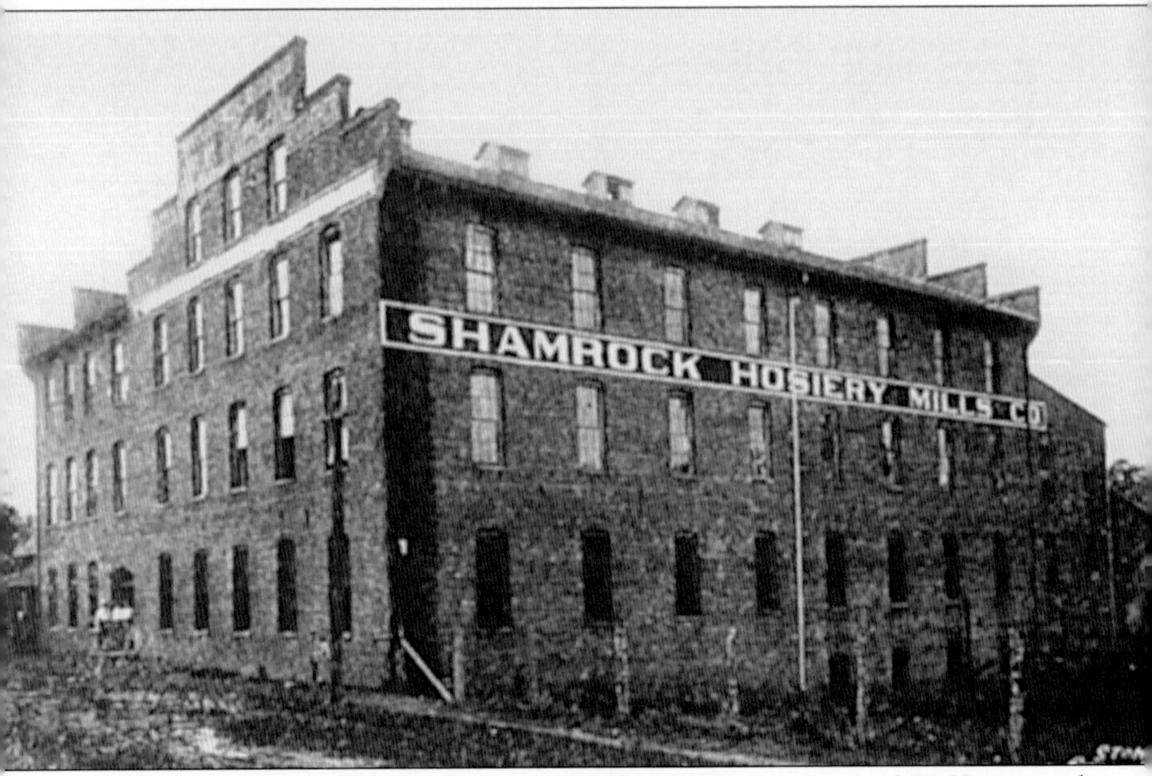

Shamrock Hosiery Mill, Located at 226 North Marshall Street. J.W. Hanes was the proprietor. In 1914, the mill was renamed Hanes Hosiery. (FCL)

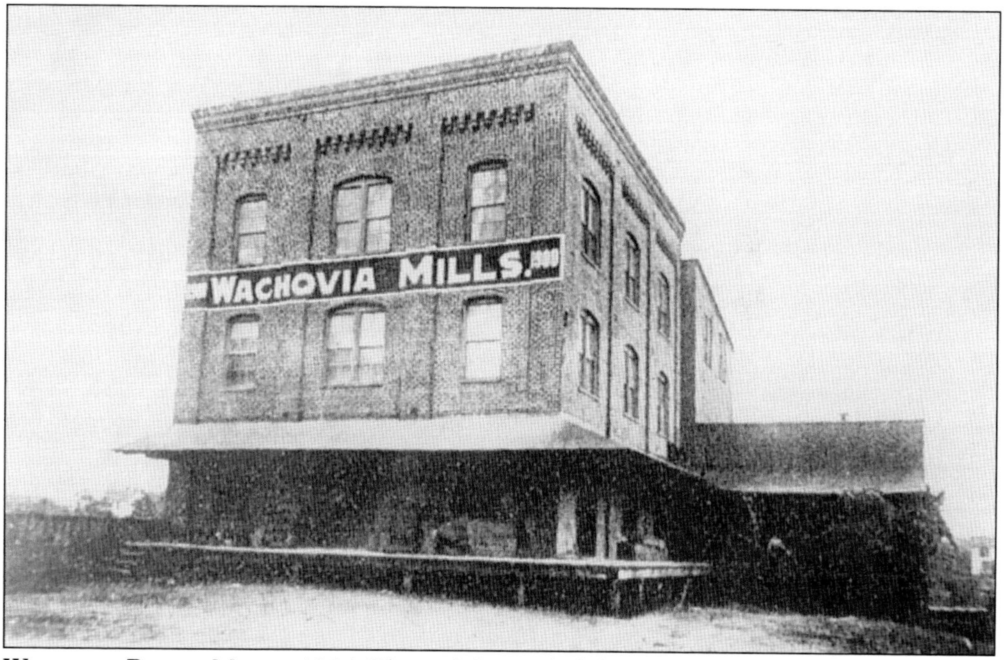

WACHOVIA ROLLER MILL IN 1904. Their ads boasted of electric power, and the mill was located at 533 Church Street in Winston-Salem. (FCL)

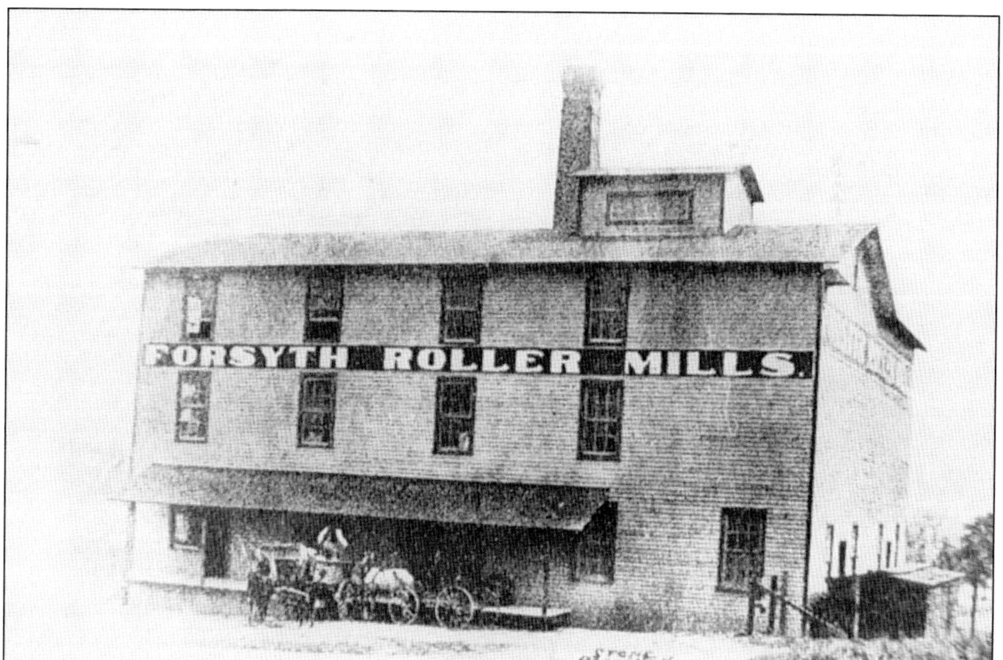

FORSYTH ROLLER MILLS, C. 1900. E.A. Holton was the president, J.E. Griffith, vice president, W.A. Lemly, treasurer, and A.L. Butner, secretary and manager. This mill was located at 1003 Liberty, in Winston-Salem. (FCL)

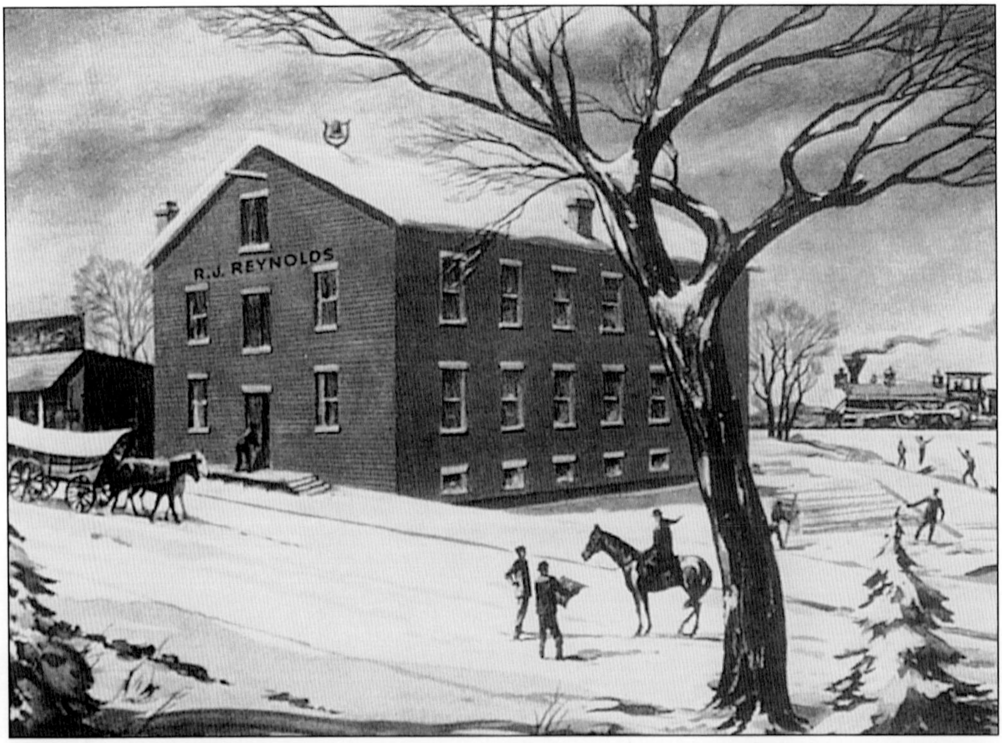

R.J. REYNOLDS'S FIRST FACTORY. In 1874, R.J. Reynolds started his first "Little Red Tobacco Factory" between Chestnut and Depot Streets just below Second Street. He paid the Moravian Church $388.50 for lot number 139. In the first year, 150,000 pounds of plug tobacco were turned out. (FCL)

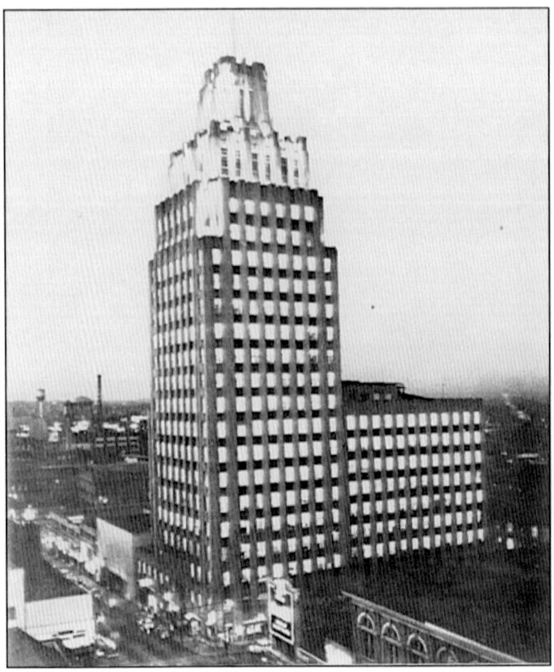

THE NEW R.J. REYNOLDS BUILDING. It was built in 1929 by Shreve and Lamb on the site of the Town Hall. Shreve and Lamb also used this architectural theme in their design of the Empire State Building. (FCL)

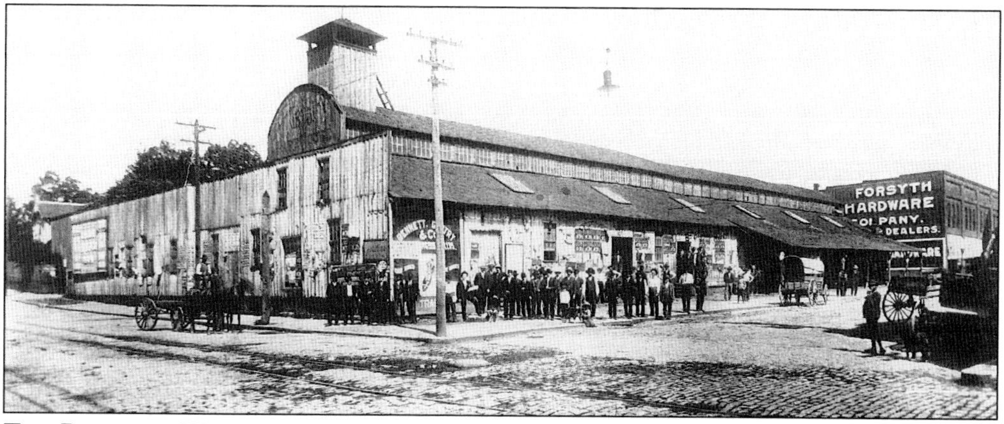

THE PIEDMONT WAREHOUSE AT FOURTH AND TRADE STREETS IN WINSTON-SALEM. It was erected in 1873 and was the first tobacco warehouse. At the time of this photo, the building was being auctioned, and would soon be torn down in 1905 for the building of the Masonic Temple. (FCL)

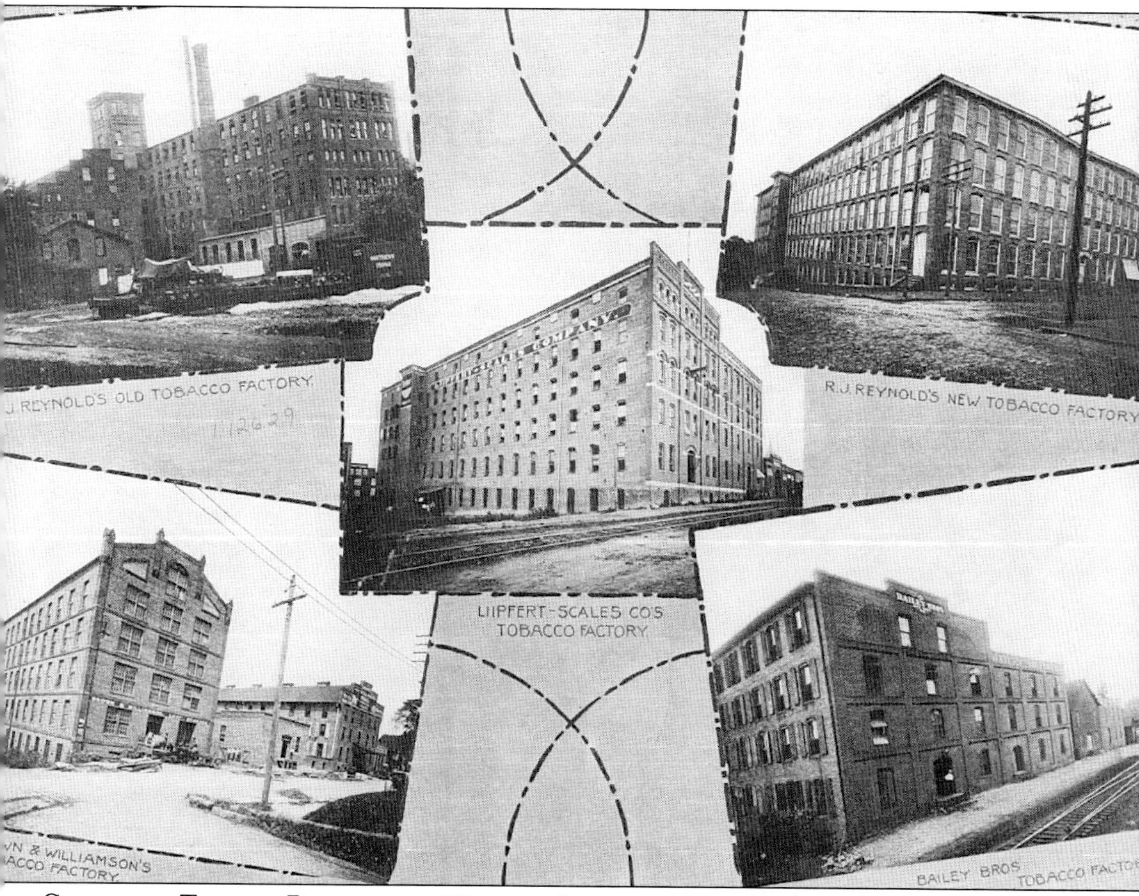

COLLAGE OF TOBACCO BUSINESSES IN WINSTON-SALEM, C. 1900. Clockwise from left to right are as follows: (top, left) R.J. Reynolds old tobacco factory, R.J. Reynolds new tobacco factory, Lipfert-Scales Co.'s tobacco factory (center), Bailey Brothers tobacco factory, and Brown & Williamson's tobacco factory. (FCL)

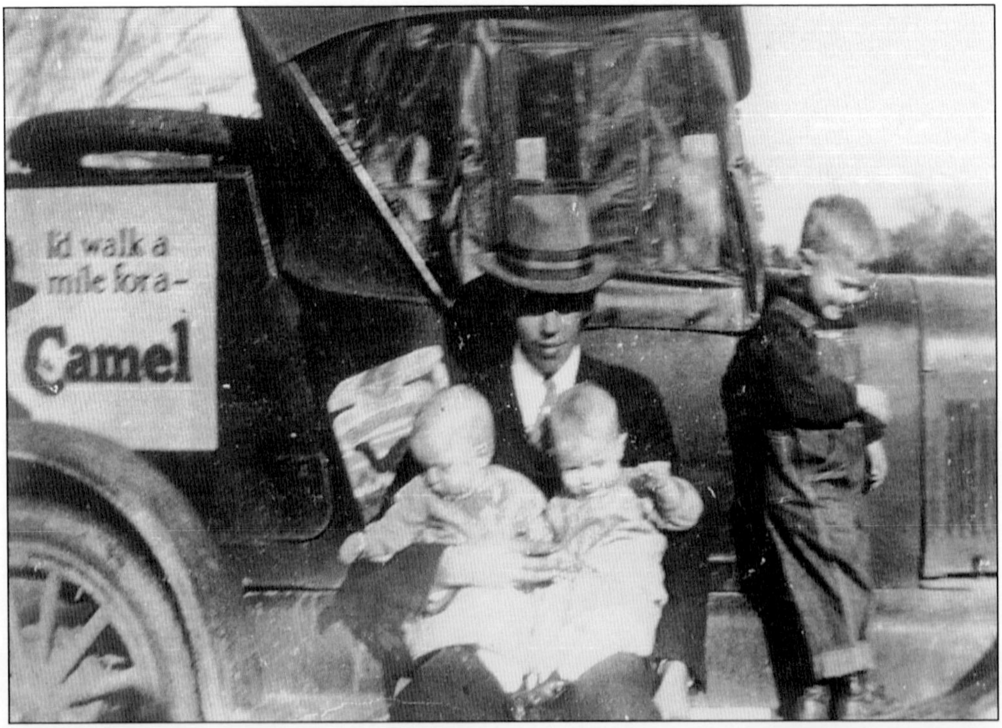

Gene Stanley, Cigarette Salesman for R.J. Reynolds. Here he is taking a break with twins Jim and John Stanley. His son Bill is standing on the running board of the 1927 Model T. Ford. (JC)

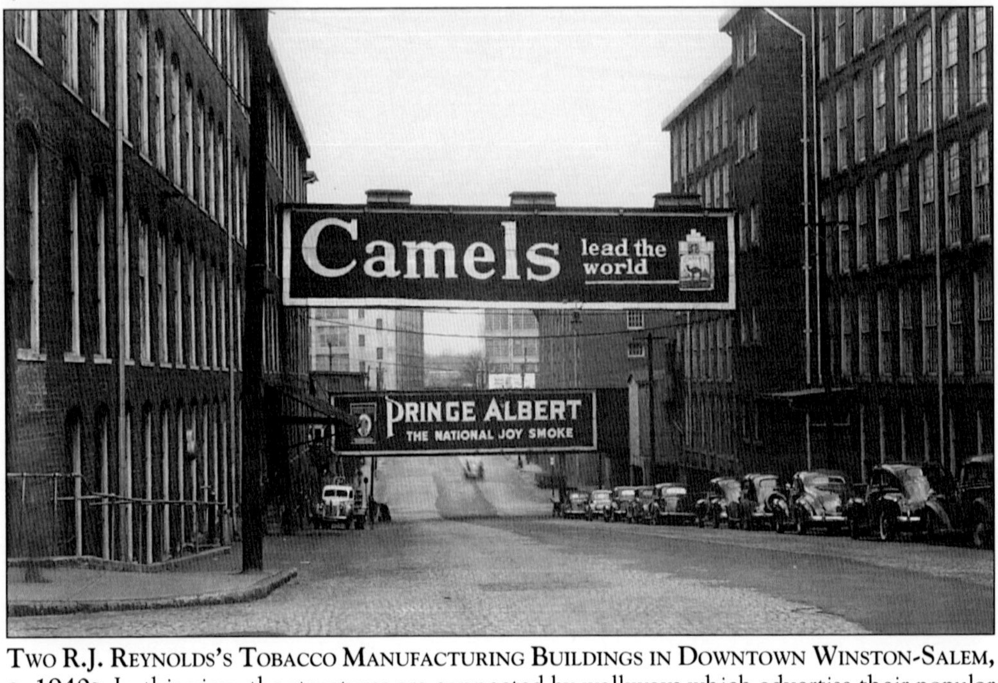

Two R.J. Reynolds's Tobacco Manufacturing Buildings in Downtown Winston-Salem, c. 1940s. In this view, the structures are connected by walkways which advertise their popular products. (JC)

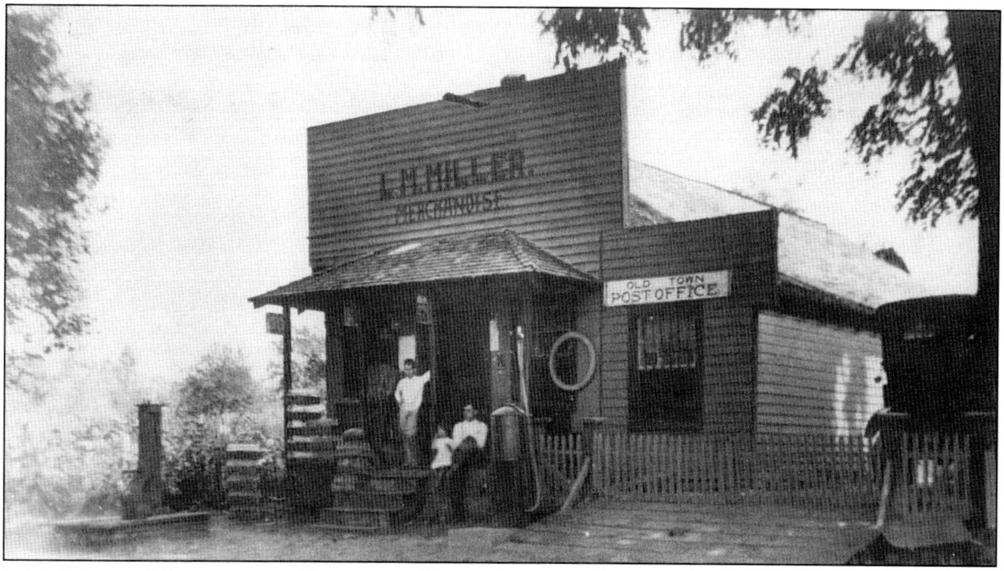

L.M. MILLER MERCHANDISE STORE AND POST OFFICE IN BETHABARA, C. 1918. (FCL)

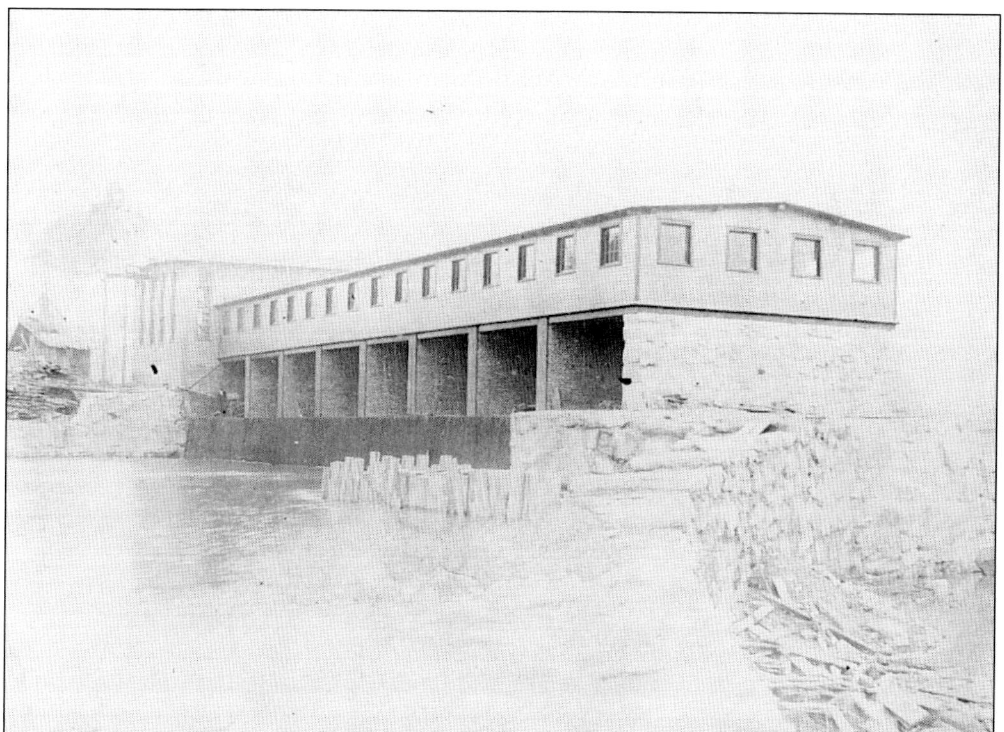

IDOLS DAM. This is a hydroelectric plant built by Henry W. Fries and his nephew on the Yadkin River near Clemmons in 1898. (FCL)

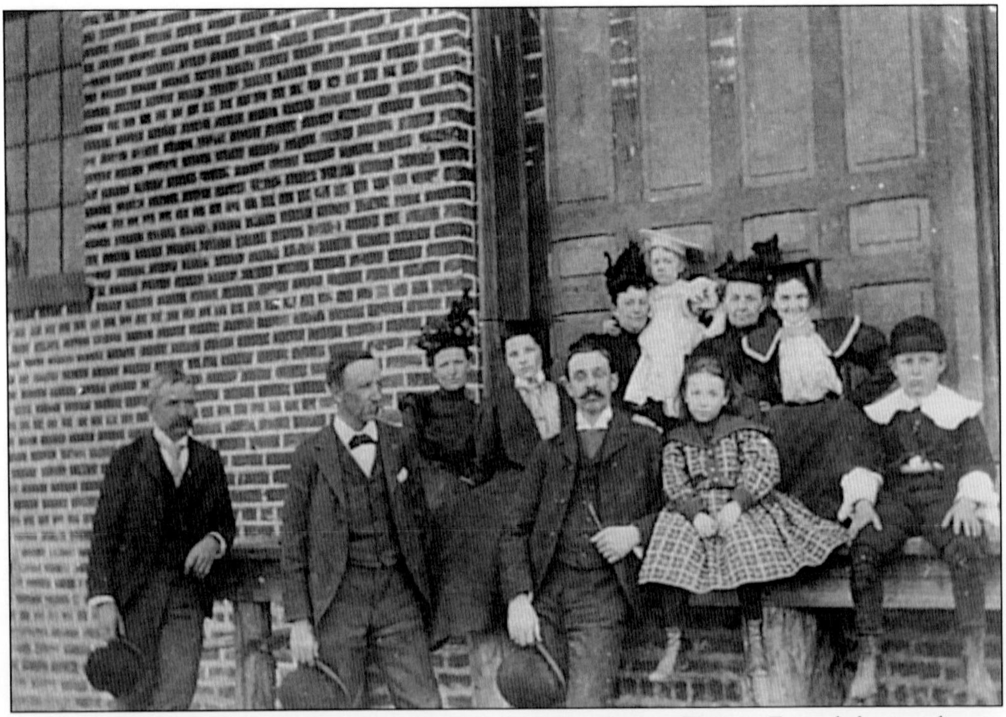

A Gathering of Fries Family and Friends at the Power Plant. From left to right are as follows: (front row, standing) Mr. Taft (electrical erecting engineer), H.E. Fries (general manager), and Mr. Claflin (electrical engineer); (front row, seated) Vivian Owens (later Mrs. Fred Noell) and Frank Reynolds; (back row) Mrs. Taft, Miss Valeska Steffen, Mrs. H.E. Fries, Anna Marguerite Fries, unidentified, and Miss Lee Beckham. (FCL)

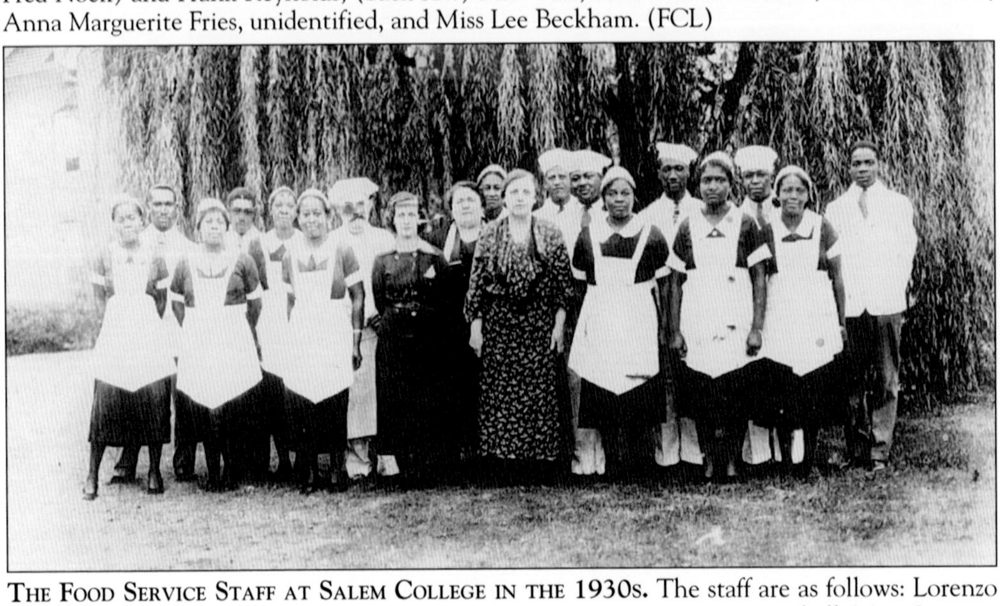

The Food Service Staff at Salem College in the 1930s. The staff are as follows: Lorenzo Johnson, Wynonna Murray, Walter Brown, Edith Lemly Page, Harry Campbell, Mary Ingram, Russell Crew (chef), Clarence Page, Emma Stewart, Margaret Davis, Blanche Stockton, Gertrude Pierce, Gus Brunner (baker), Ida Perry, Lucille Henderson?, George Amos, Van Delia Warren, Roger Moore, and Carola Price. (GPM)

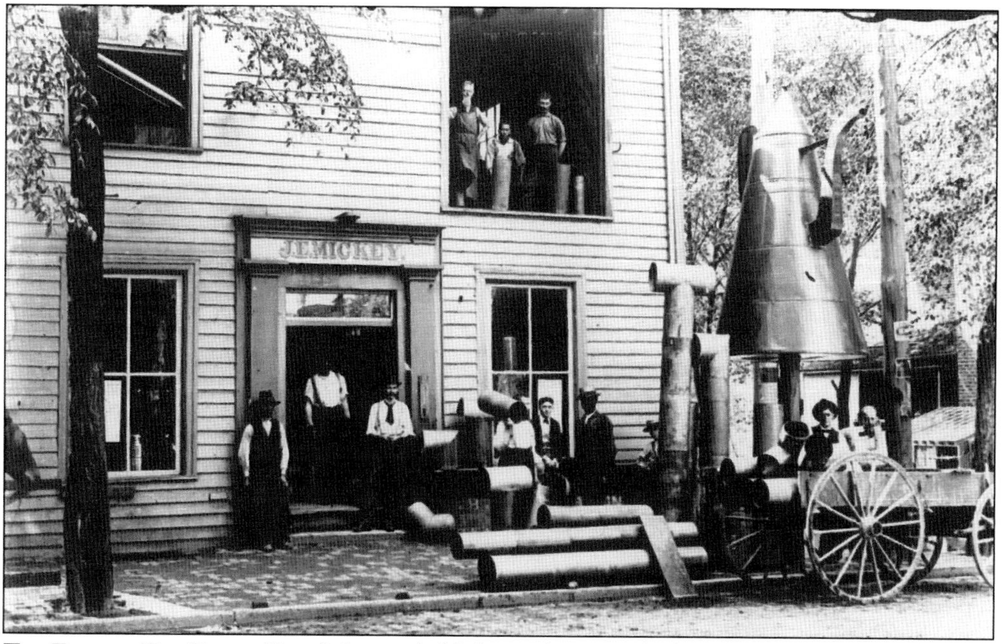

The Famous Tin Coffee Pot. It has probably been photographed more than any other landmark in Forsyth County. Built in 1858 by Julius Mickey, it was placed outside their tinsmith shop on South Main Street. (FCL)

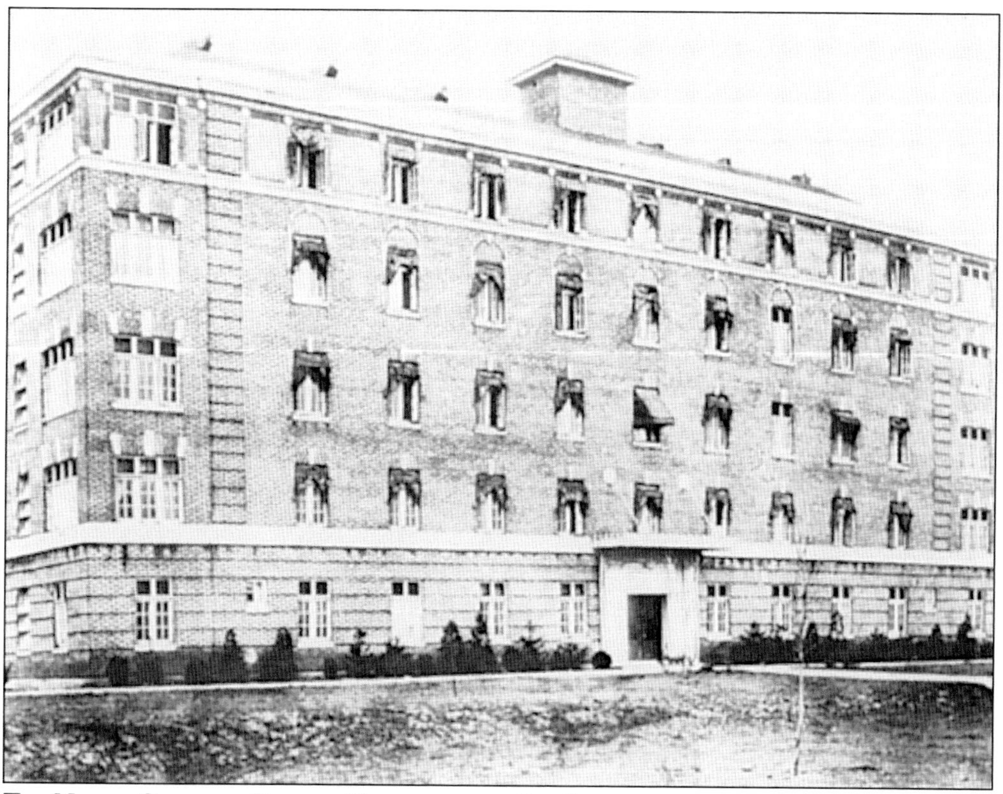

The North Carolina Baptist Hospital upon Its Completion in 1923. (FCL)

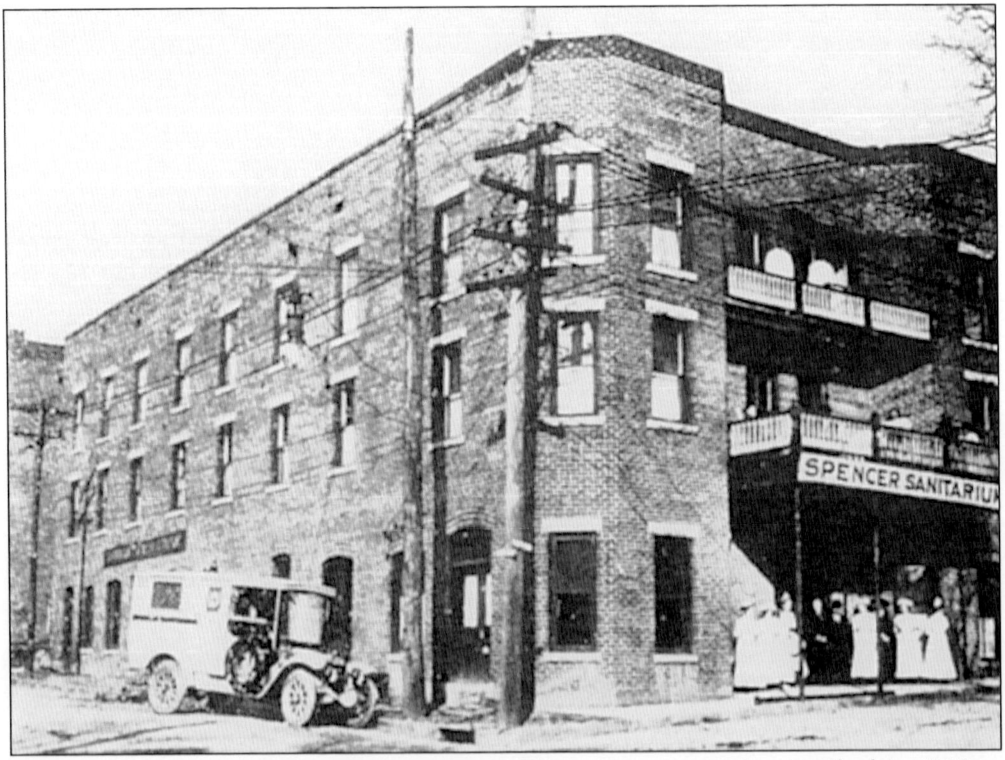

NURSES IN THEIR STARCHED WHITE DRESSES. These nurses were photographed in 1913 at Spencer's Sanitarium, located at Liberty northeast corner and Second Street. The administrators were as follows: W.O. Spencer, president; P.W. Davis, vice president; H.W. Spaugh, secretary and treasurer; and Miss H.G. Kelly, superintendent of nurses. (FCL)

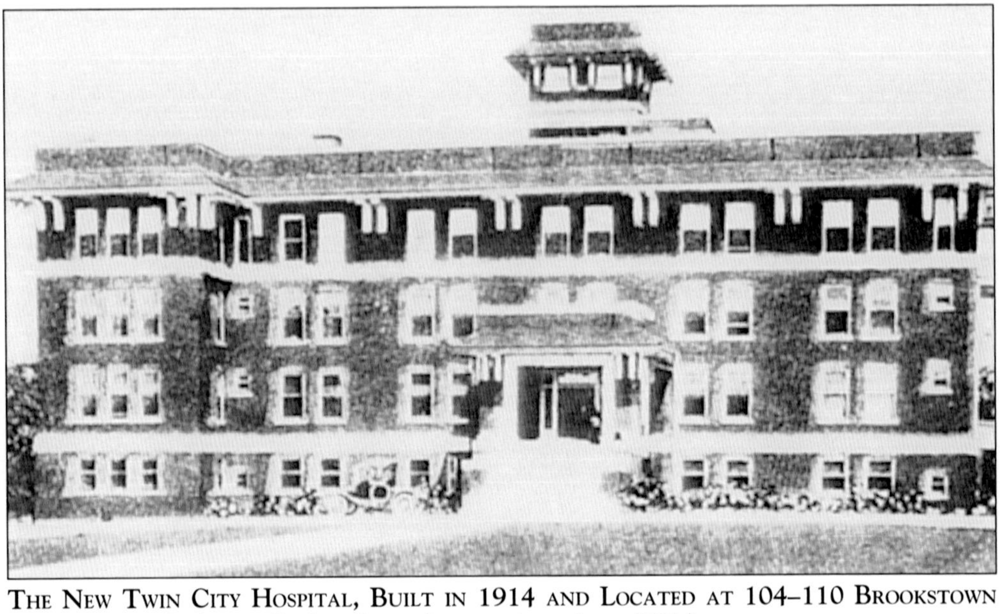

THE NEW TWIN CITY HOSPITAL, BUILT IN 1914 AND LOCATED AT 104–110 BROOKSTOWN AVENUE. Miss Catherine Rothwell was the superintendent. (FCL)

Augustus Fogle. He was born in 1820 in Salem, North Carolina, and served for 20 years as steward of the Salem Female Academy. During the Civil War, he overcame the many hardships of providing food for the resident students by traveling around the countryside searching for food. In his later years, he served as the fourth sheriff of Forsyth County, where after six years in that position, he was elected mayor of Salem. His sons, Charles A. Fogle and Christian H. Fogle, founded the Fogle Brothers Company, erecting many of the first buildings in Winston's infancy. (FCL)

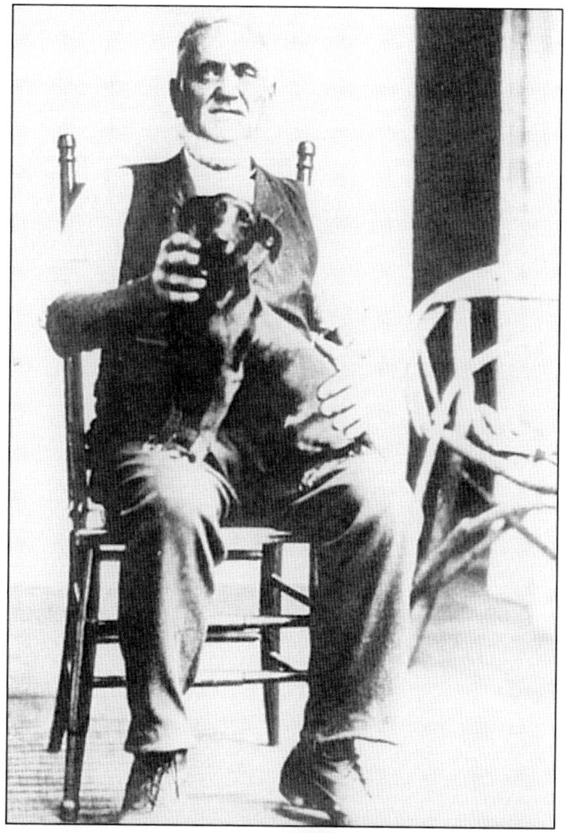

Before Automation. Crates, barrels, and wooden boxes of all sizes had to be built by hand in order to ship the many tons of R.J. Reynolds tobacco products out of Winston. Sons, nephews, and brothers worked alongside their fathers in the many construction workshops. (FCL)

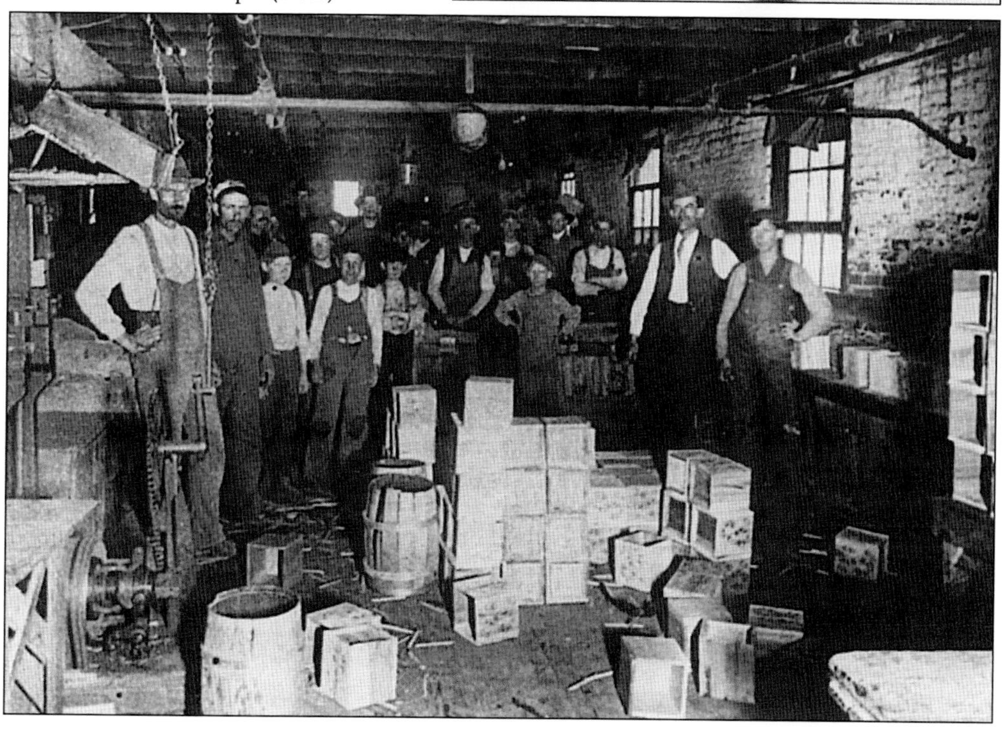

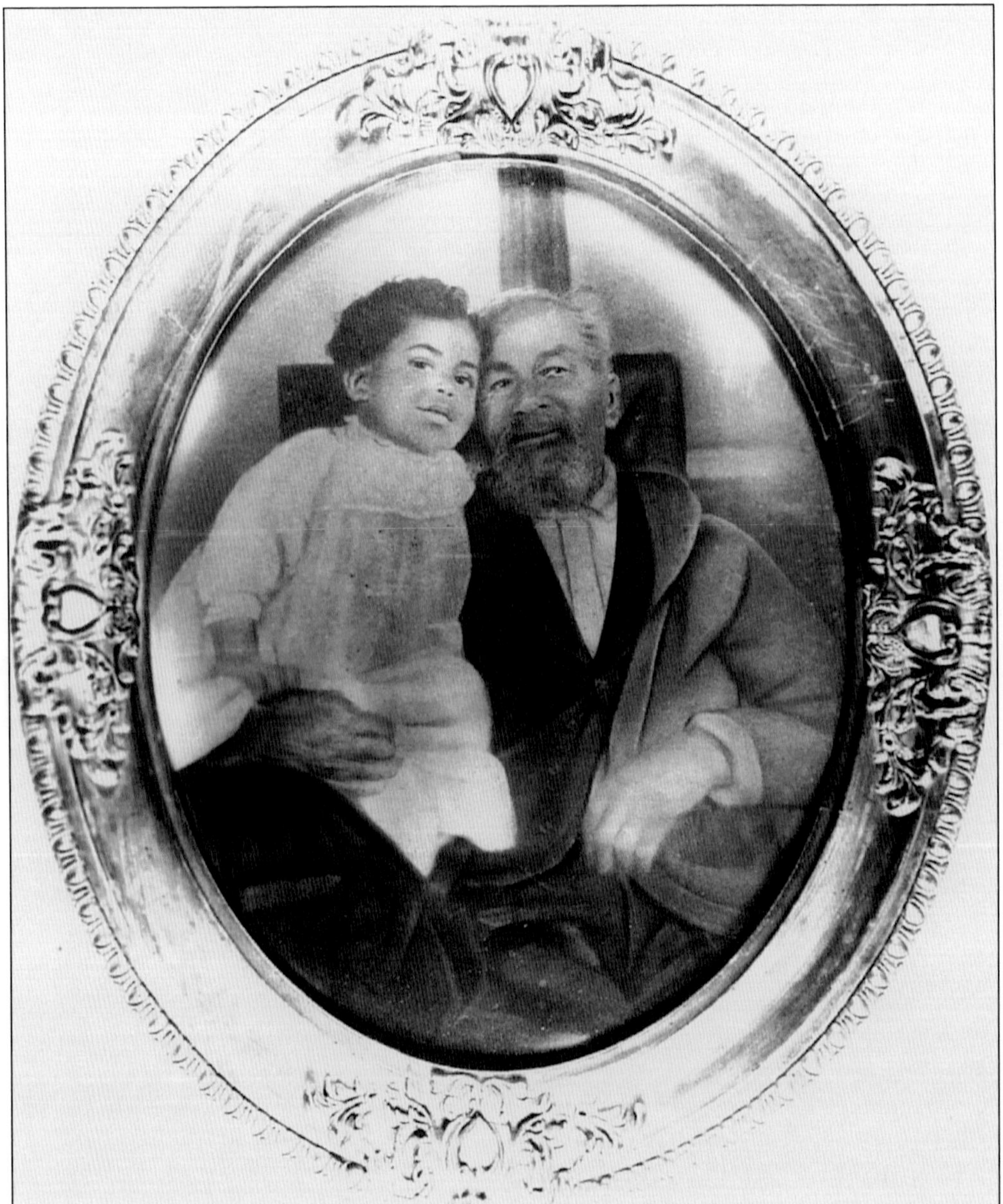

A Photograph of Washington Fries (Born in 1836) and an Unknown Child. As a slave, Washington belonged to Frances Fries and worked at the wool mill. In later years he worked as a barber. (CC)

SAMUEL FRANKLIN VANCE (BORN JANUARY 19, 1864, AND DIED DECEMBER 4, 1936). He was raised in the Belews Creek Township by his parents, John Franklin Vance (born March 25, 1825) and Sarah Barham Vance (born March 1, 1831). Samuel qualified as a teacher at age 17 and continued his studies while teaching at Vance schoolhouse. Vance later went to work for Sach Brothers, managing the lumber department. He served 6 years as appointed clerk of the superior court and 12 years as the assistant postmaster of Winston. He also was vice-president of Carolina Coal and Ice and the director of Merchant's National Bank of Winston-Salem. On December 19, 1901, he married Sallie E. Fulton, who was born on October 26, 1874, and died on February 11, 1944. (FCL)

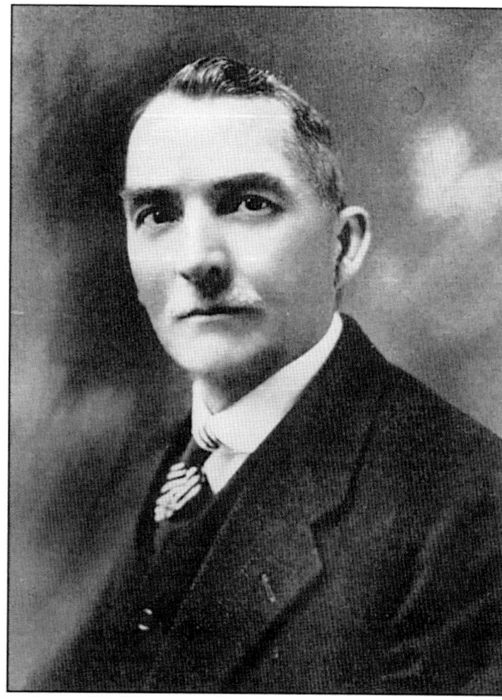

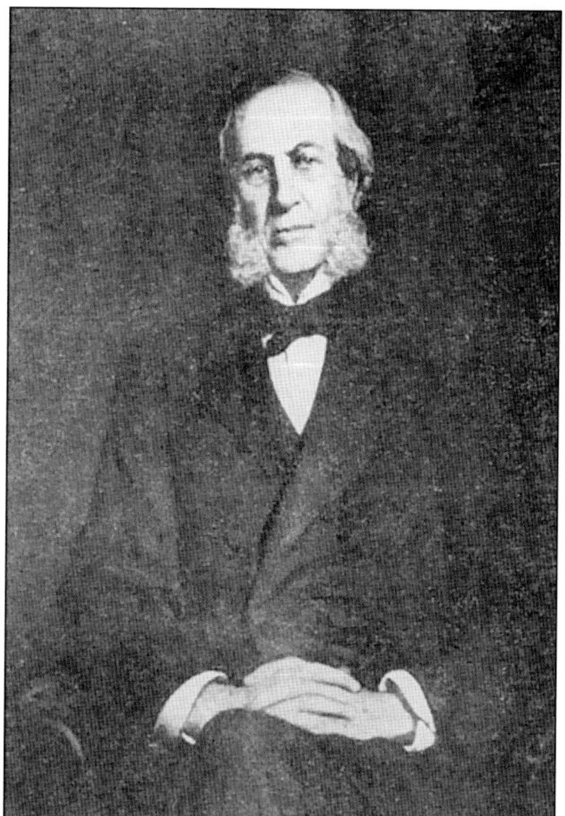

JOHN FOX SLATER. He was born on March 4, 1815, possibly in Connecticut, and died March 7, 1884, in Norwich, Connecticut. At the age of 17, Slater entered the family woolen and cotton mill textile business. Upon the death of his father, he inherited a small fortune. After the Civil War, Slater made his next fortune as an industrialist. In 1868, Slater founded the Norwich Free Academy, located in Norwich, Connecticut. By 1888, over half of his railroad investments were funding the Slater Endowment. As a result of Slater's philanthropy, normal schools could be built in the South. Simon Green Atkins, being slave-born and well educated, crusaded for educational equality for African Americans as early as the 1890s. In 1892, he persuaded the Winston community leaders to found the Slater Normal and Industrial School, which opened that year with just a handful of students. In 1925, this school became Winston-Salem State University. (FCL)

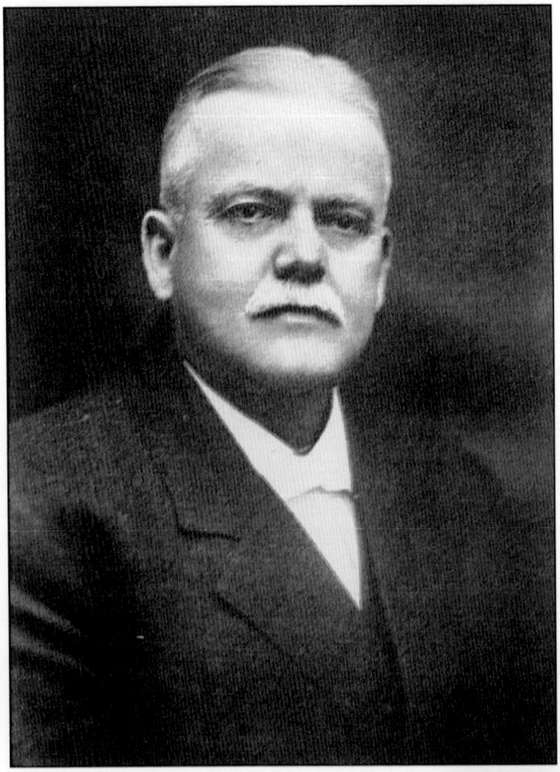

Dr. David N. Dalton. He was a much devoted and respected county physician who practiced medicine in Winston and the surrounding area for over 35 years. He was born about 1860 to David Nicholas Dalton and Melissa Rives. In 1887, he married Louisa Wilson Bitting, and together they had three children. After graduating from University of North Carolina in 1877, he continued his education at New York University, graduating with a medical degree in 1881. From 1882 to 1884, he practiced medicine in Walnut Cove, North Carolina, and then moved to Winston to set up his own practice, where he remained until his death in 1928.

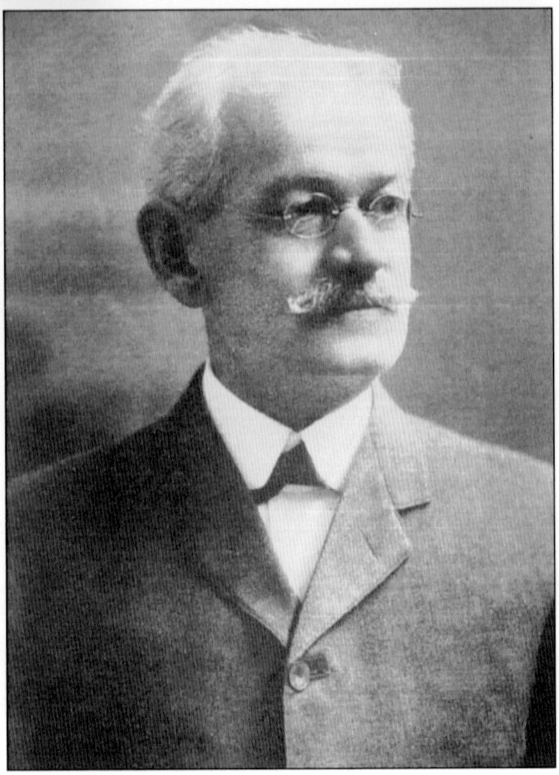

Henry Theodore Bahnson, M.D. He was born on March 6, 1845, in Lancaster, Pennsylvania. In 1858, after attending the Salem Boys School, he attended the Moravian Institute of Naxareth Hall in Pennsylvania and the Moravian College and Theological Seminary at Bethlehem, Pennsylvania. After serving in the Civil War, he again continued his education and in 1867 graduated from medical school at the University of Pennsylvania. Before starting his practice in 1869, Bahnson traveled abroad and studied at the University of Berlin, Prague, and Utrecht. In 1917, he became the surgeon for the Southern Railway, then later served as chief surgeon of the Winston-Salem Southbound Railway Company. In 1870, he married Adelaide de Schweinitz, and in 1874, Emma C. Fries. He died on January 16, 1917. (FCL)

WALTER READE JOHNSON. He was born in Stokes County on October 14, 1884, to James Thomas Johnson and Regina Edwards. After attending rural schools and Dalton Academy, Johnson taught a school term at Cornith. Unsatisfied with his livelihood, he entered University of North Carolina in 1906 and studied law. After graduating in 1909, he set up his own practice in Winston. In 1910, he married Miss Lou Milholland of Iredell County. (FCL)

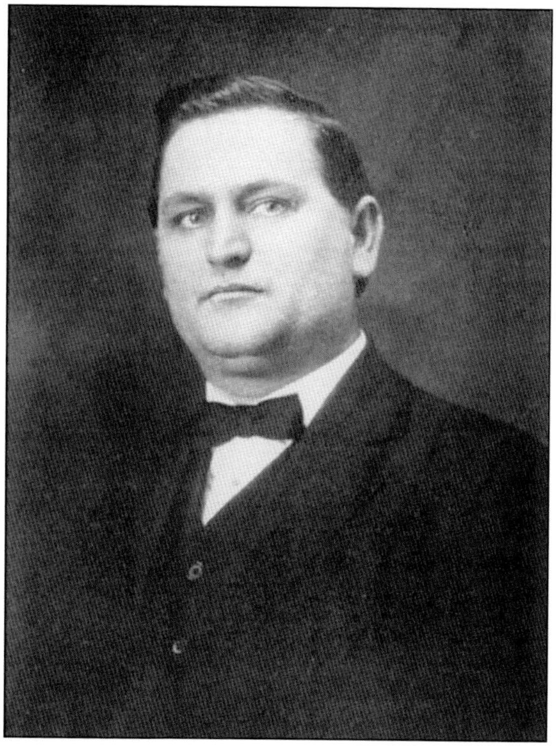

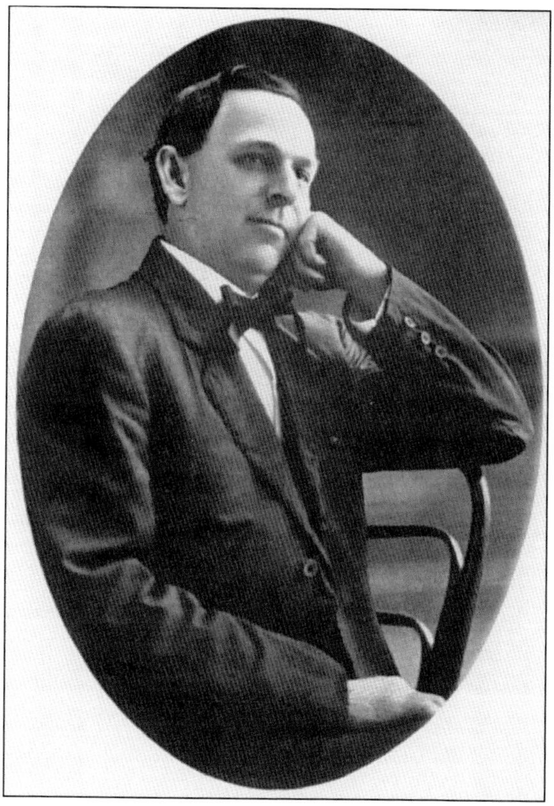

ELLIS H. SPAINHOUR, M.D. He was born on August 3, 1871, on a farm in Old Richmond to Pamelia Charity Grabbs of Bethania and William Windom Spainhour of Stokes County. After attending district schools, the Dalton Institute, and the Pinnacle Academy, all of which were located in Stokes County, he entered Baltimore Medical College. He received his degree in 1898. When smallpox broke out in Winston, Spainhour accepted the dangerous position of city health officer and immediately moved his practice from Old Town to Winston. He was instrumental in controlling the epidemic and saving hundreds of lives. (FCL)

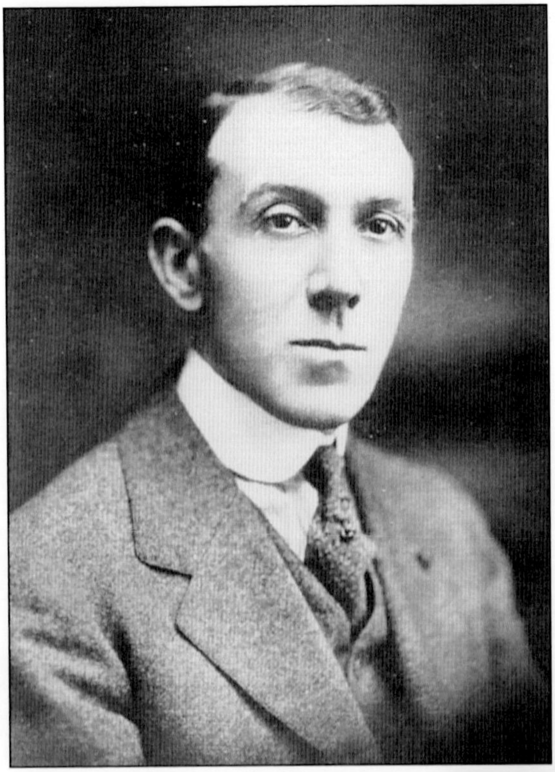

Thomas Maslin. He was born June 19, 1874, and died May 24, 1954. After graduating from Baltimore College, he came to Winston and accepted the position of bookkeeper in the Wachovia Land and Trust Company. He resigned in 1910 and began the Merchant's National Bank, of which he eventually became president. In 1906, he married Miss Martha Maney of Nashville, and together they had four daughters.

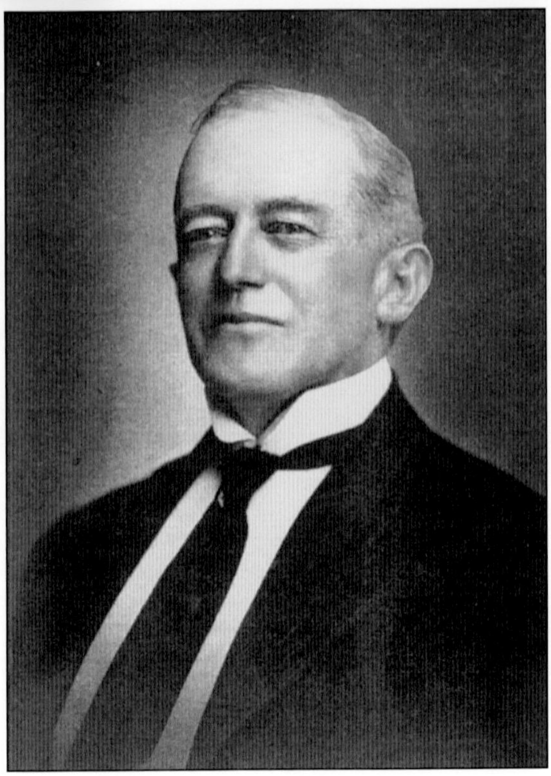

William A. Lemly. He was born around 1846 to Henry A. and Amanda Conrad Lemly. At age 17, he interrupted his studies at the Salem Boys School to join the Confederate Army. He was captured in April 1865 and released in June 1866. At age 19, he was elected cashier of the First National Bank of Salem and remained in this position for 13 years. Upon the death of the president of the bank, who was Lemly's uncle, First National was reorganized as Wachovia Bank. Lemly became president of Wachovia Bank, after the death of the bank's president, Mr. Bowman. Ill health forced Lemly to resign as president, and he died in 1928. (FCL)

GARLAND E. WEBB. He was born c. 1855 in the Mangum township of Orange County to Col. Robert Fulton Webb and Amanda Magnum. At age seven, Webb was enlisted as a drummer for the Flat River Guards, a group organized by his father at the outbreak of the Civil War. By the virtue of this service, Webb became the youngest enlisted soldier on either the Northern or Southern sides. After receiving his education, Webb spent ten years as a tobacco auctioneer in Durham, and in 1886, he began a five-year stint as an auctioneer for A.B. Gorrell in Winston. Webb was also mayor pro-tem, mayor, vice-chairman of the Winston School Board, secretary and treasurer of the Tobacco Association of the United States, and served on the board of aldermen. (FCL)

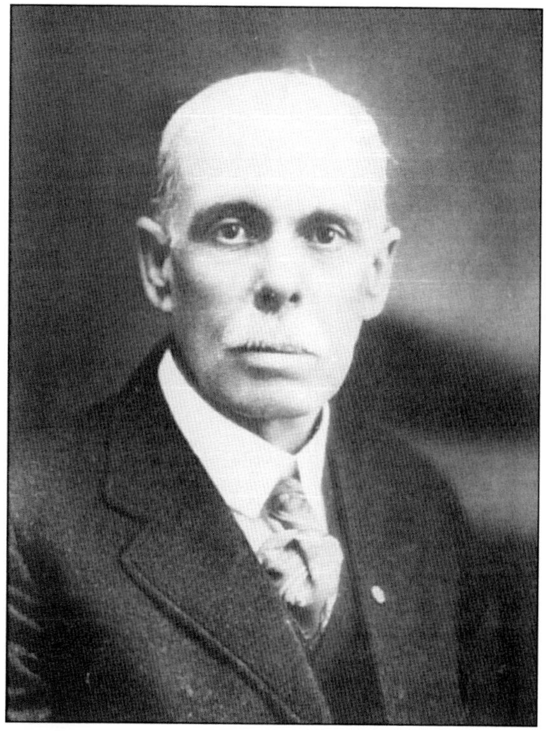

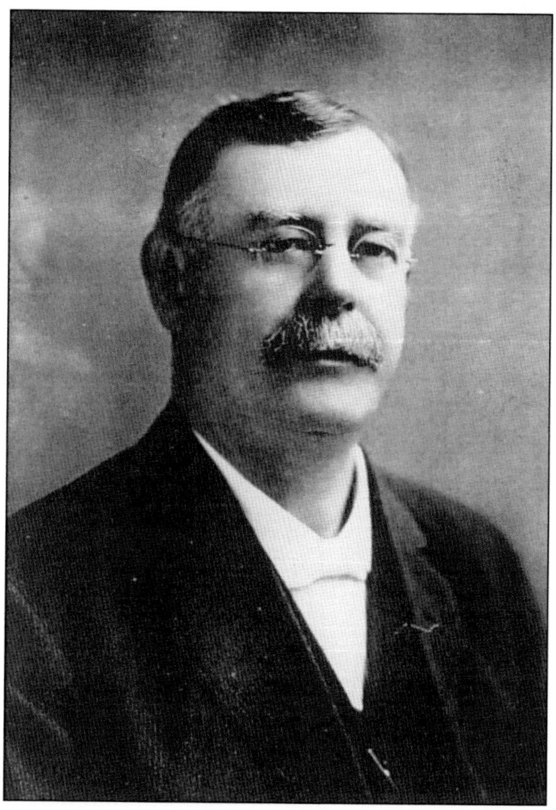

DEE RICH, SON OF CALVIN UPDEGROVE AND BETTY TENNESSEE WILLIAMS RICH. He was born in Mocksville about 1862. After high school, at age 18, he moved to Winston, where he worked for the tobacco business of Bynum, Cotten and Jones. After four years with Bynum, Cotten and Jones, he was employed by the R.J. Reynolds Tobacco Company, where he served as the manager of the rolling and casing department. Eager to rise in the company, Rich spent his extra time acquainting himself with the financial aspect of the company by assisting the company's bookkeeping department. Upon the death of the bookkeeper, Rich became head of the accounting department. From bookkeeper, Rich was promoted to cashier, then made treasurer and director of the company. (FCL)

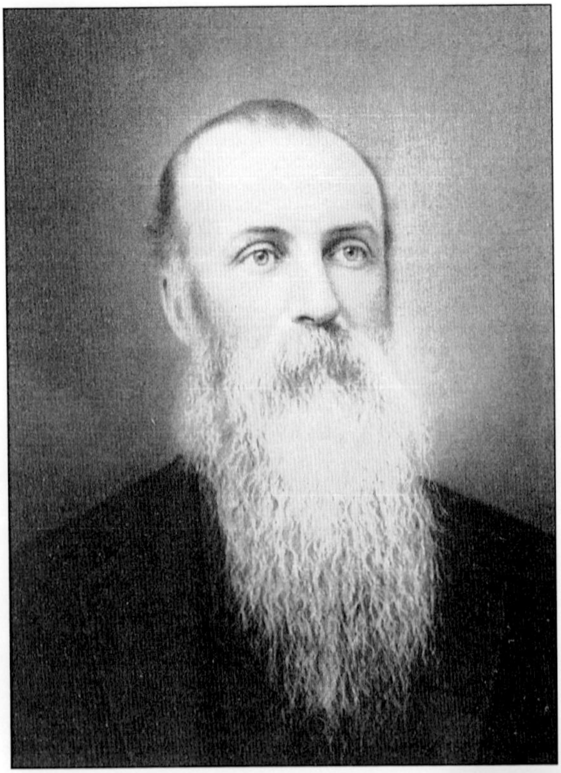

Sihon A. Ogburn, a Member of One of the Oldest Families in Western North Carolina. He was born March 17, 1840, in a log house 5 miles north of Salem to James Edward Ogburn and Sarah M.H. Tatum. On October 17, 1865, he married Mary Jane Tise (pictured). Before R.J. Reynolds started his "Little Red Factory," Sihon, together with his father and brothers, became the first pioneer tobacco manufacturers in Forsyth County, North Carolina. They raised, cured, stemmed, and twisted their own tobacco into their well-known "pigtail twists," which were sold to the retail merchants in Old Salem and and the counties of Forsyth and Stokes. (FCL)

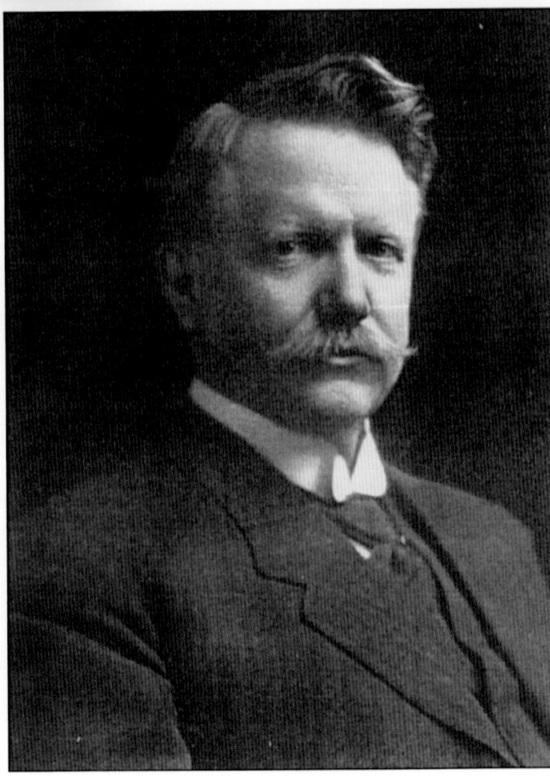

Francis H. Fries. He was born November 7, 1846, in Salem to Francis L. and Lisetta Maria Vogler Fries. After being educated by private tutors and attending the Salem Boys School, Francis entered his father's offices at the age of 15. He continued his employment at Fries Cotton Mill throughout the Civil War. In 1866, he furthered his education at the University of North Carolina. He returned to Fries Cotton Mill in 1868 where he invented and patented many modern-day machines. His career carried him on to serve as director of Fries Manufacturing and Power Company and North Carolina Midland Railroad Company. He also served as president of Arista Mills, director and president of Fealty Building and Loan, and president of People's National Bank of Winston. Fries married Miss Agnes Sophia de Schweinitz on August 24, 1886. He died June 5, 1931. (FCL)

WILLIAM POINDEXTER HILL. He was born on October 8, 1847, in Germanton, North Carolina, to John Gideon Hill (Forsyth County's first sheriff) and Susan Frances Poindexter Hill. At age 14, William enlisted in the Junior Reserve. After the war, he taught in Henry County, Virginia, as well as in Stokes and Forsyth Counties. As a business leader, he organized and also served as vice-president for the Oakland Manufacturing Company (later the B.F. Huntley Furniture Company) and the Huntly-Hill-Stockton Company, which operated the city's first ambulance. He married Miss Elizabeth Ogburn (born December 9, 1856, and died April 3, 1943), daughter of Charles B. and Tabitha Moir Ogburn. He died January 30, 1920. (FCL)

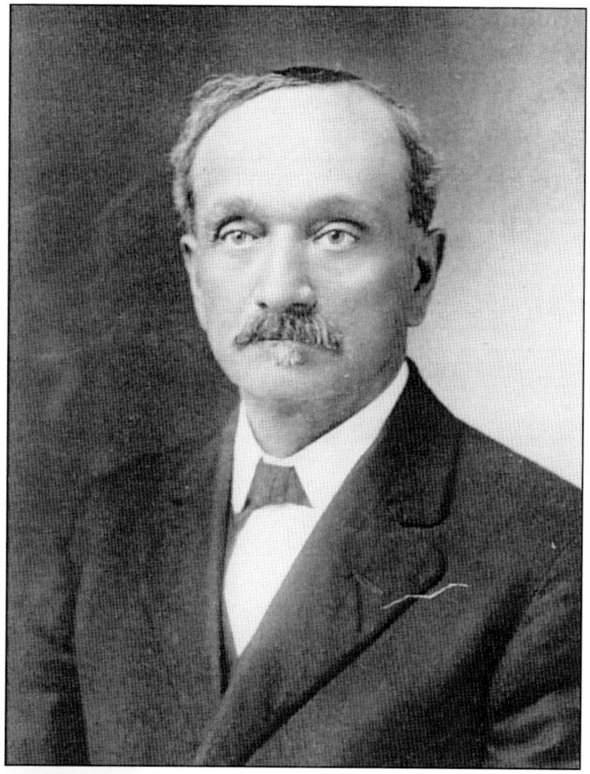

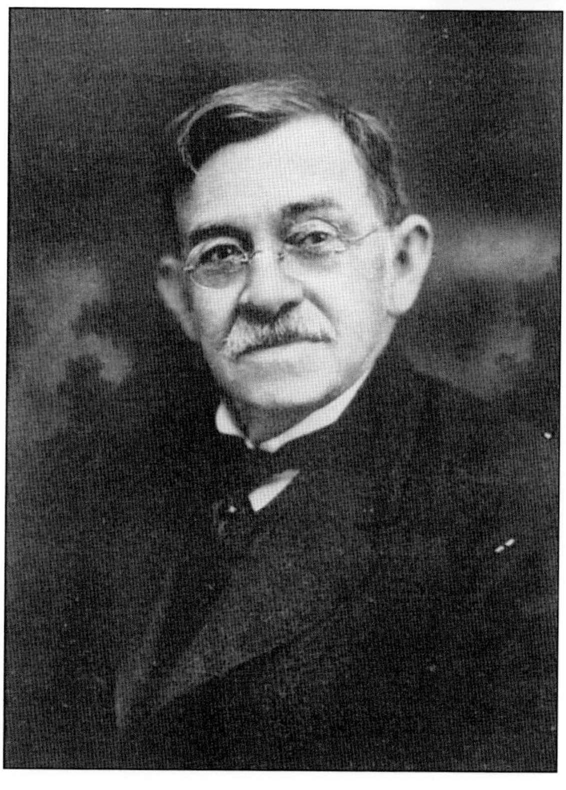

JAMES ALEXANDER GRAY. He was the first vice-president of one of the largest banks in North Carolina, the Wachovia Bank and Trust Company of Winston-Salem. James was born January 2, 1846, to Robert and Mary Millis Wiley Gray. His father had the distinction of buying the first lot in the town, located at Third and Main in Winston. James Alexander attended the free school, Winston High School, the Boys School at Salem, and Trinity College. At the close of the war, he concentrated his energies in leading Winston to become a commercial center. He helped organize the Wachovia National Bank and eventually became its president. When this bank and the Wachovia Loan and Trust Company were consolidated, Gray became its first vice-president. His wife, Aurelia Bowman, was born August 15, 1848, and died August 20, 1914. James A. Gray died in 1918. (FCL)

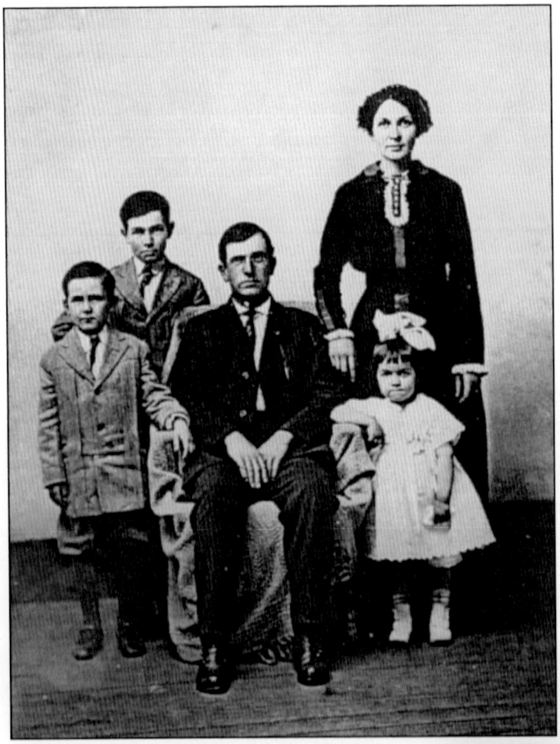

John H. Grubbs. He was born about 1870 on a farm in the Middlefort Township of Forsyth County to John and Flora Jones Grubbs. John lived at home until the age of 20, while being educated in local schools. He learned the merchant trade and continued in this career for ten years, whereafter he set up a building contractor business. This became one of the most competent and reliable businesses during the early 1900s. He married Ida M. Cobler of Surry County. (FCL)

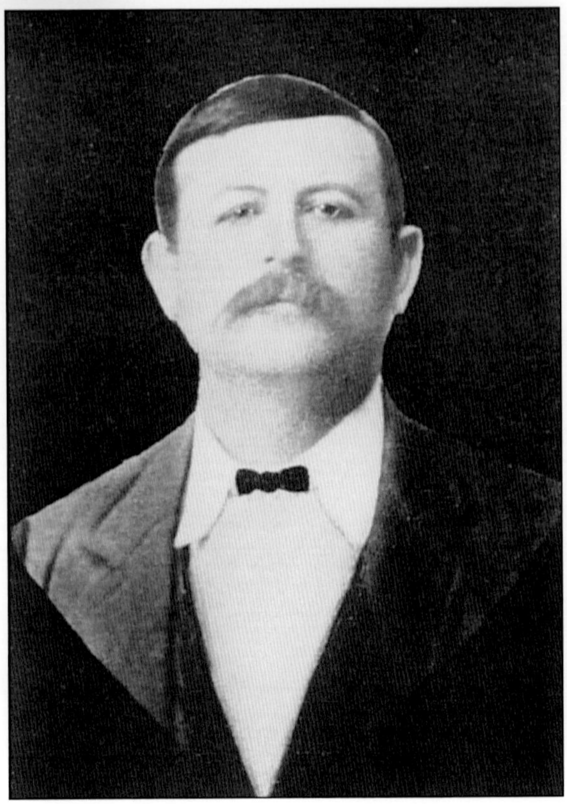

Joseph H. Phillips. An active figure in the lumber industry in Winston-Salem, he was born in Waughtown on September 3, 1866, to Crawford Tatum Phillips and Lucinda Spach. In 1884, he married Virginia Willard and later married Carrie Pardue. He began his professional career in the mercantile business, and subsequently entered into the lumber business. With limited capital, Phillips bought a portable sawmill and a tract of land. For several years he used his mill in converting timber into merchantable lumber. In 1893, he sold his mill and began dealing in lumber in Winston. He eventually established lumberyards in Centerville and West Highland. He died April 10, 1917. (FCL)

WILLIAM G. CRANFORD. He was born in June 1861 in Rowan County to Wilburn Cranford and Elizabeth Todd. Orphaned at the age of six, William was taken to the home of Jeremiah Raeber, a local miller and farmer. At the age of 21, he learned the blacksmith trade, and in 1886, he formed a partnership with a blacksmith named Ed Spach. During the early 1890s, Cranford began the study of veterinary surgery. By actively attending lectures and having a natural inclination for the work, he rapidly became widely known for his veterinary abilities. In 1895, he married Miss Josephine "Jessie" E. Tally of Forsyth County. William G. Cranford died July 28, 1934. (FCL)

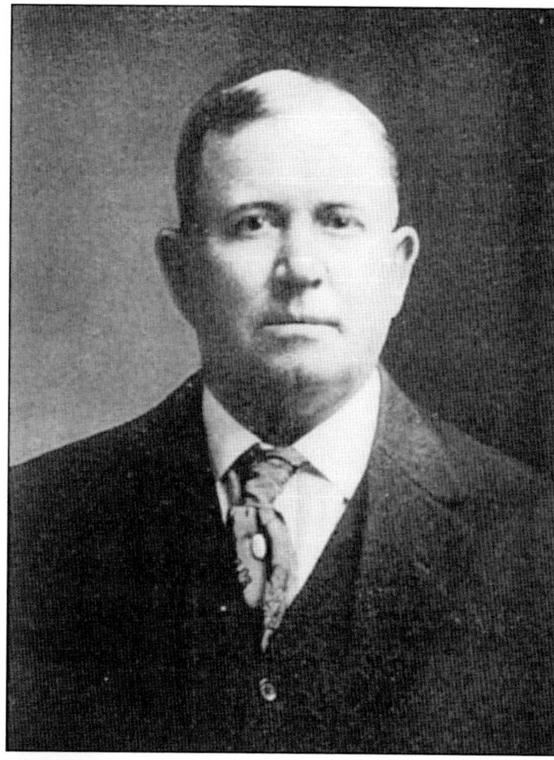

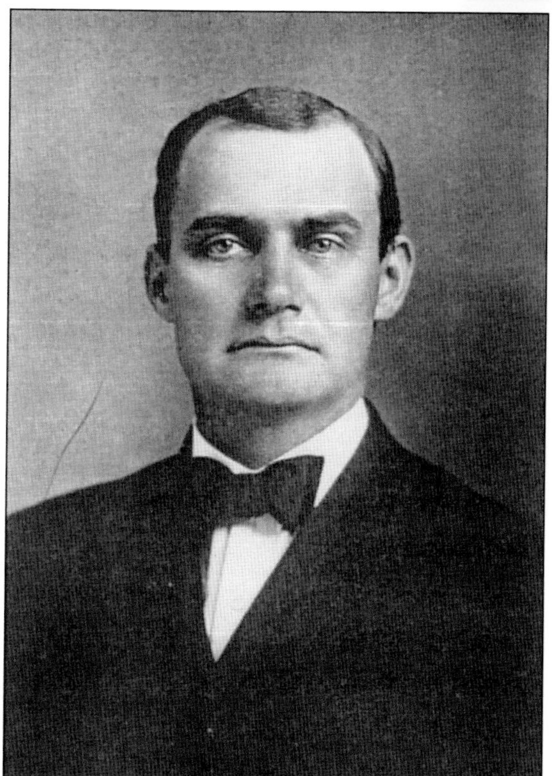

NIXON L. CRANFORD OF RANDOLPH COUNTY. He was born to Martin and Jane Cranford. After completing his education at Oak Ridge Institute, he taught school for two years before moving to Winston. In Winston, he clerked for the Taylor Brothers for five years. In 1908, he married Miss Jennie Clingman of Yadkin County. From 1913 to 1918, he was employed by the IRS. While dividing his time between teaching, the mercantile business, and public service, Cranford diligently honed his skills as a newspaper man. Nixon L. Cranford soon became president of the *Winston-Salem Journal*. Cranford died January 23, 1930. (FCL)

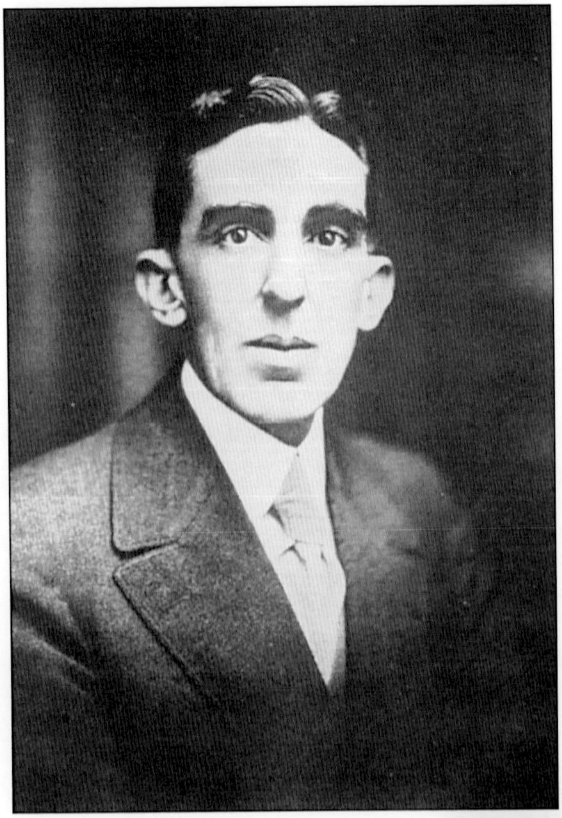

George D. Hodgin. He was born on October 24, 1867, to Stephen and Lucy Moir Hodgin. Upon moving to Winston in 1868, his father entered a partnership with N.D. Sullivan and conducted business under the name of Hodgin & Sullivan. George's professional career began with a position at the First National Bank, and later he gained experience in professions such as tobacco manufacturing, real estate, and life insurance. He was also an organizer of the Realty Exchange, and in 1906, he bought 200 lots in what is known as Liberty Heights. He also developed property near Granville School to the west and Lewis Heights to the north.

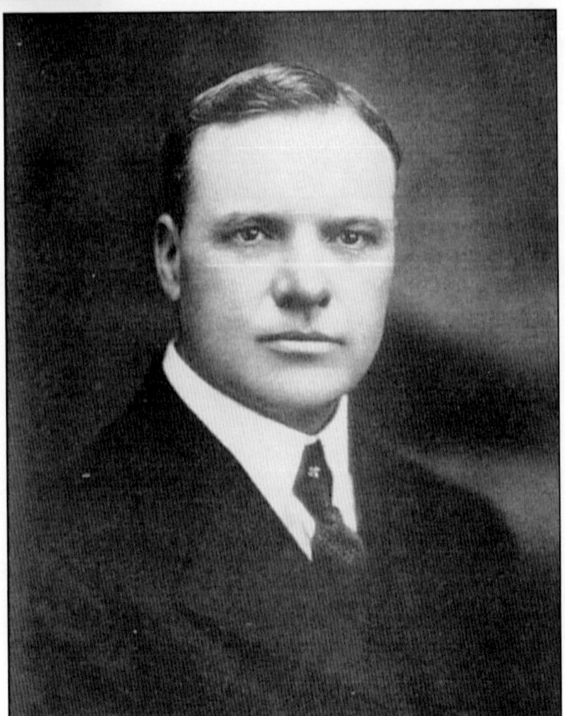

William Bethel Speas. He was born November 20, 1875, in Forsyth County to John S. Speas (born April 11, 1847) and Mary Frances Doub (born July 1847), whose father, Rev. John Doub, founded Methodism in the Pfafftown area of Forsyth County. After finishing preparatory school at Oak Hill Institute, William went on to graduate from the University of North Carolina in 1901. He entered his first teaching position in 1901 in the Vienna Township and then in 1902 taught at Clemmons High School. During this time, he married Louzana Long of Old Richmond. In 1903, Speas was chosen as the county superintendent of Forsyth County Schools, a position he held for over a decade. In 1919, he was elected president of the Forsyth County Teacher's Association. (FCL)

JAMES STUART KUYKENDALL. He was born September 8, 1871, in Maryland. In 1899, after experiencing success in the mercantile business up north, he relocated to Greensboro to work in the mercantile and real estate businesses. In 1907, Kuykendall was elected to the Greensboro Chamber of Commerce and was instrumental in bringing through North Carolina the National Automobile Highway from New York to Atlanta. In 1909, he accepted the position of secretary and treasurer of the board of trade in Winston. On June 23, 1909, he married Ruth Wharton. In 1912, he became secretary and treasurer of the Standard Building and Loan Association. James Stuart Kuykendall died January 28, 1961. (FCL)

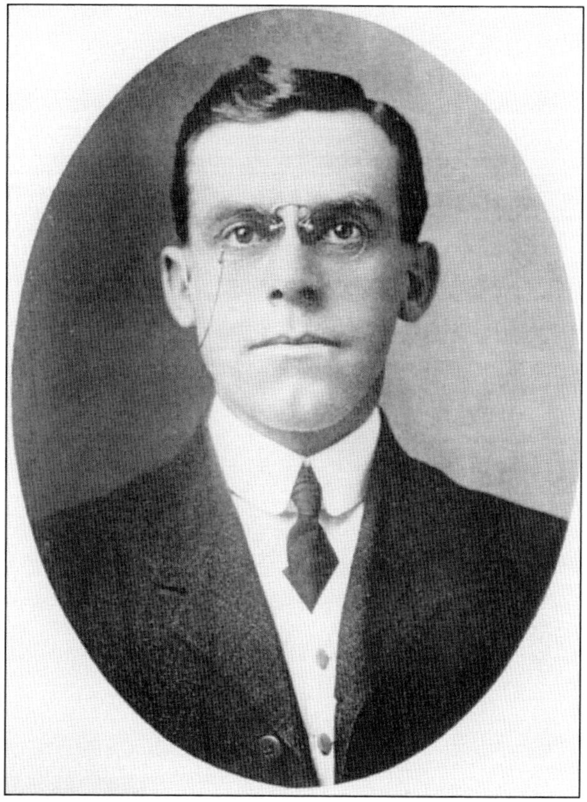

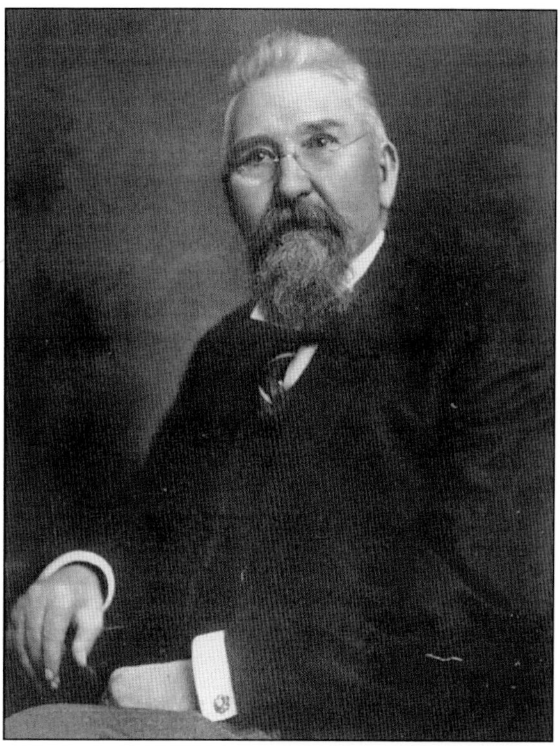

RICHARD JOSHUA REYNOLDS. His life story practically encompasses the evolution of the tobacco industry. He was born July 20, 1850, to Hardin W. and Nancy Cox Reynolds of Patrick County, Virginia. Bringing his knowledge of tobacco and $5,100 capital to Forsyth County, Reynolds began his first tobacco factory in 1875. Reynolds's company, in its first year, manufactured 150,000 pounds of tobacco. By 1919, he had built 43 great modern buildings. That same year, the "Prince Albert Special" railroad pulled 35 cars of R.J. Reynolds products daily from Winston-Salem for distribution across the countryside. Through the efforts of R.J. Reynolds, Forsyth County cradles one of the largest tobacco manufacturing companies of its kind in the world. In 1905, he married his cousin Mary Catherine Smith of Mt. Airy. (FCL)

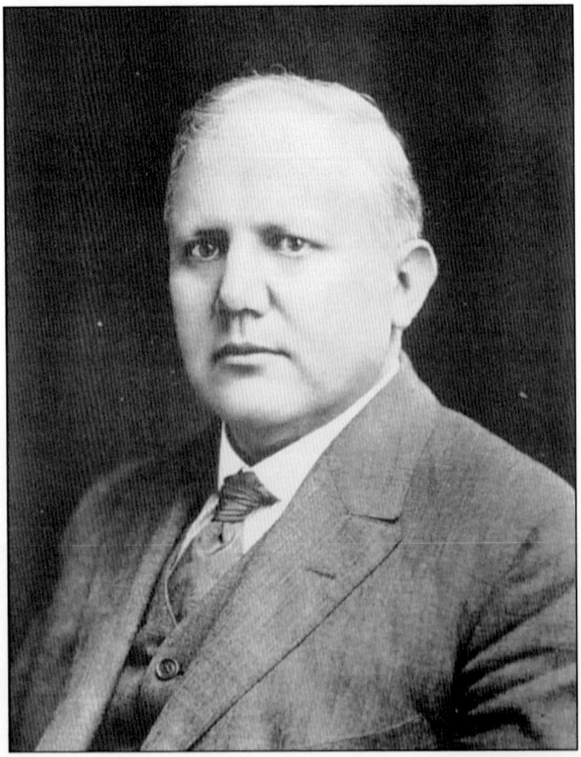

Henry Fries Shaffner. He was born September 19, 1867, in Salem to Dr. John Francis and Caroline Louisa Fries Shaffner. He began his education at Mrs. Welfare's Select School, and later attended the Salem Boys School. He completed his education at the University of North Carolina in 1887. In 1901, he married Agnes Gertrude Siewers. In 1897, he served as secretary and treasurer of the Wachovia Loan and Trust Company until 1911, when it merged with Wachovia National Bank. After the merger, he served as one of the vice presidents. Shaffner was also secretary and treasurer of Salem Water Supply Company, a member of the board of commissioners of the town of Salem for several terms, and after 1913, a member of the Board of Alderman of the City of Winston-Salem. He died on December 3, 1941. (FCL)

Dewitt Harmon. Born on July 10, 1865, he was raised in Kernersville by his parents, Julius Sheldon and Antoinette Kerner Harmon. At age 18, he qualified as a teacher and taught his first term in the Pine Grove School in Kernersville. He then taught three terms at the Moravian School in Nazareth, Pennsylvania. Eventually, he became employed as a chain and stake bearer with the engineering corps during the construction of the Richmond and Danville Railroad. As a result of his high mathematical skills, he was soon promoted to assistant engineer of the road maintenance department. In 1897, he erected the Kernersville Roller Mills. He served for several years on the board of commissioners of Kernersville and the local school board. In 1912, he was appointed by legislature as a member of the Highway Commission of Forsyth County. He died on October 29, 1944. (FCL)

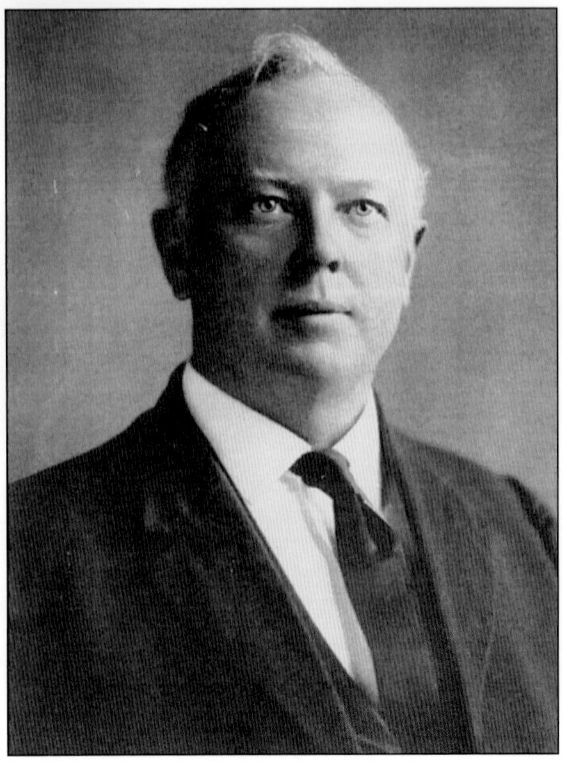